PLUME ℗

The Women's Financial Survival Handbook

PURSUING A CAREER

ESTABLISHING CREDIT

CHOOSING A BANK

BUDGETING INCOME

BUYING STOCKS, INSURANCE,
HOUSES, AUTOS

STARTING A BUSINESS

COLLECTING SOCIAL SECURITY

PROTECTING ASSETS

PROVIDING FOR OLD AGE

AND MUCH MORE

D1569225

GAIL PERKINS AND JUDITH RHOADES

WHAT DO MEN KNOW THAT WOMEN DON'T?

All too often the answer is: How important the mastery of money is in the world we live in.

Women have a lot of catching up to do if they are to take their rightful place in that world.

This is the book to help them do it.

ABOUT THE AUTHORS

GAIL PERKINS is currently editor and head writer on a major California magazine. Previously she was on the staffs of a number of magazines and newspapers, enjoyed success as a freelance writer, and while in college won numerous awards for her writing. She lives with her husband and two children in Costa Mesa, California.

JUDITH RHOADES is a syndicated financial columnist with fifteen years' experience in the securities industry, the last ten as a stockbroker. In 1974, she was awarded the *Glamour* Magazine Job-Style Achievement Award as an outstanding woman in business. Currently, she is a student in law school. The mother of two, she also resides in Costa Mesa, California.

The Women's Financial Survival Handbook

by Gail Perkins and
Judith Rhoades

A PLUME BOOK
NEW AMERICAN LIBRARY
TIMES MIRROR
NEW YORK, LONDON AND SCARBOROUGH, ONTARIO

NAL Books are available at quantity discounts when used to promote
products or services. For information please write to
Premium Marketing Division, The New American Library, Inc.,
1633 Broadway, New York, New York 10019.

Library of Congress Cataloging in Publication Data
Perkins, Gail.
The women's financial survival handbook.
(A Plume book)
Bibliography: p.
1. Finance, Personal. 2. Women — United States — Economic conditions.
1. Rhoades, Judith, joint author. II. Title.
HG179.P366   332.024'042   79-27156
ISBN 0-452-25231-8

PLUME TRADEMARK REG. U.S. PAT. OFF. AND FOREIGN COUNTRIES
REGISTERED TRADEMARK—MARCA REGISTRADA
HECHO EN FORGE VILLAGE, MASS., U.S.A.

SIGNET, SIGNET CLASSICS, MENTOR, PLUME, MERIDIAN AND
NAL BOOKS are published *in the United States* by
The New American Library, Inc.
1633 Broadway, New York, New York 10019, *in Canada* by
The New American Library of Canada Limited, 81 Mack Avenue, Scarborough,
Ontario M1L 1M8, *in the United Kingdom* by The New
English Library Limited, Barnard's Inn, Holborn, London, EC1N 2JR, England

First Printing, March, 1980

1 2 3 4 5 6 7 8 9

PRINTED IN THE UNITED STATES OF AMERICA

This book is dedicated to all the women who shared their stories with us and to all the women who we hope will learn from these stories. It is also dedicated to our families and friends, who understood why we disappeared for a year.

Acknowledgments

We are indebted to the following people and companies that generously supplied us with much of the information which is included in this book: Judithe Goldberg, certified financial planner, Newport Beach, California; Velma Shaw, stockbroker, Bateman Eichler, Hill Richards, Inc., Newport Beach, California; Ronald Gable, certified financial planner, Fountain Valley, California; Roger J. Berg, Luthern pastor, Newport Harbor Lutheran Church, Newport Beach, California; Kathi Carroll, Jaci Carroll Services, Waterbury, Connecticut; Ann Jones, Ann Jones Personnel, Kansas City, Missouri; Jane Ray, Career Clinic, Seattle, Washington; Margaret Rinton, Lynda Adams, University of California at Irvine, Government Publications Department; Ruth Urban, Abigail Abbott Employment Services, Newport Beach, California; Mary Wick, Mary Wick Personnel Agency, Tulsa, Oklahoma; Peggy Cruel, Working Women United Institute, New York, New York; American Express, Public Relations Department, New York, New York; Bureau of Consumer Protection, Federal Trade Commission, Washington, D.C.; Ron Hawthorne, assistant public relations director, Bank of America, Los Angeles, California; Elinor Lawrence, former president of California Women's Savings and Loan, Westwood, California; National

Association of Commissions for Women, Washington, D.C.; Office of Consumer Affairs, Federal Reserve Board, Washington, D.C.; S. Lees Booth, National Consumer Finance Association, Washington, D.C.; Leonard Cautela, Burson Marsteller, New York, New York; American Bankers Association, New York, New York; Richard Leahy, assistant vice-president and assistant director of industry relations, AVCO Financial Services, Newport Beach, California; Commercial Credit Corporation, Baltimore, Maryland; Loan Department, Wells Fargo Bank, Newport Beach, California; Los Angeles Federal Savings and Loan, Los Angeles, California; Patricia Mellor, head bookkeeper, Bank of Newport, Newport Beach, California; Robert G. Norris, vice-president, manager, Bank of Newport, Newport Beach, California; Diana Nichols, financial control officer, Bank of America, San Francisco, California; Bruce G. Olson, vice-president, Bank of Newport, Newport Beach, California; Julian Block, attorney, tax editor of Research Institute, New York, New York; Copley News Service, San Diego, California; Agent Nancy Vanderpool and Agent Patricia Bedell, Equitable Life Assurance Society of the United States, Santa Ana, California; Agent Myra Z. Laundy, Pacific Mutual Life Insurance Company, Newport Beach, California; Agent Linda van den Brink of PCC Financial Services, Pacific Mutual Life Insurance Company, Newport Beach, California; insurance brokers Thomas Garvey and Robert Milum of Milum/Garvey, Newport Beach, California; David L. Biehl, Bailard, Biehl and Kaiser, Personal Money Managers, Menlo Park, California; Federal Home Loan Bank Board, San Francisco, California; Norman F. Frahm, real estate agent, Laguna Beach, California; Leonora Oppenheim, Ruth Benson, realtor, Whittier, California; Michael Bilyk, national sales manager, Pacific Southwest Division, Chicago Title Insurance Company, Los Angeles, California; Joanne Holbert, Crocker Bank, Regional Headquarters, San Diego, California; Toni Quezada, assistant vice-president, International Mortgage Company, subsidiary of Kaufman Broad, Irvine, California; Michael Wells, Crocker Bank Loan Department, San Francisco, California; James C. Wickline, attorney, Chicago Title Insurance Company, Los Angeles, California; American Safety Foundation of America, Public Relations Department, American Safety Foundation of America, New York, New York; John Britton, director of public affairs, Hertz Corporation, New York, New York; Patricia Kelly, sales representative, Johnson and Sons, Lincoln Mercury, Costa Mesa, California; Runzheimer and Company, Financial Survey Department, Runzheimer Park, Rochester, Wisconsin; Roy Fairchild, New York Stock Exchange, New York, New York; Mary Kay

Higgins, regional sales manager, Merrill Lynch, Pierce, Fenner and Smith, Inc., Santa Ana, California; Securities Industry Association, New York, New York; Wilfred Duval, investment counselor, Newport Beach, California; James A. Kaplan, Gifford Fong Investment Counsellors, Santa Monica, California; Roland Kelly, Argus Investment Counselling, Newport Beach, California; Emeritus Institute for Lifelong Learning for Older Adults, Saddleback College District, Mission Viejo, California; Western Gerontological Society, San Francisco, California; Anne Crotty, attorney, trust officer, Security Pacific National Bank, Los Angeles, California; Robert Hanson, senior vice-president, trust officer, Title Insurance and Trust Company, Los Angeles, California; Jennifer Hardy, trust officer, Security Pacific National Bank, Newport Beach, California; Geraldine Sandor, attorney, Newport Beach, California; William A. Schmidt, attorney, Newport Beach, California; Robert Frank, President, Anchor National Financial Services, Phoenix, Arizona; Dr. Pamela Bigelow, executive director, Tustin Women's Law Center, Tustin, California; Paul E. Garber, attorney, Monrovia, California; Roger D. Renfro, president, Corporate Benefits Consultant, Tustin, California. A special thank-you to Eunice Sollars, our fearless and faithful typist, who is typical of the Everywoman we have referred to in this book. She has been in the position of a divorcée and is more recently widowed. A teacher by education, she changed careers in mid-life and has been financially responsible for herself for many years. To all "Eunices" everywhere, we say "Thank you" for giving the old cliché "Never underestimate the power of a woman" a new credibility.

Contents

Foreword

This book is written for the "Everywoman"—the feminist woman, the total woman, and all the women somewhere in between: the wealthy woman, the low-income woman, and the multitude of middle-income women; the married woman, the single woman; the woman who is employed outside the home, the contented homemaker, the divorced woman, the widow; the woman attending school, the young woman, the mid-life woman, the mature woman; the Everywoman—you—in the hope that it will improve your life by motivating you to become aware of your financial situation.

This is not a book that is going to show you how to make a million dollars in the stock market or how to invest your money in gold or protect your inheritance. This is a book to help educate you towards taking charge of your financial life, by offering tips on budgeting your income, purchasing a home or a car, types of insurance you should have, establishing credit, getting a job and other financial basics—in general, how to cope financially, whether you live from paycheck to paycheck or own your own oil well.

Even with the vast knowledge that is becoming more and more available to women in regard to finance, there is no ironclad formula that will automatically enable you to become financially sound or that will guarantee you lifelong security. Each woman's financial and personal situation is unique. Your main goal should be: to begin to be aware of your financial situation (where your money is going and why), to get proper advice, and to establish realistic financial goals for yourself. The attitudes of "Don't worry your pretty little head about it" and "I'll think about that tomorrow" are as out of date for today's woman as the attitude of "Keep her barefoot and pregnant." Whether married or single, you must learn to look to yourself for your financial security. This does not necessarily mean that every woman must go out and get a job, but since the average wife will be a widow for five to ten years, the divorce rate is rapidly approaching one out of two marriages, and many young women are not including marriage in their plans, all women must become realistic and educate themselves financially. To paraphrase the French statesman Talleyrand, "War and finance are much too serious to be left entirely in the hands of men." When it comes to money management, as poet James R. Lowell said (and the women we talked to would agree), "One thorn of experience is worth a whole wilderness of warning."

1

Dollars and Sense

As an enlightened woman you are no doubt proud of your awareness. You consider yourself up to date on numerous issues and take pride in the progress women have made and are making. If you are typical of many women, however, your financial position seems to be in last place in the great race for equality. In the past, women have often been shut out of the financial picture or have been preoccupied elsewhere. They have often had (or wanted) to leave their financial security in the hands of someone else. Also, because of a lack of information available on the new laws and benefits that affect "female finance," women have not always been cognizant of the best way to go about managing their money.

With more and more women earning their own money, they realize they must have a greater say in financial matters since they have come to realize it is no longer "the hand that rocks the cradle that rules the world"; it is the hand that holds the checkbook. You as an aware woman are beginning to want a piece of the action. You wish to attain a greater financial awareness for yourself. For those of you who have been handling the family finances, you realize it is time to increase your financial knowledge. Test yourself on the following quiz. If you are unable to answer even one of the questions, you will find this book important to your financial future and worth saving for reference.

1. Do you know what the initials CFP stand for?
2. Do you know why your car insurance is higher if you are a single woman?
3. Do you know where to go for advice on money matters?
4. Do you know what type of insurance a woman should carry?
5. Do you know the definition of a mutual fund?
6. Do you know the safest way to earn interest on your money?
7. Do you know why it is important to establish credit in your own name?
8. Do you know how to avoid being without assets if you are widowed?
9. If you were forced to take over the family finances, would you know where to begin?
10. Do you know what to look for when purchasing a car?
11. Do you know how to start your own retirement plan?
12. Do you know the logistics of getting a job?
13. Do you know how to set up and stay on a budget?
14. Do you know how to make sense out of the stock market?
15. Do you know which Social Security laws apply especially to women?

Finance is the most basic of subjects; money is needed in order to buy the requirements of life—food, shelter, clothing. Money is also needed to pursue life's pleasures and to secure your future. When you look at the subject as a whole, it can be overwhelming. But if you break it down to parts of a total sum, finance becomes less complex. We can learn about finance by taking the time to study it, through classes or books. Financial knowledge is an ongoing study. It needs to be constantly updated. Many magazines and newspapers now run regular features and columns on money and money management. It is important for a woman to keep herself up to date on the latest financial information.

All of us need help at times with how to spend, save, or invest our funds properly. Very few people can accomplish this alone. Even the greatest economic wizards require the services of another expert on occasion. As a woman who wishes to be aware of her finances you should know the experts you can go to for assistance, whether you have a small, large, or (like most) medium income. Choosing someone to help you financially is somewhat like choosing a doctor. You may have to shop around in order to find someone you have confidence in, someone you feel comfortable with. Just as doctors have different specialties, so do financial experts. Listed below are various categories of financial experts who can be of aid to you:

Certified Financial Planner (CFP)—can be found in the Yellow Pages under "Financial Consultants." A CFP will look at all your assets and liabilities and help you to prepare a budget, help you decide how to invest your money, and, in some instances, help you invest it. Brokerage houses sometimes have CFPs on their staff. CFPs are usually paid per consultation or by commission. (See budget chapter for more information.)

Stockbrokers—Any reputable New York Stock Exchange member firm has trained its brokers in the knowledge of all forms of investments, including stocks, bonds, and insurance. Some are even qualified to help you do tax planning. A stockbroker is basically a sales professional and earns her/his living by selling the particular products her/his firm endorses.

Accountants or Tax Consultants—These are professional people trained to do your bookkeeping and to keep you advised of the newest tax laws. Accountants are usually paid by the hour, and tax consultants, per income tax return. A bank or savings and loan officer can recommend one to you.

Insurance Brokers or Agents—An insurance broker sells numerous insurance products from various companies. A broker has agents working for her/him. There are also companies that employ agents to sell only their policies. A chartered life underwriter (CLU) is qualified to do a form of estate planning. Insurance is broken down into two broad categories: life and disability; fire and casualty. You can arrange to have your policies examined by an insurance consultant. The duty of a consultant is to analyze your existing policies and tell you where you are lacking or overinsured. The consultant cannot sell you anything. All fees for insurance policies are included as part of the premium you pay on policies purchased.

Investment Counselors—can invest your money in stocks, bonds, or real estate. They will also maintain your financial records and prepare figures for income tax purposes. Investment counselors are paid a percentage of the assets you have to invest. These fees could well be deductible for income tax purposes. Stockbrokers generally recommend investment counselors. The fees are in addition to the ones which are paid to the stockbroker.

Bank/Savings and Loan Officers, or customer service representatives—can describe the various services that are available to you, from a simple checking account to a home loan. They will often help you with financial problems as a free service. Springing up over this past half decade have been savings and loans and banks founded and managed by women for women. Besides the normal banking and savings and loan activities, they feature classes to educate women in finances.

Lawyers—A lawyer is basically someone who knows the law. What this has to do with your finances becomes important when you are going through, or contemplating, a divorce. Also, a lawyer helps you prepare your will and a trust if you want one. She/he devises estate plans, sometimes with the help of an accountant, so that your retirement days can be simplified and so that when you die, your estate will not be eaten up by taxes. Sometimes you need a lawyer to help you get out of debt. Lawyers' fees are usually on an hourly basis. Law clinic or Legal Aid fees are by consideration. You can call your county bar association for lawyers who specialize in family law or go to a clinic if you are unable to afford a private lawyer.

After you have found an expert to help advise you, just what type of advice are you apt to receive? One such expert, Ronald Gable, a CFP, had this to say, "There are only three ways to assure your financial future—inheritance, which only happens to a chosen few; bank robbery, which is a rather desperate approach; or sound financial planning. I strongly advise the latter."

Gable teaches financial awareness classes for women. He feels that "people tend to handle their finances in 'pockets,' a little here and a little there. Because of emotions, lack of knowledge, fears, and prejudices, they fail to handle their financial situations properly." He advocates long-range planning and avoiding any type of insurance or investment program which contains gimmicks, such as "guaranteed ways to increase your money, which usually contain too many ifs.

In his opinion, *all* women, whether married or single, should become aware of their financial situation. He advises the financial novice to gather all facets of her finances together and sit down with someone who knows how to coordinate them. He also feels a woman should learn basic banking information. For example, "a bank is a good place for a checking account, but I prefer a savings and loan for a savings account, as you will earn more interest and you are not as apt to withdraw it." Gable also feels that married women and never-married women are in the most secure financial position. "Divorced and widowed women are in a more vulnerable one since they are faced with immediate money problems from the very first day their marital status changes."

He strongly advocates that married women be involved with the family's financial planning. "Women should no longer leave all the financial decisions to their husbands and should not allow their husbands to shut them out. If they don't handle the money, they should at least be aware of how much there is and where it is going."

Another financial expert, Velma Shaw of Bateman Eichler, Hill Richards, Inc., has been a stockbroker for twenty-four years. She has also been, at one time in her life, a divorcée. She spends much of her professional life teaching financial awareness to women, especially women who have been divorced or widowed. One of the problems she has seen over the years is that women tend to seek advice after the fact and do not equip themselves with beforehand knowledge. She recommends that a woman not mix her money and her social life. "Don't turn to some friend you see socially to handle your money. Keep your financial advisers as business acquaintances." Velma feels if a woman is fortunate enough to be left with an income and decides not to handle the money herself, she should employ the services of an investment counselor or consider putting her assets into a trust and having her money managed by a professional. "Since no two women's financial situations are alike, a woman should seek the knowledge and advice that will increase her financial awareness and in turn increase her financial assets."

The following list of dos and don'ts should help increase your financial awareness:

Do

1. Consult an expert to help set your financial awareness goals.
2. Set up a budget for living expenses that includes an emergency fund.
3. Establish the habit of saving—start a savings account even if it is only $10 a month (or less).
4. Take the time to make out a will.
5. Familiarize yourself with financial terms and phrases.
6. Establish credit in your own name whether you are married or single.

7. Make certain you have life insurance and disability insurance on yourself, especially if you are head of household.
8. Get into a retirement and medical plan where you work, or establish one on your own.
9. Find out what services are available at various banks and savings and loans near you. Select the ones that have the most to offer you.
10. Consider taking a money management class.

Don't

1. Go to someone whose advice will enrich his/her own pocket at the expense of yours.
2. Be afraid to learn more about your financial situation. When it comes to money, ignorance is not bliss.
3. Make hasty decisions. Take the time to evaluate the pros and cons of any financial decision.
4. Turn to friends for advice. Learn from their mistakes and successes, but don't depend on them to do your financial planning.
5. Forget to read all parts of any contract you sign, and remember, by law, you have three business days (excluding Saturdays, Sundays, and holidays) in which to cancel any signed contract which the salesperson asked you to sign in your home.

These dos and don'ts tie in with what the financial experts we interviewed feel are the ten most common Money Mistakes:

- The mistake of not setting up and sticking to a budget.
- The mistake of not establishing a savings plan.
- The mistake of not keeping adequate financial records.
- The mistake of not making out an up-to-date will and estate plan.
- The mistake of neglecting an insurance program.
- The mistake of not setting long-range financial goals and objectives.
- The mistake of shying away from professional advice when it is needed.
- The mistake of going too far in debt. Credit cards can be hazardous to your wealth.
- The mistake of doing your own taxes when you do not have the knowledge.
- THE MISTAKE OF NOT EDUCATING YOURSELF FINANCIALLY.

This last and most glaring mistake of not educating yourself can be found in the stories of women we spoke with.

Helen Parsons, a divorcée, is forty-three years old and has two grown children who have moved away. Helen, always supportive of her husband, stood by while he was struggling to climb the ladder of success in the securities industry. At the height of his career, he walked out on her and moved in with his young secretary. He did not want Helen to get a lawyer for their divorce, promising he would "take care of her." She believed him. Emotionally and physically the experience took its toll. Helen had not worked outside the home and had to go out and find a job to support herself since her husband ended up not supporting her. He also tried to get her to sign documents turning real estate interests over to him. Helen snapped out of her grief at that point and obtained a lawyer so that there could be no signing of documents without close inspection (to protect her interests) and to obtain a settlement. Helen told us, "My case has been tried, and we were ordered to return to court in several months for another look at my husband's financial status. At least with the help of my lawyer I've been able to face reality, and I am beginning to pick up the pieces of my life, both financially and emotionally. I should have faced reality a long time ago."

Celia Adhamson's husband, Earl, suffered a major stroke that left him without any comprehension of numbers. Celia was suddenly thrust into the position of having to take care of all money matters for the first time in her life. She could not even balance her checkbook. In desperation Celia told the teller at the bank about her plight. The teller passed her on to the bank's customer service representative. The representative gave Celia step-by-step instruction on how to balance her checkbook. Celia asked and was given answers to a multitude of financial questions, some of the simplest nature. The representative acquainted Celia with the booklets and pamphlets the bank offered free to its customers. Celia was so "turned on" to money matters once she found they were not "over her head," as she had always believed, that she enrolled in a financial course at a college near her home. The course covered budgeting, credit, bank accounts, etc. Celia also found out that some chapters of the National Organization for Women offer workshops for women who find themselves in similar situations, with special emphasis on older women's financial problems. (Consult your phone book for the chapter near you, or write National Organization for Women, 425 Thirteenth Street NW—Suite 1048, Washington, D.C. 20004.

"I never dreamed there was so much help available for women in regard to financial matters. There is no excuse for a woman being 'money ignorant,' and I found out you are never too old to take charge of your own financial situation." Celia is seventy-eight years young.

When Cheryl Stanius was divorced and left with two children, she had a job which paid quite well, but in her words, "I had never had to make any type of financial decisions, and I had no idea where to begin. I wrote to a financial newspaper columnist for some ideas on money management. Her answer was very helpful:

"'Money management broken down in its simplest form really calls for some basic knowledge translated into practice. You'll be able to learn as you go along, one decision at a time. If you have a decision to make, make it without being afraid that you have made a mistake. A budget is a basic foundation to thoughtful money management. [See chapter on budgets.] Additionally, be thoughtful about bargain hunting. Ask yourself, "Can I afford it?" not "Do I want it?" Open an account at a bank where you can have not only checking facilities but credit card privileges as well. Pay off any bills which might be overdue to save the heavy service charges. Also, current bills should be paid on time to avoid late charges. There are other avenues to explore, but the ideas stated here represent the basic essentials of learning to think financially.'"

These horror stories about the dangers of financial ignorance could go on and on; suffice it to say—take the time to learn about finance. It's your future that's at stake.

2
Getting a Job

For many women, getting a job is a necessity. For others, it is a desire, and for some, it is a means of filling a void created when children leave home. Whatever your reason for seeking a job, it is a very big step. You will find that you'll spend more time at your job than you will at home or anyplace else. It would be nice if you could spend that time doing something you like. This chapter should help you cope with that often traumatic experience of getting a job by familiarizing you with the steps you will need to take.

One of the first things you must remember is the dreadful fact that women are often discriminated against when being considered for a job, promoted less often than men, and are often stuck in "woman-type jobs" that pay less than "man-type jobs." For example, today nine out of ten women will work at some point in their lives, yet 79 percent of them will end up in clerical work. Women account for 99 percent of all typists, but only 1 percent of women repair them. On the average, typewriter repair work pays more than typing work. On the other hand, 99.7 percent of electricians are men. Electricians earn an average of $330 per week, while a stenographer's pay averages $159 for the same period.

A publication you may be interested in when preparing to get a job is the U.S. Labor Department's booklet *Occupations in Demand* (available from any office of the U.S. Employment Service or your public library or by writing Consumer Information Center, Pueblo, Colorado 81009). The booklet states that in traditional women's fields (whatever that means) the greatest need is for secretaries, bookkeepers, nurses, and telephone operators. That didn't surprise you, did it? Other skilled workers mentioned that are the most in demand are auto mechanics, carpenters, plumbers, bricklayers, welders, machinists, and short-order cooks. This booklet tells where these jobs can be found. The facts and figures clearly show women are paid less than men in every line of work. Dr. Joyce Brothers says that considering wages, it costs $5,000 to be a woman. That is how much less the average woman earns than the average man. Not only that, women's relative income position has deteriorated in most occupation groups during the last twenty years.

Among clerical workers, the average salary of women in 1974 was 59 percent of that of men employed in clerical work; the proportion was 69 percent in 1962. This is a continuation of a long-term downward trend from 1956, when women clerical workers' salaries were 72 percent of men's. This trend is consistent in each occupational category; women's relative incomes indicate that earnings are still considerably less than men's. The 1977 statistics showed that men and women in the labor force had almost the same amount of schooling, and more women than men had completed high school. Obviously we have not progressed as far as the media would lead us to believe.

This all could be turned around overnight if women throughout the country simply refused to work until they were paid the same wages men would be paid for the same jobs and promoted as often as men would be. It would also be nice if, as the song says, "it rained pennies from heaven." It simply isn't going to happen. As long as women have themselves and others to support, they cannot always obey their consciences.

This chapter is not meant to ignore these discriminatory facts and offer lighthearted pie-in-the-sky advice. We are simply telling you how it is for a woman who is entering or reentering the work force. Whether you are able to take a stand against sex, wage, age, or promotion discrimination, only you can determine. We will offer some pertinent information to help you prepare for and obtain a job. The rest is up to you.

PREPARING TO GET A JOB

If you decide you want to get, or must get, a job in the future or if you would like to get a better-paying job than you have now, there are several things you should be doing to prepare yourself.

Many junior and four-year colleges are now offering vocational planning classes especially for women. There, through a series of tests and questionnaires, you will be able to find where your interests and skills are concentrated. You will also be apprised of where the jobs are, how to go about finding one, and how to develop marketable skills. You will learn to compose a résumé and receive tips on making job interviews a success.

On the basis of the information you learn in class, you might have a better idea of what type of job you'd like and are suited for or what future classes you might take to develop a marketable skill if you don't already have one. A lot of this will, of course, depend on whether you are looking for a job or a career. If you are lucky enough to be just starting out and income is not a major concern, you can get started on planning a career based on your talents and interests. If you are looking for a job to give you immediate income, this type of class can give you a realistic outlook on looking for and getting that job.

If you discover you do not have any marketable skills other than housekeeping (and you don't want to perform housekeeping duties on a daily basis for someone else), you should begin to obtain some specific skills (typing, bookkeeping, computer programming, etc.). Your state or community college is an excellent resource for training if you live near enough one to make attending it practical.

In many communities there are trade schools at which you can (for a fee; sometimes quite a large fee) learn a skill. Be wary of any agreement you sign at a trade school. Read it over carefully. Check with the Better Business Bureau if you are in doubt about the reputation of the school. Make sure the skill you are learning is not being taught on outmoded equipment. For example, if you are learning radiology, check with a hospital as to the type of equipment they use.

Patty Coffman spent $500 to learn a skill in the computer industry at a trade school. Upon applying for a job after graduation, she was told that the skills she had learned were ten years out of date. Needless to say, she did not get the job.

If you are interested in going to a four-year college to take some classes or to earn a degree in a particular field, do some research first at the library or with your counselor to see what job opportunities in that line of work exist. In California, for example, it is no longer feasible to obtain a teaching credential, because teaching jobs are very scarce. Ten years ago every other college student in California majored in education, believing it to be a very marketable skill.

You may already have a marketable skill you are unaware you have, something you have always thought of as a hobby or something you have done on a volunteer basis that can be literally put to work.

Dorothea Simmons had been a schoolteacher's wife for many years. She had always corrected and edited class papers for her husband, Carl. When Carl died unexpectedly, shortly before his retirement, Dorothea did not think she had any marketable skills. While looking in newspapers and magazines for any possible sign of a job for which she was qualified, she found several ads for manuscript editors. "It dawned on me that's what I had basically been doing for years—and with so many people feeling they are great authors, I pick up enough work to augment my income."

Nancy Roberts was reared in New Orleans and cultivated some superb cooking skills but considered them a hobby. When she and her husband were divorced, she was at her wit's end as to how she could adequately support herself and spend time with her young son. A friend of Nancy's asked if she would make a dessert for a dinner party she was having. At the dinner party one of the guests asked about the dessert. After being given Nancy's name, she called and asked Nancy if she would make several of the same desserts for a large party. From that first dinner party, Nancy eventually started a small catering business, which is thriving today.

Sometimes volunteer worker skills can turn into a paying job. Heather Olney had been a volunteer worker in a small hospital for several years. Each year her volunteer duties increased as the hospital grew in size. While glancing through the classified ads, she saw a want ad for a hospital position which required the skills she had been developing as a volunteer. She obtained an interview and took a résumé which showed the extent of her volunteer capabilities. Armed with a recommendation from the hospital administration, she got her job.

We do not want to imply that getting a job is as easy as just putting some hobby to work for you, but we do want to emphasize that women traditionally tend to underestimate their abilities and do not always recognize their talents. You should take them into consideration when assessing your skills.

Before applying for a job you must obtain a Social Security number, if you do not already have one. A Social Security card may be obtained at your local Social Security office. You should apply there for your card several weeks before you need it, for it usually takes about four weeks to receive your card. The number on your card is used to keep a record of your earnings; consequently, you will need just one Social Security number during your lifetime.

The Social Security law requires that you furnish evidence of age, identity, and citizenship or alien status when you apply for a Social Security number. If you need help in obtaining any documents, get in touch with any Social Security office. There are a variety of documents that can be submitted as evidence of your age and citizenship. A birth certificate or church record of birth or baptism is preferred as proof of your age and place of birth. If neither of these records is available, one of the following documents can be used to show your date of birth or age:

School record
Church record
State or federal record
Insurance policy
Marriage record
Military discharge papers
Delayed birth certificate
United States passport
Any other record which shows
    your age or date of birth

To show evidence of identity (you are who you say you are):

Driver's license
State identity card
Voter's registration
School identification card
Work badge or building pass
Military ID
United States passport
United States identity card

Credit card if your signature is shown
Library card with signature
Any other document which shows either
    your signature or your photograph

If you were born outside the United States or are an alien, check with the Social Security office to see what documents you must furnish.

If you have lost your original Social Security card, contact a Social Security office to obtain a duplicate. While it is only necessary to know your number, carrying your card is an excellent idea. You should also contact the Social Security office if you change your name—to get a new card showing your new name (you will keep the same number). Once you are working, your employer will be required to give you a statement of the Social Security contribution deducted from your pay. This is done at the end of each year or when you stop working for that employer. These deductions are reported on your W-2 Form and will help you maintain your Social Security record.

FINDING A JOB

When you feel you are prepared, one of the best ways of going about finding a job is to tell everyone you know that you are looking for a job. You will be surprised to find how many people know of people who know of people who are looking for an employee.

Another way is to consult the classified ads, of course, or to pound the pavement and leave your name at a lot of places that are hiring or may be hiring in the future. If you have been taking classes at a college or business school, it will often have a job placement service you can utilize.

If you have tried any or all of the above methods to no avail, you may be forced to go through an employment agency. We do not mean to imply that this should be the last resort, but you should be aware of a few facts when seeking employment through an agency. As with any other kinds of businesses, there are reputable and not-so-reputable employment agencies. You should ask to see a business license when selecting an agency. When filling out any form you are asked to complete, be careful of what you sign. Read it over thoroughly (it is wise to take it home and read it, then bring it back the next day).

There are fee and nonfee employment agencies. A fee agency is one that charges the employee (you) a fee for finding a job, and a nonfee agency is one that charges the employer for finding an employee; naturally the nonfee would be more advantageous to you.

A fee agency can take a big chunk out of your paychecks, but if you are unable to obtain a job any other way, it might be worth it. We are of the personal opinion that you shouldn't have to pay to get a job (you might be interested to know that the United States is the only country where it is still legal to charge an employee a fee). There are federal regulations now, however, that set limits on what you can be charged by an agency by stating the percentage of your salary that can be charged as a fee. Be wary of an agency that wants you to "sign a little piece of paper for the files," or you may find you owe the agency some money, and be very explicit about what types of jobs you will not take. If you are not very definite about this, you will waste your time by being sent out on interviews for jobs in which you are not at all interested or suited for.

There are a growing number of employment agencies (or personnel agencies, as they are sometimes called) that are specifically geared to women, especially women who are reentering the job market. We contacted several of these agencies throughout the country to gather advice for women seeking employment.

According to Ruth Urban, manager of Abigail Abbott Personnel Service in Southern California, there are lots of jobs available, but the problem is finding *qualified* women to fill them. She feels many women do not adequately prepare themselves to enter the work force. In addition she feels that with all the mature women returning to the work force, employers need to be made aware of the advantages of hiring the more mature woman since "Hiring is done from the pit of the stomach and is very subjective. If the employer is used to a twenty-five-year-old sitting at the receptionist desk, it's difficult to talk him in to a forty-year-old woman. We find, however, that once hired, the mature woman becomes a valuable employee."

Mrs. Urban also notes that some women do not list all their qualifications. Priscilla McLean was one of these women; she had been fund raising chairman for several years for a charitable organization in her city. She had directed and trained as many as 150 individuals on how to canvass and solicit money and was responsible for collecting tens of thousands of dollars. When her husband, Art, died in an automobile accident soon after their divorce, her alimony ceased. During her first interview at an agency she told the interviewer she had never worked before and ended up with a menial file clerk job. In telling this story, Mrs. Urban pointed out that any woman with the skills that Priscilla used in her charity campaign should have made those qualifications known to the interviewer. It might well have led to a higher-paying and more challenging job, such as a paid fund raiser.

If you do not have a specific skill, Mrs. Urban advises that the best way to find a job which might lead to a career is to get your foot in the door as a trainee in an entry-level position—stuffing envelopes if necessary. "Remember, employers first supply goods and services and then career development if you're lucky. Typing may be the only way to get in this door, whether you like it or not."

Some pointers for your initial interview at the agency:

1. Go dressed as if you were to have an actual interview with an employer.
2. List *all* your qualifications.

One final suggestion from Mrs. Urban is that a woman take jobs through temporary services such as Kelly Girl. "It may be the simplest of tasks, but it at least gets you inside the door, acquaints you with the job market, and gives you an opportunity to see what type of job and firm you would like to deal with. It can often lead to a full-time job with one of the companies you have filled a temporary position for."

Mary Wick of Mary Wick Personnel Agency in Tulsa, Oklahoma, also told us she would advise a woman going back to work to take jobs through a temporary agency.

"The jobs aren't as demanding, and it's a great way to brush up on your skills and get used to a job again. It's also a good way for a gal fresh out of college or secretarial school to find out what type of firm she would like to work for."

Ms. Wick feels more and more women are progressing from clerk typist (in Tulsa that position pays around $500 a month) to executive secretary, then on to administrative assistant (which pays $1,300–$1,500 a month). She has also seen many women enter sales, especially real estate sales, in the last few years. "Though the salary is usually commission only, women are making nice livings from sales and are finding they are very good at it. A woman who goes into sales should make certain she also has a sales contract."

She emphasizes as well that women should brush up on their

skills before seeking employment and have a nice appearance. However, "It is hard to sell a nice appearance without skills."

Kathi Carroll manages the Jaci Carroll Services Office in Waterbury, Connecticut. Waterbury is a city of approximately 100,000
people. Most of the jobs available to women in this area of the
country are light-industrial or clerical work. "Unfortunately, if you
can't type, it's difficult to get a job. A woman simply must have a
skill, and typing is a skill."

One case history Kathi related to us was of a woman in her late
twenties who was a college graduate but had never worked. After
she was divorced, she needed a job. The employment agency placed
her in a job as a personnel clerk at a large corporation. As she
became more accustomed and proficient at her work, the company
began giving her salary increases and promotions. Recently the
corporation sent out an announcement naming her its new director
of personnel. This was the same woman the agency had placed several
years before as a clerk-typist and whose only training was a liberal
arts college degree.

"This is an exception to the rule, however, so I would advise a
woman to learn typing and bookkeeping. I hope the job market for
women will change; but we are in a transitional period, and like it or
not, if you have basic office skills, you can usually get a job."

Ann Jones has a professional placement agency in Kansas City,
Missouri. She told us that if a woman lives in a metropolitan area
and has no skills, she suggests going to a large corporation for employment. Although companies such as American Telephone or other
large utility companies do not use an employment agency or personnel service as a means to hire employees, Ms. Jones said that she
has directed women to their personnel departments. Since these
kinds of companies train employees to do a certain job, they help a
woman acquire a skill.

She also agrees that if a woman wants a career in a specialized
field, she may have to type just to get her foot in the door.

WHAT TO LOOK FOR IN A JOB

What you look for in a job depends on why you are seeking a job:
(1) You are supporting yourself; (2) you are supporting the family; (3)
you are helping support the family; (4) your children are grown, and
you would like to go back to work. Your demands of what a job must

offer will decrease in strict proportion to your increased needs for money. A job you wouldn't consider taking if you didn't need the money becomes the job you take if you do. There are, however, some features of a job you would be wise to take into consideration:

Is the company reputable? (Check through Better Business Bureau or a similar organization.)

If you are the sole support of yourself and/or your family, fringe benefits should be considered when deciding on a job.

Does the company offer an adequate medical and/or dental plan? (See insurance chapter.)

Does it offer a retirement plan? (See retirement chapter.)

Does it have a credit union? (This is not a must, but it can be very helpful when you need to borrow money.)

Does it offer a paid vacation and medical leave, and if so, after how long?

A job with a large company or corporation usually offers a lot more in the way of benefits than, for example, a small dress shop. Even if the salary you are offered in a small firm or business is larger, consider what you will have to pay to purchase your own medical/disability and retirement plans and see if you would actually be ahead.

As strange as it may sound, having a job can be expensive, and this is one aspect you should consider when you are going to work. It is also important to figure out how much these expenses will chip away at your paycheck if you are in need of a job for your livelihood.

First of all, if you are married, your and your husband's income will most likely be taxed at a higher rate when yours is added to his. Also, you will no longer be a deduction on his income tax form, although you can be claimed as an exemption on the paycheck for withholding purposes.

Additionally, if you don't have a second car, you will probably need one unless you have convenient public transportation. There will be car-related expenses, such as gas, oil, insurance, wear and tear, and replacement costs.

You will, no doubt, need a more extensive wardrobe than you now have and a gross of pantyhose. Also, you can expect an increase in your clothes-cleaning bill. There will also be the matter of eating lunches out, unless you have the time to pack your own. This can get very expensive. Baby-sitting, and if you're lucky, cleaning lady expenses, can put a sizable dent in your paycheck. You will also find yourself eating dinner out more often and purchasing prepared foods, which are more expensive. The deductions for local, state, and federal taxes will also decrease your disposable income. (See "Budgeting Your Income" chapter).

In some cases it can literally cost you money to go to work, but anticipating what your expenses will be will help you know what minimum salary you will need to have to meet these expenses and still make money. Isn't that the point of getting a job?

FILLING OUT A JOB
APPLICATION FORM

When you apply for a job, you will be asked to fill out a fairly standard job application form. It will vary slightly from place to place; but basically firms will request the same information, and unless you are blessed with a fantastic memory, there are certain documents and facts you should take along with you to make recall easier.

First, of course, you should take your Social Security card or number and your driver's license with you. Take along your employment record (a list of where you have worked, from exactly when to exactly when, for whom you worked, your reason for leaving, your starting salary, and your final salary). Without these facts jotted down, it can be very time-consuming and nerve-wracking to try to remember. The applicant is often asked to list references other than relatives, so you may want to have some names, addresses, and phone numbers jotted down.

By law (the Equal Employment Act), a job application should not ask for your sex, your age, your marital status, who's going to care for your children while you work, your race, or your religion. However, most forms do ask for your sex, your age, and your marital status. You can refuse to answer, telling the prospective employer it is unlawful to ask, but you should be aware that you may not get the job. Once in a great while a future employer may find it rather refreshing for someone to take a stand; but for the most part, he/she will label you as a troublemaker, and who needs a troublemaker in the organization? Only you and your financial status can decide if you are going to stand up for your rights and risk not getting the job, or if you fill in the blanks and get the job, you may be able to help change the system from the inside.

One very annoying question often asked on a job application or during an interview is: "Who will care for your children while you are at work?" Obviously it is nobody's business, as long as you are at work every day, but it may still be asked. Feel free to say, "None of your business," and apply elsewhere, but if you really do want that particular job, an adequate reply would be: "Since I am as conscientious at home as I would be on the job, my children will be well cared for."

Often when seeking a job, the applicant is asked to take a battery of tests. For some women this is an absolute trauma, as testing days may have been twenty and, in some cases, thirty years ago.

The tests comprise, if you have never worked before, a spelling and simple math test plus a test designed to see if you know the alphabet (that you can file CAPITAL expenditures under "capital"—which has to do with money—and not "capitol"—which has to do with cities). You may also be asked to take a typing and shorthand test or to demonstrate your skills on an office machine. In some cases you may be given these same tests through an employment agency. No company today is supposed to administer general intelligence tests unless they are justified by the position being applied for. If you feel you are being overtested, you can complain, but you probably will not get the job. The way to combat testing phobia is not to be caught off guard. Go to your local library, or borrow your fifth-grade child's math book and speller. Read a secretary's manual for proper English usage. If you will take the time to follow these simple suggestions, you'll pass those tests with flying colors. Or at the very least you won't be unprepared!

THE RÉSUMÉ

If you are applying for a job as a bank teller, clerk, or typist, you will probably be asked to fill out only a job application, but if you are applying for a position as a secretary, a management position, or a job in a creative field (or in any area which may require a lot of prior experience), you will be asked for a résumé. More and more places of employment do request résumés. A résumé is a written statement of your personal and employment qualifications.

Your résumé should reflect and sell you. There are some dos and don'ts when it comes to résumés. A résumé can "make or break you" because it is the first image of you to a projected, prospective employer. Try to keep it to one page (see sample) if at all possible. If not, get heavy bond paper, and type on both sides. It has been our experience that employers do not read résumés more than a page long. A résumé should *always* be typed. It must be neat (it does not have to be the original, but make sure the copies are clean, clear, and legible).

It should contain the following information or variations of the following:

YOUR NAME

YOUR ADDRESS

TELEPHONE NUMBER

YOUR CAREER OBJECTIVES: What you want to be when you grow up, so to speak.

POSITION DESIRED: Or applied for.

SALARY REQUIREMENT: It is best to put "negotiable" but if you must have a minimum monthly income, do not be afraid to say so.

PROFESSIONAL QUALIFICATIONS: Where you have worked and in what position, but not details—they can go in your job application; a résumé should not look like a job history—only job highlights.

EDUCATION: Where you went to school; degrees earned.

HONORS AND AWARDS: It may seem odd to include that you were Miss Congeniality in 1966; but this gives a bit of a picture of you, and if you happen to be applying for a position that involves dealing with people, being Miss Congeniality may be important.

OUTSIDE INTERESTS OR HOBBIES: This is to let prospective employers know something about you, the person.

REFERENCES: You can either list two or three nonrelatives or put "Available upon request," which is often preferred and saves space.

SPECIAL QUALIFICATIONS: Speak eighteen languages fluently, can drive a limousine; available on weekends—any information that makes you a little different from someone else.

When composing a résumé, don't falsify, but make what information you put in sound impressive. Use active terms "responsible for," "head of," "served as."

Sylvia Dawson
16th Street
Newport Beach, CA
(714) 223-4161

EDUCATION   Ohio State University, Columbus, Ohio
                         B.A. Social Sciences   December 1977
                         GPA 2.95

                         Course work in Communications; Sociology;
                         Psychology; Survey Research; Data Analysis.

EXPERIENCE   Customer Service Representative   1/78-2/79
                         Blue Shield of Central Ohio
                         Columbus, Ohio

                         Analyzed medical insurance claims in order to
                         discuss and explain coverage information effec-
                         tively to Blue Shield subscribers.

                         Part-Time Administrative Office Assistant
                         6/76-8/77
                         Creative Arts Printing Company
                         Cleveland, Ohio

                         Assisted in compilation of purchase orders and
                         tracing delinquent accounts.

HONORS/CONTINUED   Dean's List. Completed Blue Shield Corporate
EDUCATION   Training Program. Honorary ratings in all course
                         work completed.

REFERENCES   Will be furnished upon request.

SONYA SAWYER
1352 Oleander Drive
Costa Mesa, CA 92626
(714) 541-8211

VOCATIONAL OBJECTIVE: A position at the executive secretary or administrative assistant level which will enable me to use and further
develop my creative and organizational skills.

EXPERIENCE:
ADMINISTRATIVE ASSISTANT, St. Michael's Presbyterian Church,
Newport Beach, Ca., 1978-1979. Assistant to the Director of
Children's Education. Responsible for public relations with 650
pupils, their parents, 150 teachers, and the church committee
structure in a program involving over 50 classes weekly. Develop
and implement special programs; design, lay out, and produce all
department publicity. Create displays and special effects. Non-
paying position.

TEMPORARY OFFICE WORK, Timely Temporary Service, South Gate, Ca.;
General Tire & Rubber Co., Los Angeles, Ca.; Stauffer Chemical
Co., South Gate, Ca., 1955-1959.

Did temporary office work, including bookkeeping (accounts
payable, accounts receivable, payroll), PBX-receptionist, and
general office duties.

Familiar with a variety of business machines, including the IBM
Selectric II typewriter, ten-key adding, posting, addressing and
folding machines, postage meter, ditto and mimeograph, dry mount
and laminating presses, and the A.B. Dick 321 Offset Duplicator.

VOLUNTEER EXPERIENCE: 1958-1979. Chairman, Children's Education Committee, St. Michael's Presbyterian Church, Newport Beach, Ca.;
Chairman, Ways & Means Committee, Jr. Ebell of Newport Beach, Ca.;
President, Southern California Council of Alpha Phi Alumnae;
and others.

Served as president and/or chairman of various volunteer groups
involved in organizing community service projects, educational
programs and fund raising.

Have done artwork for school, church, and charitable organizations
such as displays, flyers, posters, and program covers in addition
to free-lance work, including gift items and displays. Taught
crafts to senior citizens and children. Made classroom instructional materials at the Newport-Mesa Unified School District
Instructional Media Lab.

EDUCATION: California State University at Long Beach:
Bachelor of Arts with honors in Social Science,
Minor in Physical and General Science

REFERENCES: Available upon request.

In both cases the women who were applying for jobs had limited experience. Sylvia Dawson had just moved from Ohio to California, she was fresh out of school and too young (twenty-three) to have acquired much of an employment record. Her strongest asset was her excellent school record, which she emphasized on her résumé and she feels it helped her to obtain a position after only a few weeks in Southern California. Sonya Sawyer's case was a little different since she decided, at age forty-four, to reenter the job market after her children had gone to college. Having been employed outside the home only in the early years of her marriage, Sonya was a bit concerned about how to "sell" herself on her résumé. Consulting a friend of hers who was employed in a personnel department, Sonya was advised to list her very active volunteer participation on her résumé. As it turned out this volunteer experience was responsible for her obtaining a part-time job in the production department of a local newspaper, which soon worked into a full time position. In both cases the women's first contact with their future employer was a concise and well-organized résumé.

If you would like your résumé to receive more attention than the average one, and if you have a little money to spend, there are some alternatives to the one-typed-sheet style of résumé.

Edie Vanian told us she feels she got her job because of her résumé. "I was qualified all right, but so were several other people. I think the ingenuity of my résumé got me the job." She had her picture taken and prints made. She then purchased heavy bond, colored paper and created a "book" type of résumé by folding the paper in thirds and placing her picture in the first third, her typed résumé in the second, and a handwritten letter in the third. Even though she left her résumé at eleven different firms, she took the trouble of handwriting each letter, gearing it to that particular firm.

"Since I was applying for a job in an art-related field, I feel my out-of-the-ordinary résumé helped show what I could do."

Creating an unusual résumé, especially if the position is an unusual one, can be beneficial to you; but, remember, do not present one that is going to take too much of a potential employer's time, and stay away from a "cutesy" approach.

THE JOB INTERVIEW

After you have filled out your job application, you will probably be personally interviewed either at that time or at a later date. If you are applying for an executive job or a job that entails a lot of responsibility, you may have a "screening-out" interview. This is an interview in which the interviewer questions you, forms an initial opinion, and decides whether or not you are qualified for a second interview with the person or persons who have the authority actually to hire you.

During the interview it is important that you have a well-groomed appearance and retain eye contact with the interviewer. Don't look away or lower your gaze. Also, take charge of the interview without being bossy. Don't be intimidated. You are dealing with another person on a one-to-one level. Express yourself well, and speak so you can be heard. It can be very annoying to an interviewer to have to strain to hear someone speak.

Generally you are asked the same type of questions at each interview, worded in various ways: Why do you want this job, and what can you bring to it? What salary do you expect? Why did you leave your last job? What are your long-range career plans? Tell me about you, the person. Is there anything else you'd like to say?

Here are some possible answers to these questions, to have in mind. (Tailor them to your own situation, of course.)

Why Do You Want This Job, and What Can You Bring to It?

The answer, of course, is obvious—for the money and/or self-fulfillment—but that isn't what the interviewer is really asking. He is asking what you know about the firm and what is unique about *you* that you can bring to the job. In preparing an answer, you will want to have some knowledge of the firm (such as what exactly it does and its reputation in its field). You can get some background information by reading trade journals, asking around, checking at a library.

Karen Selza told us that she credits her beforehand knowledge of the company she works for as the major reason she got her job. "I was applying for a job in public relations for a computer company. I had been in public relations work before, but not at a computer company. Before I applied for the job, I went by and picked up a copy of the company's annual report. I also read up on the computer industry as a whole and familiarized myself with computer terms (which can boggle the mind). I called a stock brokerage house to find out if the company was listed (a public company). I also asked a friend in the computer industry what sort of reputation the company had within the trade. I then had the background knowledge to formulate what I could say when asked what I could bring to the job (based on the type of firm it was). The person who interviewed and subsequently hired me was very impressed, not only that I knew so much about the company but that I had taken the time to find it out. He felt if I were that thorough before I even got the job, I would be just the type of employee he was looking for. Of course, if I had not remained conscientious, I would not have kept the job. So far I have had several promotions."

What Salary Do You Expect?

This is an extremely difficult question. If you name too low a figure, it sounds as if you do not value your own work. If you name too high a figure, you may price yourself out of a job. You may want to respond by getting the interviewer to name a figure, so that you can negotiate from there. "What salary range did you have in mind for this position?" Remember, nine out of ten prospective employers will speak in terms of annual salary, not monthly or weekly.

If you are asked what you were receiving when you left your previous job, you may legitimately add 20 percent over your previous salary to allow for benefits you were receiving. If it was a very low salary, don't lie about it, but allude to the fact that you now have more experience.

If you have not worked before, you don't have much bargaining power unless you do some research on what that particular type of job pays. (Local classified ads that list salary for your type of position could be a place to start.) If you feel you are put on the spot, you can simply say, "To be perfectly frank about it, I don't have an exact figure in mind; but I want to be paid enough to reflect that my work has value, and I will expect to receive an increase within ninety days if my work is satisfactory."

Why Are You Looking for a New Job?

This can be a tricky question, so be careful how you word your answers. You really don't want to say, "I was bored out of my skull," "The boss was a fanny patter," "Too much work, too little pay," or "My co-workers were all gossips."

Why *are* you changing jobs? Are you relocating? Do you need more of a challenge? Did you feel you had gone as far as you could go there? Did you decide to take a new career direction? Was the office too far from home? Did you feel, realistically, that you were underpaid?

These can be some valid reasons to give. A good rule of thumb is to tell the truth; but word it nicely, and have your answers in mind ahead of time.

What Are Your Long-Range Plans?

What's really being asked here is: Are we going to hire you only to have you quit in three months—or if the least little thing goes wrong?

If the person interviewing you seems to be the very confident type, you might want to toss off, "I hope to have your job someday," but this can be dangerous. Better to answer in a way that will let him know that you do not consider this job as just a stepping-stone, but part of a definite plan of advancement that could take place within his company. "Right now I'm very excited about being hired as a copywriter, but I would like to move up to feature editor, then editor, then publisher. That way I will know all aspects of the various jobs."

Tell Me About You, the Person

This is really the most important question of the interview. He's really not interested in the fact that you were Aunt Evalyne's favorite niece; he's trying to get to know what type of person you are.

Here is where your résumé can come in handy. Rather than rattle on trying to find a subject he's interested in, refer him to your résumé. He has probably looked it over, so you can safely ask, "Is there any information you would like me to expand on?"

If not, *briefly* tell him your background and your hobbies but do not go into a lot of personal information. "My husband went through mid-life crisis and ran off with his young receptionist, and I need a job."

Generally you should limit what you say to around five minutes, to make it clear that you can express yourself, but no so long that you sound like a nonstop talker.

If you haven't been previously employed, now is your time to emphasize how many committees and organizations you have been in charge of. He may take this into consideration when deciding whether or not to hire you.

Gayleen Pfister disagrees with this, however. She was basically a housewife who stayed home for twenty years, brought up her children, and had recently completed some additional courses in journalism which complemented the degree she already held.

"With my nifty résumé a friend had helped me compose (after reading that volunteer and church work would now be considered job training), I went out to knock 'em dead. I quickly learned that they couldn't care less about any previous experience other than a paying job. On top of that, in every job interview I was asked to take a typing and math test, which I failed miserably. I was, or thought I was, an intelligent woman, but I just hadn't dealt with the business world. Being very good with people and able to write, I thought I'd be perfect for a public-relations-type job. But that was not the case. What it boils down to: I was forty years old, with no marketable skills. In desperation I went to an employment agency, and in my case, that was a disaster. Fortunately I had a husband to support me, so I could hold out for something in the field I wanted— newspaper, public relations, or magazine work. I made that fact abundantly clear to my counselor at the agency (I thought), but she still sent me out on unbelievable interviews, describing them as having something to do with my field. One time I was sent out to an accounting firm under the guise that I would be interviewing customers and writing up their answers. I was immediately plopped down in front of a complicated-looking adding machine. I gave away the fact that the job wasn't for me when I asked how to turn on the machine. I finally told the man who was to interview me that I wasn't qualified for the job. If it hadn't been for his kindness, I would have been in tears. He even called the agency and voiced his displeasure to them for subjecting a client to what I had had to go through. When I returned to the agency, I told my counselor in no uncertain terms never to subject me to that type of situation again. I ended up taking a job on the staff of a magazine selling ads and doing a little of everything but was never paid, as my boss turned out to be dishonest. I had to pay the employment agency for finding me the job, however. I later found I could demand a refund, which I did, and needless to say, I quit the job.

"I did, however, gain experience while on the magazine. I met another woman writer, and we formed a partnership. We began to write and publish in local magazines. From there I eventually got an editorial job (for pay) on a magazine. Looking back on it all, I find it's quite funny. But at the time it was a very traumatic experience."

Is There Anything Else You'd Like to Say?

This is a question that can immediately cause you to draw a blank, but it can be an opportunity to reiterate important points you want the interviewer to remember and to mention anything you might have forgotten. (This is where researching a company before your interview can be important.)

"I am extremely proficient in math, so I could also do the billing."
"I speak several languages, so I could deal with your non-English-speaking customers."

This is also the time for you to find out a few things about the job if they have not been covered. Exactly what is your job title, and more important, EXACTLY WHAT IS YOUR JOB? Often job titles do not fit the job. "Corporate secretary" sounds impressive, but it might mean you make coffee and sharpen pencils for the people on executive row. Naturally you don't want to whip out a big list of functions you won't perform (like making the coffee), but make sure you know what is expected of you for the most part before you take the job. You will also want to know the promotion and salary review policies and just what position you can attain in the company with your background.

Terminating the interview will usually be done by the interviewer as he/she is used to having to move people along, but if an uncomfortable silence develops or if the interviewer is a bit non-committal, a closing line could be: "When would be a good time to call you to find out your decision?" This way you are not only ending the interview but finding out what's the next step.

A follow-up letter ("Thank you for your courtesy, and once again, let me say how very interested I am in this job") is always a good idea. Even if you do not get the job, your courtesy is important. "It was very nice meeting and visiting with you, and I hope you will keep me in mind in the future." Who knows? Maybe the person who got the job will not work out. You may be next on the list.

Some of the things you may observe at an interview can indicate to you if you really want a job with that particular company. Women we have talked to have mentioned everything from observing fighting among the employees to the telling of off-color jokes as reasons why they did not take a particular job.

At any rate, every interview makes the next one easier, until you reach that ideal situation where you, the job, and the interview come together in a perfect combination. Remember, when you accept a job, it might as well be a marriage "for better for worse from nine to five every day," and if it's a job you'll feel uncomfortable with, it will show at work, in your after-hours personality, and in your personal relationships.

MATURE WOMEN AND THE JOB MARKET

We all know women face sex and wage discrimination, but do mature women (thirty-five and over) face additional discrimination—age discrimination? Consider these facts:

In 1975 (latest statistics available) nearly one-third of all women workers were forty-five years of age or over. The labor force participation rate of mature women has risen dramatically since 1950, although the rate has stabilized somewhat since the late 1960s.

Increases in labor force activity have been particularly pronounced for married women. Women who drop out of the labor force when they marry or start a family have increasingly sought to return to work when the youngest child begins school or when family responsibilities have lessened.

Mature women, however, are still less likely to be working than other age groups because they encounter many obstacles in the job market as they seek to enter or reenter the labor force. They often find employers unwilling to credit their previous work experience or their activities during the period they were out of the labor force as evidence of potential. Consequently, with rusty or outmoded job skills, little or no recent experience, inadequate counseling, or a lack of job contacts, they frequently must settle for low-skill or low-paying jobs which require little or no specialized training and which afford limited opportunity for upward mobility. These entry or reentry difficulties are reflected in mature women's occupational status and earnings, in their higher incidence of poverty, and in the length of their unemployment.

The average income from earnings and all other sources for women aged forty-five years and over was only $4,342 in 1974. This figure, however, refers to all reported income, including earnings from part-time jobs. Also included is income from all sources other than earnings, for those women who did not work at all. Among the women over thirty-five who worked year round full time, the average income was $7,773 in 1974, substantially lower than the $14,817 for men forty-five and over and about the same as for women twenty-five to forty-four years ($7,856). With the increasing age of mature women there is a greater likelihood of their having low incomes or of their not being able to find jobs at all.

Yes, indeed, mature women face discrimination. It is usually well hidden—prospective employers, for example, will not say, "You are too old." They will tell you, "You are overqualified." Don't let them get away with it. Ask exactly what they mean by "overqualified." Point out that statistics show that when a mature woman does obtain a job, she has a lower incidence of absenteeism than a younger woman, that she is not going to have to be called home for a sick baby, that her generation does not consider work a four-letter word. Depending on how desperately you want or need the job, ask yourself, "Do I really want to work for someone who doesn't care how good an employee is at her work, but only that she is twenty-five years old, with an ample bustline, or for a company that will hire a man in place of a woman and pay him more?" If you really do feel that you have a case, that you have been discriminated against because of age, you can report the firm to the Labor Board, the Fair Employment Practices Commission, the American Civil Liberties Union, the Status of Women Commission in your state (addresses appear in credit chapter).

Jane Ray is the director of the Career Clinic in Seattle, Washington. She spent fifteen years as a personnel director of a corporation before entering the employment agency field.

We asked her how she handled subliminal discrimination against older women. She told us, "I won't let it happen. I tell the employer right away that if he won't hire a mature individual, I don't want to waste my time or his by sending a woman for an interview. I sometimes feel that I'm a social worker at heart. I too have been divorced and had to return to work. Often I see women who have been married twenty years and now need to return to work for the first time in their lives. They feel they have no skills whatsoever. I have to find those skills out of Scout work, hospital volunteerism, or P.T.A. activities. I find in Seattle there are more office positions that cannot be filled because of the lack of qualified people than in any other city, so the mature woman here at least has a chance. The Pacific Northwest is also ripe for women who want careers in management, especially in the insurance field.

"Though discrimination does exist, if women would not look down on typing, they could more easily find a job. It still is a very effective tool for getting your foot in the door. Then you can help shove that door open further for other women, especially the mature woman."

STARTING YOUR OWN BUSINESS

With the increase in women returning to or entering the work force and not always being able to find a job, many of them are considering starting businesses of their own or going into partnerships and starting businesses with another person. Even women who are already employed are opting to start their own businesses.

Since the subject of starting a business could be a book in itself, we will just lightly touch on the subject and suggest that you beg or borrow the U.S. Small Business Administration's booklet *Starting and Managing a Small Business of Your Own*. It is invaluable. To obtain a copy, write:

Superintendent of Documents
U.S. Government Printing Office
Washington, D.C. 20402
Send $1.35

Along with the many helpful ideas offered by the Small Business Administration in this booklet, it suggests that when you are thinking about starting a business, you pick the field you know most about or a field you like.

You can start by writing out a summary of your background and experience. Include jobs you have had, schools you have attended, and your hobbies. Then write down what you would like to do. Try to match what you would like to do with what you have done. If you do not like the business you choose, your lack of enthusiasm may lead to failure.

In making a selection, remember that the more experience and training you have had which can be put to direct use in operating a particular enterprise, the better your chances of success since many small business fail each year. So pick the field you know most about. The best way to obtain knowledge of a business is through actual experience in it.

Lucille Brookson had always loved house plants and had a real green thumb. Her friends began to bring her their wilted and weary house plants, and Lucille would tenderly nurse them back to health. With her children in school all day, Lucille had toyed with the idea of starting some kind of business. Feeling that there were getting to be too many plant shops, she had dismissed her first idea of opening one. A friend suggested that, instead, she open a plant hospital. Lucille did just that and was quite successful, and since some of the plant shops in her town went out of business, she now offers plants for sale.

"I suppose in a monetary way I'm not a rousing success, but I have been able to pay the rent on my shop, meet expenses, and make a small profit. If I didn't have other income, I wouldn't be able to support myself, but I am seeing the business grow, if you'll pardon the pun, and I am very contented making money out of a hobby I love."

Before you even consider starting a business, there are a few statistics you should know: Out of all new firms started, about one-third are discontinued within one year; about 50 percent are discontinued within two years; and approximately two-thirds, after five years. After this the discontinuation rate drops rapidly, so your chances of success improve the longer you stay in business. Younger businesses tend to be discontinued first, with the largest single cause of business failure attributed to poor management. According to Dun & Bradstreet, Inc., a corporation which supplies credit and financial information on business, lack of managerial experience and aptitude has accounted for around 90 percent of all small-business failures.

If you are planning to start your own business, it is vital that you take a course in business at a college near you. Many colleges are now offering courses geared exclusively to starting your own business that cover such subjects as what types of business have a high success rate, managing a business, and figuring expenses, overhead, and interest.

When thinking about starting a business, you may want to weigh the advantages and disadvantages of working for someone else or of having your own business. When you work for someone else, you do your work and get your salary. You usually have insurance benefits, paid vacations, and overtime. You also have to be there on time, answer to someone else, and follow the rules. With your own business you can come and go when you wish (but you will find you put in more hours for less pay than you ever did working for someone else). You do not have group insurance, paid vacations, and paid overtime.

When you are employed by someone else, you are one cog in the wheel. When you work for yourself, you are the wheel. But you are also responsible for buying, selling, hiring, firing, profit and loss. The buck stops at your desk.

If, after knowing all this, you still want to own your own business, remember when you are figuring what you need to get started, your available money should exceed the estimated initial cash by a safe margin. This is because you not only need money to get started but also need enough to carry the business until it becomes self-supporting. In some instances this may be four to six months, in many cases, much longer; the average is two years. Getting the money to start a business is, of course, your first priority. One of the principal causes of failure among businesses is inadequate financing.

The main sources of money are: (1) the commercial bank; (2) the Small Business Administration; (3) private banking; (4) your own money. As we said, we are only briefly touching on some of the factors that are involved in starting a business, but when you are seeking financing, bear in mind a few considerations.

If you are thinking of taking a loan at a bank, you would probably have a better chance if you go to a bank you have dealt with for several years (see our Banking Institutions chapter). You will have to have a good credit rating and be able to qualify for a loan.

The Small Business Administration will make loans to new businesses. Information may be obtained from your nearest field office. For addresses and telephone numbers of the field offices, look under "United States Government" in your telephone directory.

You also may know of a private loan source that would like to back a small business, yet not have the hassle of running it. If you make this kind of agreement, get everything in writing: Is the person going to be a silent partner and share in the profits, or are you going to repay the money, at which time your debtor will no longer have any involvement in the business?

You may possibly have your own money, or you and a friend may each have an amount of money you can pool to form enough capital to start a business. If you value your friendship, get everything in writing. Many a friendship has ended when it turned into a partnership.

Figuring how much you need to start a business can vary too widely even to list a ball-park figure. Here is where the Small Business Administration can be invaluable. Its booklet contains a worksheet chart to help you figure what you will need to start a business. Some other decisions you will be faced with when starting a business are: location of the business, obtaining a license, insurance, purchase of supplies and equipment, keeping the books, banking, and, of course, making the business a success. You should talk to as many independent business people as you can find to gain some insight.

Your decision to go into business may not depend entirely on financial reward. The potential return on investment may be overshadowed by your desire for independence, the chance to do the type of work you would like to do, or the feeling that you can be more self-fulfilled than you would be if you worked for someone else.

Such intangible considerations must not be overlooked. Nevertheless, you cannot keep your own business open unless you receive a financial return (or at least meet expenses) on your investment. But whether you start your own business or become employed by someone else, joining the work force will drastically change your life.

3
Keeping the Job

When you obtain a new job, you will also have some new problems: If you are a homemaker, coordinating your home responsibilities with your job responsibilities can produce a multitude of complications; if you are working for the first time, you will encounter new responsibilities. One of the main dilemmas faced by working mothers is that of finding adequate child care. While on the job, you may encounter unpleasant situations such as job and sex discrimination and sexual harassment.

In this chapter we will discuss these as well as other problems women face when entering the work force and offer some possible solutions.

But just what does this have to do with finance?

The answer is simple. Having a job has to do with having available money, and if you quit your job for any of the above reasons, it will naturally result in a loss of that income. The majority of women who do terminate their employment do so for one or more of these reasons. If some of the situations you may run into when you get a job can be examined and dealt with in advance, you may be better prepared to handle them when they present themselves . . . and more often than not, they will.

ADJUSTING TO A NEW ROLE

We feel strongly that if you are a married woman who has spent most of your married life as a homemaker, you should be aware, when entering the ranks of working wives, that your working will make tremendous adjustments in your life and in your husband's. There are several psychological adjustments husbands are faced with when their wives are employed outside the home. One of these adjustments is that many men feel consciously or subconsciously threatened when their wives go to work. Just exactly what do they feel threatened about?

Roger J. Berg, a Lutheran pastor who does a great deal of marriage counseling, says that a lot of men can't freely put into words what they feel threatened by, and the ones who can talk about the problem list vague worries, such as: "She'll become too independent," "She'll be working with a lot of men," "She may feel she should be the boss because she is earning a paycheck," "She might leave me," "She'll expect me to help with the housework," "She won't give me the attention she did before she went to work."

Pastor Berg feels that the wife's reason for going to work and the state of the relationship are major factors in how readily a husband adjusts to her new role. "If there is a loving relationship between the couple, the husband wants his wife to be happy, and if she's happy working, he will be able to adjust. It may take some time and some understanding. On the other side of the coin, if the wife feels deeply about her husband, she will allow him the time to adjust. Often the situation works itself out. However, I see husbands who don't ever seem to adjust and wives who will not allow them time to adjust. Consequently, I see some marriages break up over dual careers. Who's to say where the fault lies—with him for his stubbornness or with her for her impatience? But since no one person makes a marriage and no one person breaks up a marriage, it is not fair to say that women's going to work is what is causing the divorce rate to increase. The name of the game is a loving relationship and proper communication. Once adjustments are made by both parties, two career couples often have a better relationship than they did before."

Sharon Golson went back to work as an illustrator after her children were in school all day. Her husband, Stanley, didn't care much for the idea; but he knew they could use the money, and he realized Sharon was too gifted to waste her talents. He felt he could handle Sharon's returning to work, but when she received several promotions and raises within the first year (which put her income almost up to what it had taken him twelve years to achieve), he became resentful.

"Where he had been helpful before, even when I didn't work outside the home, he suddenly stopped doing anything around the house," she told us. "His attitude was that housework was my job and I should stay home and do it. When I started being sent to overnight conferences, we had a showdown. He told me to quit the job, and I told him I loved him very much, but I was not going to quit my job. For a couple of months our relationship was very strained. Then, when my name started appearing in magazines, and we were able to go on a long-awaited cruise and buy a much-needed second car, Stanley's attitude began to change. His objections to my working seemed to lessen. He once again began to help me with the children and the housework. Looking back on it now, Stanley says at the time he felt I would leave him—what did I need him for? I had income, an active life, and a satisfying career. Only when he realized that after I obtained all that, I didn't leave him did he begin to feel less threatened."

Men are not the only ones who feel threatened by women's going to work. Women themselves sometimes do. According to a woman psychologist, who prefers not to be named, "Women still have fears about competing with men, that men will not find them attractive, and fears concerning whether or not they can make it in a man's world. They sometimes are afraid of getting out in the business world at all. When a woman does get out, she comes face to face with the very real facts that women have been kept down professionally by men; they have been underpaid, underpromoted, and relegated to traditional women's jobs."

She also told us that a woman "has to make a decision of taking a stand against discrimination or taking the money and running. She fears the aggressiveness she sees in herself and sometimes longs to go back to being an innocent. Reading about discrimination is one thing; being faced with it is another. A working woman also has fears about whether or not she is going to succeed—a fear men have had to face for years. The only thing a woman can do is to decide what *she* can personally do about such discrepancies as being passed over for a promotion (complain loud and long to the right party) and salary inequalities (find out what a man in her position is receiving and protest to the management), then go on and do the best job she can do and not worry about appearing aggressive. It's been considered a plus in men for years. A secure man doesn't fear an 'aggressive woman,' and who would want any other kind? And a secure woman doesn't care if she is labeled aggressive."

The only advice we can give you is: When you are in the transitional stage from homemaker to working wife, it is important that you and your husband be responsive to each other's needs and allow time for the adjustments to take place and job-related problems to be solved.

Job Discrimination

After you find a job, or even when you are trying to find a job, one of the first problems you have to confront is sex discrimination. If you apply for a job, meet the qualifications, and then discover a less qualified man was hired instead of you, you may well have been discriminated against.

Once you are employed, it is disheartening to discover that you are getting paid three-fourths as much as the guy sitting next to you who has the same type of job. How often, too, is a woman passed over for a promotion in the corporate ladder?

Shirley Gleason was a bookkeeper for a restaurant chain for ten years. She was coordinating several restaurant payrolls and had a great deal of responsibility, but when a job as head bookkeeper opened up, instead of her being promoted, a male accountant, fresh out of school, was brought in for the job. When Shirley asked for an explanation, the head of the company told her he "just couldn't envision a woman in that job."

"I could have fought it—sued or something—but I had to look at the situation realistically. I had great company benefits, nine years in a profit-sharing plan, less than a mile's drive to and from work. I really didn't want to chance jeopardizing all that, plus this was a few years before the women's movement, and no one was listening to women."

Fortunately, the militant woman and the stand she has taken against discrimination has paved a path for all women to travel on. With the rise of the women's movement, women have developed constructive methods to combat job discrimination. There have been lawsuits instituted by women against companies they feel have discriminated against them. Though lawyers tell us these are difficult cases to prove, there are a number of instances in which women have won, been reinstated, and collected back wages. There is still a long way to go, but at least women are beginning to be listened to in matters of wage and sex discrimination and, to have some legal rights spelled out.

Another problem working women have had to face, and have been quiet about since they had no recourse, is the problem of sexual harassment on the job. Many believed it was their own personal dilemma or "woman's lot." Some believed that their actions somehow caused these situations to occur or that they should have been able to avoid them. In recent years, as the issue has begun to be discussed more openly, women have re-evaluated their positions in the work force and on the campus. What has emerged is a growing awareness of the scope and complexity of the problem. As this realisation has come about, there have also been an increasing number of court cases.

In one situation a woman complained about her boss's continual embracing of her shoulders and touching of her arms and waist. When she protested, she was told that he was just being a "friendly fellow" and she, a poor sport. But when she sued and won, he got the message and stopped harassing her and other female employees. In another, an administrative assistant at the Environmental Protection Agency (EPA) lost her job after refusing her boss's sexual advances. She sued, and the court ruled that sexual demands as a condition of employment are illegal. EPA settled out of court with a back pay award.

You may doubt that any of this applies to you because you feel you are twenty pounds too heavy and twenty years too late. Don't kid yourself. Chances are if you are a female, you will run into sexual advances or innuendos on the job at some time. And if you are fresh out of school, you can count on it. But before you mutter, "Men are all alike," be honest. Don't you know of women who use this to their advantage? We do. We have had women make no bones about the fact that they flirt and sleep with men to secure and advance their job or income. This does not, however, change the seriousness of sexual harassment.

A woman, who will remain anonymous, told us she doesn't really feel this is what she's doing. "I am single and in real estate sales. If I want to make social contacts out of my professional life, what's wrong with that?" The fact that she doesn't make "social contact" with anyone other than clients that end up buying property from her doesn't seem to bother her, and it doesn't bother us, except women like her make it even harder for women who don't want to play this game.

For just as many women who do play this game, there are many more who truly feel that they are being sexually harassed on the job. Because most women will not publicize a complaint, the public at large, and businesses in general, are led to believe that sexual harassment on the job is not a problem.

The fear of reprisal is enough reason for many women to remain quiet about sexual harassment. To refuse sexual demands may mean jeopardizing their futures, their careers, their grades. In the case of working women, the decision simply to quit a job is a luxury many cannot afford.

Prior to 1976 there were few reliable statistics on the incidence of sexual harassment. Most of the data collected since then have focused on women in the workplace. A *Redbook* magazine survey of 9,000 clerical and professional women provided the first national data: Of the respondents 92 percent had experienced overt physical harassment, sexual remarks, and leering, with the majority regarding this behavior as a serious problem at work; nearly 50 percent said that they or someone they knew had quit or been fired because of harassment; and 75 percent believed that if they complained to a supervisor, nothing would be done. In a study conducted in New York by the Working Women United Institute, 70 percent of those surveyed said they had been harassed. A U.S. naval officer who distributed questionnaires to women at a Navy base and in the nearby town of Monterey, California, found that 81 percent of the women who participated in the survey had experienced some form of sexual harassment.

Sexual harassment is difficult to define. It may range from sexual innuendos made at inappropriate times, perhaps in the guise of humor, to coerced sexual relations. Harassment at its extreme occurs when a male who is in a position to control, influence, or affect a woman's job, career, or grades uses his authority and power to coerce the woman into sexual relations or to punish her refusal.

What can you do if you are put in the position of losing your job if you don't go along with your superior's sexual advances? At the bottom line, you only have two choices—quit or sue. But if you really need and like your job, you can try: (1) being firm ("I never mix my professional and my social life"); (2) making it clear you have no intention of "going along" with his advances; (3) threatening to tell his superior and wife; or, if these do not work, (4) taking appropriate legal action. We have been told that the majority of these cases, though very difficult to prove, are usually settled out of court because the men involved do not want the adverse publicity.

The following list comprises organizations you may write, or if you live in the area, visit, to obtain counseling and referrals for legal assistance regarding sexual harrassment.

Alliance Against Sexual Coercion (AASC)
P.O. Box 1
Cambridge, Massachusetts 02139

Provides counseling and referral services concerning sexual harassment in the workplace and on campus. A literature packet is available for a $2 donation.

Cambridge Women's Center
46 Pleasant Street
Cambridge, Massachusetts 02139

Sponsors a Women Against Violence Against Women (WAVAW)
Project; provides counseling and referral services.

Cleveland Women Working
1258 Euclid Avenue
Cleveland, Ohio 44115

Membership organization for women office workers; provides counseling and referral services, monitors employment trends, makes
recommendations to government agencies, and operates a speaker's
bureau.

9 to 5
YWCA
140 Clarendon Street
Boston, Massachusetts 02116

Provides counseling and referral services for women experiencing
employment-related problems; monitors employment practices in
the major industries; conducts surveys on employment opportunities for women.

Vocations for Social Change (VSC)
353 Broadway
Cambridge, Massachusetts 02139

Assists victims of sexual harrassment in the workplace with job counseling, legal options, and employment compensation.

Working Women United Institute (WWUI)
593 Park Avenue
New York, New York 10021

Conducts research on sexual harassment in employment; conducts workshops and educates the public and employers on this issue. Staff available for speaking engagements. Send for checklist, $1 prepaid.

For a solution to job discrimination or sexual harassment on a more immediate basis, you may take your problem to your local Equal Employment Opportunity Commission (EEOC). There you will be required to fill out a questionnaire, see an interviewer, and specify charges. From your information the EEOC will decide whether or not you have a case. Whatever monetary loss you feel you may have suffered because of sexual harassment or job discrimination will be included in a lawsuit filed in your behalf.

The matter of sexual harassment is a very serious subject, and there is no justifiable reason for a man sexually to harass a woman on the job, but if you are constantly being approached for sexual favors, a good long look at your behavior and your appearance may be in order. Though a woman's mode of dressing should not result in crude behavior by men, some women almost seem to invite sexual advances by the way they act and dress.

What to Wear Where

We are not going to insult your intelligence by telling you to dress in good taste. You know that. There are numerous magazine articles and books that go into great detail on rules of dress for women at the office. We beg to disagree with many of them, however, when they emphasize over and over that a woman must *always* be tailored at the office. A woman should dress in an up-to-date manner and be well groomed, but if you look best in a blouse with a ruffle at the neck, wear it. Of course, plunging necklines and out-of-date mini-skirts are no-nos, but as far as ironclad rules go, we feel that's up to you. Your line of work and the type of woman you are should also dictate your mode of dress.

When you are applying for a job, or after you get the job, how you dress can be very important. Some women are the tailored type, and some aren't. We are a case in point. One of us is only comfortable in tailored clothes; the other prefers a more feminine look. A rule of thumb should be: Wear (within reason) what projects *you* and what you find comfortable and functional on the job. Whatever style of clothing you choose, look like a woman of today. Nothing dates a woman faster than clinging to the look that was popular in her heyday.

Personnel agency manager Ruth Urban told us after she was widowed and had to go back to work, the first woman who interviewed her remarked that she looked fine for staying home, but not for entering the job market, and told her to update her image.

Your appearance is just one of the aspects you will be concerned with when you go to, or return to work. You will find, most of all, time becomes your enemy.

Sectioning Your Life

Sectioning your life can be of significant value in allotting you time for *yourself*. Block out weekly time for work, for chores, and for family and weekly time for yourself. Some obvious solutions to small, mundane time problems that often escape you will help you accomplish this. Even though they are very simple, they may help you find a few extra minutes which could add up to a few precious hours that you can spend any way you wish.

For example, one woman we talked with said that she saved precious morning time by going through her wardrobe over the weekend and selecting her clothes for the coming week. (She had no small children, but this could be applied to a child's wardrobe as well.) Weekend clothes selection allows her time to launder that blouse with spots on it instead of finding it dirty in her closet the morning she plans to wear it. "Figuring out what I'm going to wear for a week saves a good half hour of 'daily morning plowing through the closet' time."

Another simple solution for saving time is to throw in a load of laundry at night instead of waiting to do it all on weekends. (Have your family use the washing machine as a clothes hamper for white clothing.) Doing your laundry at night seems obvious, but you would be surprised how many women wait till their day off to catch up on it. As you will see in reading the case histories in this chapter, working women we have met have devised some interesting solutions to the problem of not enough time.

Janet McMahan told us that having to be at work at 7:00 A.M. was causing her a multitude of problems. "I'm the type that always felt my housework should be done before I left the house. I was getting up at five to make certain the house was in good shape and still be at work by seven. Being a night person by nature, I became unbelievably irritable. I finally rearranged my thinking. Since I got off at four, the obvious time to straighten up the house was when I came home from work, not before I went. It took me awhile not to feel 'undone' at work, knowing the beds weren't made, but having that extra hour's sleep in the morning soon made me forget about it."

Planning and creating exciting meals when you are working are one of the most time-consuming problems you will face. One of our friends spends one afternoon each weekend preparing main dishes and freezing them for the following week. If your idea of heaven isn't spending Sunday afternoon in the kitchen, there are some alternatives you may have overlooked: Microwave ovens and crock-pots are, of course a working woman's best friends.

Grocery shopping for a week or two weeks at a time is a great help. Jotting down the main dish on the kitchen calendar helps remind you what menu you had planned for that night (and also what to take out of the freezer that morning).

Simple timesaving solutions may sometimes be overlooked in meal preparation, such as moving your dinner hour from six to seven. Just because you've always eaten at an earlier time doesn't mean you can't change your dining habits.

Coping with Housework

You've probably read numerous articles in the vein of "Now that you have a job, you should feel worthwhile and fulfilled." So why are you so tired?

You're tired because you don't have one job—you have two jobs. Whether single or married, every woman who is employed has two jobs: her outside job and the job of keeping up a home. If you are married and have a husband who helps with the housework, and some do, you are indeed fortunate. The main complaint of the majority of married women who are employed (and half of all women in the United States are employed), is that they do not receive enough help from their husbands with housework or child care. Even if a woman earns as much as, if not more than, her husband, and no matter how important her job is, she is still likely to be the one mostly responsible for the home and children.

On the average, an employed wife puts in four to five hours a day on housework, in addition to her eight hours on the job; on top of that many wives feel guilty that it is not enough. No wonder you're tired!

It is surprising how many women say, "My husband never helps me with the housework," but questioned whether they ever asked him to, they reply, "Well, no. I shouldn't have to." Husbands are notorious for not noticing what needs to be done around the house. When Janie McClelland was finally able to get her husband to help with the housework, she had lost seven pounds and was so run-down she wound up with a very bad viral infection. She told her husband, Doug, that she needed *help;* it was impossible for her to sell real estate, take care of the house, and keep the children well and happy. Doug promised he would help but said she had been so efficient he had never even thought about offering to help.

Couples who do share more equally with the housework and children, however, still run into problems when they both work. Weekends are often spent catching up instead of being spent together.

"It's very easy to drift apart when you both work," Sonja Johnson told us. "My husband, Brian, and I got so we only saw each other very briefly before work and after work. By the time we prepared dinner, ate, cleaned up, gave the children some attention (helped with homework and discussed their problems), it was our own bedtime. Weekends were spent getting the yardwork caught up, grocery shopping, doing laundry and a major housecleaning. We not only had no time for each other but were so tired we began to fight all the time. I had to do some real soul-searching. I loved my job, but I knew something had to give. I seriously considered quitting, but Brian felt that was unfair. Instead, we sat down and rebudgeted our time. We figured if I weren't working, I wouldn't be bringing in any money at all, so even if we hired some help, we would still be ahead.

"We employed a woman to come in a half day a week and do the big jobs—vacuuming, the week's laundry, windows, bathrooms, changing linens, et cetera. We also hired a neighborhood boy to do the yards. Then we took a good hard look at the children's responsibilities. We had always had them clean their rooms and make their beds, but since they were now twelve and fourteen, it was time to update their chores. I had been of the opinion that after being in school all day, they shouldn't have to come home and do a lot of work, yet I was at work all day and still had to come home and work. Four people were living in the house. It was not fair for two people to have to do everything. The outcome was a new schedule for the children that included some meal preparation, grocery shopping, and doing a little more cleaning of their rooms than tossing things under their beds. We began eating out on Wednesday nights, even if it was takeout. This seemed to break up the long week of dinner rush hours. Each one of the four of us was assigned a weeknight to be responsible for dinner. I also invested in a crockpot and am eyeing a microwave oven for the future. It was amazing the difference these changes made in our family life. Weekends we have some time for recreation and, more important, each other. It is well worth not having quite as much money to spend."

This all worked out well for Janie, but what if you are married to a man who, when it comes to helping with the housework, hasn't in the past, isn't now, and probably won't be in the future—even though you have tried everything from killing him with kindness to killing him . . . period. You basically are looking at three rather harsh alternatives. None of them is particularly fair, but as we have said before, we're telling you how it is—not how it should be.

Keeping Your Job and Doing All the Housework

He doesn't help with the housework, but you're not ready to end your marriage over it. Yet you are developing an ulcer. Change your attitude. He's not going to help, so either stop being so particular about the house yourself, hire someone to help you, or just do the best you can. Whether your husband will help you or not often depends on the reason why you are working. If he doesn't want you to work, he probably won't make life easier for you, housework included.

Quitting Your Job

Many women seem to be able to handle simultaneously a job, a husband, children, and housework, but some women feel that something or someone doesn't get a full share. This was Fern Staley's case. Fern finally decided to quit her job and stay home with Kevin, age seven, and Frank, Jr., who was nine. Several years ago, when both boys were in school part of the day, she had felt that she should re-enter the work force and help Frank, Sr., pay for their new house. After she went to work, she found that she was crabby, constantly tired, and impatient with her sons, and the house never seemed clean. Even her relationship with Frank was being strained. All things considered, Fern decided it was best to quit the job even though it meant remaining on a tight budget. She did enroll in two college classes, since she had long since outgrown the bridge circuit and the tennis, lunch, and shopping bunch. "I know having an outside job is stimulating for a lot of women, but I felt I couldn't be a conscientious wife, mother, and businesswoman all at the same time. My day will come, though. In the meantime, I love what I am doing, and my schooling will help prepare me for a better job when I do join the work force again."

Leaving Him

Sometimes nothing works. Lee Reynolds and her husband live in a large three-bedroom custom tract home in a suburban area. Mike is getting a branch of a business started 500 miles away and flies home on weekends. Lee holds down a full-time job, and she has been attending night school to earn a law degree. If the house is not completely clean when Mike walks in, he is miserable to live with during the weekend. She has asked him for some help or to agree to get someone who would share housekeeping chores to live in. Lee feels one solution would be a smaller place to live, but again Mike does not want to move. Unfortunately Lee does not see her problem lessening and is contemplating divorce.

"He not only wants me to bring in an income but wants me to be an immaculate housekeeper—and to quit law school. I know I cannot live under this pressure much longer. Being a lawyer has been a dream of mine for years. I don't feel I should have to give it up to do the housework."

Many men will never be caught doing housework. They cannot picture themselves involved with chores on that level. Often their attitude is, fair or unfair, their mothers did everything for them, and you should, too. You cannot change your husband overnight just because you want or need to work. We really feel that for the most part how helpful your husband is depends on two things—the condition of your relationship and how his mother reared him!

SOLUTIONS TO CHILD CARE

If you are going back to the work force or entering it for the first time and you have school-age children, a major problem is being sure your children are being well cared for during the time you are at work. You will quickly realize that the biggest chunk of your new paycheck will go for child care. Your costs could range anywhere from $25 to $60 a week, perhaps more. The following is a list of where to look for baby-sitting services:

Neighbor

Maybe you'll be extremely lucky and have a neighbor who just adores your young Amanda or little Paul. Of course, she'll love to sit for you and earn some extra spending money.

Baby-sitting Agency

Agencies keep a roster of women who are available for baby-sitting services. On an hourly rate, this is the most expensive way to find a sitter, but as a usual rule, they're reliable. Ask to see a business license, and request references (check the references out). You can find agencies in the Yellow Pages under "Baby Sitters."

Preschools

There are preschools which accept younger children and have extended day care for older children as well. Many churches have preschools, often called nursery schools, at their facilities. All pre-schools should be city licensed. In order to obtain a license, they have to be inspected by a local fire department. Preschools are also listed in the phone book under preschool or nursery school.

Referral

Often you will learn of a good baby-sitter by referral. Tina Levine made numerous new friends through her classes at school. One of the women gave her several names of other women who earned money by taking care of children in their homes. Tina called three, interviewed them, asked for references, and eventually found a woman who would come to her home and take care of seventeen-month-old Jennifer, enabling Tina to go to work without worrying about carting Jennifer off to a baby-sitter's.

Colleges

Through the job center at a college you might find a girl who would exchange baby-sitting services for room and board. Generally this works better if your children are older and require someone only to see that they get off to school and have supervision when they return. A college girl who is taking nursery training can be ideal. Call the college, and ask for names.

Friends

One possibility is to hire as a babysitter a friend who has children the same age as yours. The majority of Joan Mayhew's friends have children, so it was a simple matter for her to find a sitter for Don, her six-year-old, when she had to go back to work. The arrangement worked out well because Don could play with his friends and be well cared for. This can put a strain on a friendship, however. If your child gets on your friend's nerves, it can affect your relationship.

Classified Ads

Every day you see ads in the local newspaper requesting or offering baby or child care services. If you place or answer such an ad, remember to interview the applicant thoroughly and to request and check references.

Baby-sitting Cooperative

If you have a part-time job in the mornings or work days and know of a woman who works afternoons or evenings, you might want to trade baby-sitting hours.

House Sharing

You could give a woman a room in your home in exchange for baby-sitting and housekeeping services. (Perhaps the woman has a child of her own and has no desire to go back to work, but what little alimony she has is not enough for her to live on.) A job such as you offer would make it possible for her to sustain herself and her child, plus furnish your child with care in his/her own home.

Lisa Baker is a divorcée who has custody of her four-year-old daughter, Courtney. Although Lisa receives excellent child support, she works as a legal secretary and attends law school. Margaret, who is also divorced and has a child, speaks some English but is more comfortable with her native tongue. Hence, she has had trouble getting a job. She receives no child support. Margaret lives in and cares for Courtney and her own child. She also shops for groceries and does the housework. This gives Lisa the luxury of some free time to socialize, study, and spend time with her daughter. She pays Margaret quite well each month and also gives her extra fringe benefits, such as additional days off, spending money, or some new clothes. Margaret attends night school twice a week to improve her English. It's a good arrangement because Courtney and Margaret and Lisa are compatible.

Pregnant Teenagers

There are social service agencies such as the Salvation Army or the Florence Crittendon Home that care for unwed, pregnant girls through their pregnancy. These girls are available to live in your home temporarily and perform light household duties and child care for a small salary. They are not allowed to care for children under two. You will have to check your local Salvation Army or Crittendon to see if it has a home or hospital that might provide these services.

Private Day Care Nurseries

These can also be found in your telephone directory and, like pre-schools, must be inspected and licensed. You might want to do some cost comparisons before you choose a nursery. Also, check the facilities and interview the people in charge before you make any decisions.

Day Care Centers

We know there is a diversity of opinions on the subject of day care centers, but they can be the only answer to child care problems for many women. Most child care centers that use federal or state money are run to provide child care services for low-income families. The family is charged for the services according to how much it is able to pay. Check with your local welfare office to see if you qualify.

We also know there is a lot of questioning of whether there should be federally funded day care centers at all. But since day care facilities are a reality and can be of great financial benefit to a large segment of women, we hope this synopsis will be of use to you and clear away some of the confusion. We include a listing of the state agencies that regulate and license day care facilities, to enable you to have a source to contact if you want to start a center or would like more information about enrolling your child in a day care facility.

There are three major types of day care centers which are federally funded in all or part:

1. The Family Day Care Home

This serves only as many children as it can integrate into its own physical setting and pattern of living. It is especially suitable for infants, toddlers, and sibling groups and for neighborhood-based day care programs, including those for children needing after-school care. A family day care home may serve no more than six children (three through fourteen) in total (no more than five when the age range is infancy through six), including the day care mother's own children.

2. The Group Day Care Center

A center for older children, this type offers familylike care, usually to school-age children in a family residence. It utilizes one or several employers and provides care for up to twelve children who need before- and after-school care, who do not require a great deal of mothering or individual care, and who can profit from considerable association with their peers.

3. The Day Care Center

This is apt to be run by qualified professionals for groups of twelve or more children. It utilizes subgroupings on the basis of age and special need but provides opportunity for experience and learning that accompanies a mixing of ages. Day care centers usually don't accept children under three years of age unless the available care approximates the mothering in the family home. Centers do not usually attempt to simulate family living. Centers may be established in a variety of places: private dwellings, settlement houses, schools, churches, social centers, public housing units, specially constructed facilities.

Federal interagency requirements have not been set for center care of children under three years of age. If programs offer center care for children younger than three, state licensing regulations and requirements must be met. Center care for children under three cannot be offered if the state authority has not established acceptable standards for such care.

Day care facilities (family day care homes, group day care homes, and day care centers) must be approved for meeting the standards for licensing.

STATE REGULATORY AGENCIES
DAY CARE CENTERS

Alabama: Department of Pensions and Security—special regulations for centers which care for children under three years of age.

Alaska: Department of Health and Welfare.

Arizona: Department of Health—can enroll infants with special permission.

Arkansas: Department of Public Welfare—special rules for children under three years of age.

California: Department of Social Welfare—special provisions for children under two years of age.

Colorado: Department of Social Services—minimum age is two years of age.

Connecticut: Department of Health, Maternal and Child Health Section—allow only certain number of children under three years of age.

Delaware: Department of Health and Social Services.

D.C.: Department of Public Health, Bureau of Maternal and Child Health.

Florida: Department of Health and Rehabilitative Ser-

	vices, Division of Family Services—only licensed in Dade, Duval, and Orange counties.
Georgia:	Department of Family and Children Services.
Hawaii:	Department of Social Services Public Welfare Division—two years old minimum age.
Idaho:	Voluntary licensing only—two and one-half years old minimum age. Department of Public Assistance.
Illinois:	Department of Children and Family Services.
Indiana:	Department of Public Welfare—three years old minimum.
Iowa:	Department of Social Services—two years old minimum.
Kansas:	Department of Health—licensed by state Department of Social Welfare; minimum age three.
Kentucky:	Department of Child Welfare.
Louisiana:	Department of Public Welfare.
Maine:	Department of Health and Welfare—two and one-half years old minimum age.
Maryland:	State Department of Health and Mental Hygiene.
Massachusetts:	Department of Public Health—three years old, except children are accepted between the ages of two and three with approval of Massachusetts Department of Public Health social worker.
Michigan:	Department of Social Security—two and a half years old minimum.
Minnesota:	Department of Public Welfare—three years through twelve years.
Mississippi:	Mississippi does not have mandatory licensing for child care facilities. The Department of Public Welfare does maintain standards for group care of children six weeks of age and older and issues a voluntary certificate of approval.
Missouri:	Department of Public Health and Welfare—minimum age three years.
Montana:	Department of Public Welfare—minimum two years.
Nebraska:	Department of Public Welfare—minimum two years.
Nevada:	Welfare Division of Department of Health, Welfare, and Rehabilitation.

New Hampshire: Division of Welfare, Department of Health and Welfare.

New Jersey: State Department of Education—minimum two years.

New Mexico: New Mexico Health and Social Services Department.

New York: Department of Social Services.

North Carolina: Child Day Care Licensing Board.

North Dakota: Public Welfare Board of North Dakota.

Ohio: State of Ohio Department of Public Welfare.

Oklahoma: Department of Institutions, Social and Rehabilitative Service.

Oregon: State Public Welfare Division.

Pennsylvania: Department of Public Welfare.

Rhode Island: Rhode Island Department of Social and Rehabilitative Services, Division of Community Services, Child Welfare Services.

South Carolina: Department of Public Welfare.

South Dakota: Department of Public Welfare.

Tennessee: Department of Public Welfare.

Texas: State Department of Public Welfare.

Utah: Department of Social Services, Division of Family Services.

Vermont: Vermont State Office of Economic Opportunity, Day Care Operations Unit.

Virginia: Department of Welfare and Institutions.

Washington: Department of Social and Health Services.

West Virginia: Division of Social Services, Department of Welfare—family day care homes are not licensed, but are approved and supervised by county welfare departments.

Wisconsin: Wisconsin Department of Health and Social Services—licensing is for centers or homes caring for four or more children. Day care homes must be certified if care is purchased with federal, state, and local funds.

Wyoming: Division of Public Assistance and Social Services, Department of Health and Social Services.

Department of Health, Education and Welfare, Office of Child Development.

4

Establishing Credit

Credit is not a right for women or for men. Neither the doctor, the department store, nor any financial institution is under any obligation to extend credit to you. It is up to you to demonstrate that you are worthy of the privilege.

Credit is a privilege—the privilege of using money, goods, or services before you pay for them. The doctor who sends you a bill instead of asking you to pay cash for an examination is extending credit to you. So is the department store that lets you charge a purchase. Any form of installment buying is a credit transaction, as is any loan of money.

Credit buying has become such an American way of life that we mistakenly believe credit is our right. It is not, but since institutions do offer credit, the standards for determining credit should be the same for men and women. It is no secret that until very recently many credit-granting institutions discriminated against women, not because of their credit standing, but because they were women. Just as women had been denied equal job opportunities, they were denied equal access to credit. And equality without economic equality is not equality at all.

Elinor Lawrence, former president of the California Women's Savings & Loan in Westwood, California, remembers when she had to send a successful career woman home to have her father cosign a mortgage on a house.

"The fact that more and more women are seeking credit to enable them to do such things as own their own homes does not prove that it is easier for a woman to obtain a loan," she says. "What it does mean is that this trend has instituted new laws which will help a woman achieve financial independence."

The practice of credit discrimination was called into question when, during the late sixties, state commissions on the status of women began listening to alarming evidence from women who had been shut out of the consumer economy on the basis of their sex or marital status.

The states began to move, and now most of them have strong laws making credit discrimination illegal. On the federal level, Congress began to pass laws prohibiting the Small Business Administration from practicing sex discrimination and making it illegal for lending institutions to deny certain types of credit on the basis of sex. In October 1975 the Federal Equal Credit Opportunity Act became law, making it illegal for creditors to discriminate on the basis of sex or the marital status of an applicant when evaluating creditworthiness.

The Federal Equal Credit Opportunity Act does not guarantee you access to credit simply because you are a woman. What it does guarantee is that you will have the same access to credit as a man in your financial situation. A credit institution can no longer turn you down, or demand extra security or stiffer terms, just because you are a woman. Specifically the act states that "it shall be unlawful for any creditor to discriminate against any applicant with respect to any aspect of a credit transaction on the basis of sex or marital status."

The act prohibits the following:

- Refusing credit because of a change in marital status.
- Refusing a married woman a separate account even though she would qualify if single.
- Demanding financial information about a spouse when the applicant is individually creditworthy.
- Refusing a married person credit because of the credit rating of the spouse, unless the credit application is for a joint account.
- Refusing to consider alimony and child support as income.
- Refusing to consider a wife's income when a couple applies for joint credit.

- Asking about an applicant's birth control practices or childbearing plans.
- Refusing to consider income from regular part-time employment.
- Refusing to recognize the legal name of a married woman.
- Terminating or revising terms for a credit transaction because of a change in the borrower's name or marital status, as long as no change has occurred in the borrower's willingness or ability to pay.

Another important law for women that you should be aware of is the Fair Credit Reporting Act, which took effect in April 1971.

This act requires that:

- Creditors provide an explanation of the reasons for rejection of a credit application within 30 to 100 days if the applicant wants to know why credit was denied.
- Applicants for credit be provided with information from any credit records used to determine whether credit would be granted.
- Creditors cannot charge interest on disputed amounts or adversely affect a credit rating while a complaint is being investigated.

YOUR CREDITWORTHINESS

If credit is a privilege for the borrower, it is sometimes a risk for the lender. Naturally the lender looks carefully for factors that will lessen the risk. If you think the questions on a credit application are excessive, ask yourself whether you would be willing to lend your own money to a stranger without very strong reasons to believe you were going to get it back. That, in the simplest form, is the business that credit institutions are in, and that is why they pay such close attention to the following factors:

Ability to Pay generally is based on income and how an individual spends it. Income can come from salary, self-employment, business ownership, alimony and child support, investment income, pensions, or Social Security. But the most important consideration is evidence of a continuous source of income over a period of time.

A credit manager will take a close look at your income and is likely to deny an application for credit when the income is insufficient to support the amount of credit requested. Someone with a $10,000 annual income, for instance, probably would not be eligible for a $50,000 mortgage but might qualify for a $30,000 mortgage.

The Amount of Indebtedness is as important as your income. You may take home a large paycheck, but if all of it is already committed, you are a poor risk to repay a further loan.

Sound Financial Habits are also considered. Checking and savings accounts are indications of good personal money management.

Your Assets and Possessions are another factor. A lender who is undecided about your application may ask you to put up collateral— pledge something like a car or stocks as a guarantee of repayment. If you have assets that can be used in this fashion, this can be a point in your favor.

Your Credit Record is extremely important. Financial institutions will look closely at your past credit history (which is also how they check the accuracy of certain information in your application). A credit bureau report that shows a record of late or missed payments, legal action to enforce collection, defaults, repossessions, or bankruptcies can weigh heavily against you. But records of payments made on time and accounts satisfactorily closed are excellent ways to ensure further credit.

According to the Bank of America, creditors set their own criteria or standards for extending credit. These standards vary from creditor to creditor: One will extend credit; the other won't—on the basis of the same information and financial situation. The bank believes, however, that basically all creditors look for the same thing: your ability to repay the debt and your willingness to do so.

In its consumer information report, the Bank of America gets specific about what potential creditors consider. It lists the following:

Stability—how long you have lived in the area, at your present address; whether you own or rent, have a telephone; whether you own other property, have savings, investments, insurance, character, and reputation.

Income—your occupation; whether it's year-round or seasonal; your employer; how long you've worked there; how you are paid (salary, commissions, fees, etc.); how much you earn; sources and amounts of other income for debt repayment such as alimony, child support, pensions, annuities, dividends.

Age—In most cases, you must be at least eighteen, the age of majority, which is when you become legally responsible for your contracts.

Expenses—number of dependents relative to income; living expenses relative to income; life-style consistent with income.

Debt Record—how you pay your bills; how much you owe (debts outstanding); how often you borrow and for what purpose; whether you've had accounts in collection, have had repossessions or declared bankruptcy.

HOW CREDIT DECISIONS ARE MADE

Credit File Review—If you've received credit before, you will probably have a credit file at a local credit reporting agency or bureau. This bureau will be consulted by your potential creditor. Your credit file shows creditors how you've handled debt in the past, usually considered a good indication of how you will handle debt in the future.

If you've never used credit before, there will not be a credit file. Instead, creditors must rely on other indications of your ability and willingness to repay debt.

Your credit file is opened the first time you are granted credit, provided your creditor reports to a credit agency or bureau. Your file is updated as you apply for, use, and repay credit through your lifetime. It usually includes your name, address, Social Security number, phone, bank, occupation, employer, income, time on the job, employment record, number of dependents, spouse's name and employer, information of public record such as tax liens, judgments, bankruptcy; also where you have credit, the amount of credit, and how you pay your bills.

Credit Scoring—This is one of the methods used by some creditors to assist in evaluating credit applications. Credit is not automatically granted if you receive a passing score, nor is it automatically refused if you don't. Your score is the total of points earned by characteristics such as income, length of employment, etc. Scoring is based on the statistical likelihood that a person with a passing score will be a good credit risk.

Verification—Creditors will verify the information on your credit application—through credit-reporting agencies or by directly contacting the credit sources and other references you have listed.

Final Evaluation—Each credit application is judged on its own merits. No matter where you apply, the decision is based on: (1) your specific situation and the facts you give to the creditor; (2) the creditor's own criteria or standards for extending credit; and (3) the creditor's judgment of your ability and willingness to repay your debt. It's a human decision. It comes down to asking the basic questions you would ask if someone were borrowing from you: Can he/she pay it back? Will he/she pay it back?

When You're Turned Down—In most cases, it will be for one or more of the following reasons: too much debt already; too short a time living in the area or employed at your present job; income too low in relation to necessary living expenses, plus required debt repayment; poor repayment history. Denial of credit for any other reason we will discuss in more detail later.

BEGINNING YOUR CREDIT RECORD

It may sound as though you can't get credit unless you already have proved your creditworthiness, but it's far from difficult. The two most common ways of establishing a financial history are relatively simple. The first is to apply to a local department store or retailer for a charge account in your own name. Make small purchases you are sure you can afford, and pay your monthly bill promptly. This method has the advantage of being inexpensive in that there are no financing charges as long as you pay your bill in full by the due date. If you do not plan to pay your bill in full, find out how much you are being charged to finance your payments.

Most department stores and retailers are required to list the amount of finance charges on your bill. The standard clause is: "There will be no finance charge if the new balance is received by your next closing date. If you elect to pay the minimum (a percentage) payment, a finance charge will be added, computed on the average daily balance; periodic rates of ——% per month (an annual percentage rate of ——%) on balances of $—— or less and ——% per month (an annual percentage rate of ——%) on that portion of the balance over $——." Each state determines what amount can be charged as finance charges. Therefore, this can and does vary from state to state. There is no federal law setting a maximum rate that can be charged; again each state determines its own. It does make a difference where you open your account, however. For example, if you open a charge account at a Sears store in California and spend part of the year in Florida or travel a great deal, you would be charged the rate of finance charged in California no matter where you made your purchases.

When opening a charge account, you may be confused about the different types of accounts. Most stores offer budget accounts and revolving accounts. A revolving charge account is designed for your smaller purchases, such as clothes and cosmetics. You can pay these charges on a percentage basis each month, or you can pay the bill in full. If it is paid off in 30 days, there is no finance charge. A budget account probably can best be described as one you use when you are making a large purchase, such as kitchen appliances or furniture. You are then given a definite period of time to pay your balance. In most cases it is three to five years.

A second relatively simple way to establish a credit record is by opening a checking or savings account in your own name (Mary Robinson Smith, not Mrs. John Smith). It is important to open accounts in your own name because "Mrs. John Smith" is a social title, and it could refer to a succession of women. You yourself are "Mary Robinson Smith," and you should use this name when applying and establishing your own credit.

Make sure you do not overdraw this account, since the most important part of a credit history is to have a blemish-free record. When you have established your reliability, you may want to apply for a loan. Again, repay it on time. This second method takes longer and is more costly, but it is a more solid recommendation for future credit.

It takes time to build a good credit rating because lending institutions look for a pattern of responsible borrowing, which can be established only by prompt payment of your obligations over a period of time.

Here are some further suggestions that may help you establish credit. There's no way to guarantee you will be granted credit, however. That's still up to you and the creditor.

1. Know you can repay. Before you apply, look at your current income and expense situation. Will you be able to make payments on a loan, charge account, or credit card and still meet your living expenses and other obligations?

2. Borrow only what you need—not the most you can get or less

than you really need. If you take out a loan, the reason for the loan is an important consideration of the lender when extending credit.

3. Complete your credit application. It's in your best interest to provide a complete application, to be candid and honest in listing all current payments and debts—even though you may feel it will lessen your chances of getting the credit you want. Mainly it will help prevent getting more credit than you can currently handle and losing your good credit record.

4. Establish a banking relationship. Along with opening a checking or savings account for a valuable reference, you can use a savings account as collateral. This can also be one of the least expensive ways to borrow money because your savings account continues to earn interst for you during the time it is pledged against the loan. However, you may not withdraw the amount pledged until you have repaid the loan. Having bank accounts indicates good money management habits to a lender.

5. Apply for credit in your own community. Creditors are more likely to know you, your neighborhood, or your employer. They can more readily verify facts on your credit application from local sources.

6. Take advantage of special credit plans. Some creditors provide special credit plans with limited lines of credit and different qualifying criteria for first-time credit users.

7. Get a cosigner or guarantor. Sometimes, when your credit qualifications aren't strong enough for you to get credit on your own, a creditor may agree to a loan or charge account if you have a cosigner, comaker, or guarantor. This can be a relative, business associate, or friend with a good credit record who will agree to be responsible for your debt if you fail to pay. This can be sticky at times, say, if you become ill and your friend must pay your bill. Many a friendship has been broken over cosigning, but it can give you a start in establishing credit.

8. If possible, make a big down payment. Creditors may be more willing to extend credit for cars, appliances, furniture, etc. on the installment plan if you can make a large down payment. With more of your own money invested, they feel you are less likely to forfeit your investment by allowing the item to be repossessed. You may have to postpone your purchase awhile to enable you to save up the down payment, but it can be one of the simpler ways to establish credit.

For instance, Janice Kutchens, a recently divorced woman in Southern California, did just this when she decided to purchase a car. After being turned down repeatedly because of having no credit history, Janice postponed buying a car until she could put a sizable amount down.

"I took a second job at a restaurant and put every cent I earned into a car fund," she says. "It was rough, but by saving tips and salary, I had a nice down payment saved in six months. The finance companies that had turned me down suddenly seemed to feel I was a good credit risk. I have no trouble getting credit now, as I can show I am buying a car. It seems the more credit you have, the more you can get."

9. Consider layaway plans. Some stores will allow you to use layaway plans for purchases when they're not willing to extend credit. Once you've shown your willingness to make regular payments on the layaway merchandise, you may be allowed to open a charge account.

10. Request any credit accounts you now use that are in your husband's, or your and your husband's name, also be listed in only your name. As of November 1, 1976, creditors *must* comply with this request, thereby getting credit established in your name. As we said before, be sure they are Mary Smith, not Mrs. John Smith.

Equally important to establishing credit is maintaining credit once it is established. Lenders and credit bureaus do not keep inactive accounts on their books indefinitely, and you might find that your credit has lapsed, just when you need it the most.

Credit is something you earn. Once you get credit, take good care of it by making your payments on time and for the full amount. Select payment dates that coincide with your paydays. If you can't pay because of illness, unemployment, or other emergencies, contact your creditors. Visit them or call them *before* they call you. Explain your problem. Extend the same courtesy you'd expect from someone who owed you money and had trouble making the payments. Most creditors will be willing to help you work out a plan to enable you to repay your debt and maintain your credit record. Remember the lender has an investment in you. The firm is primarily interested in getting its money back. If it takes longer than planned, it is still better, from the lender's point of view, than writing off the debt entirely.

THE BUSINESS OF EXTENDING CREDIT

There are many different types of credit. You may obtain credit directly from a lender (as in a personal loan or charge account), or you may use a bank credit card and not have to pay interest as long as you pay your bill in full within a certain time, while in other cases there is no such grace period. If you apply for a bank card, you should know something about them.

Bank credit (or charge cards) are issued by thousands of banks across the country, usually through Master Charge or Bankamericard (Visa), the two largest bank charge plans. Cardholders can charge at retail stores, restaurants, service stations, airlines, and other facilities affiliated with the bank card plan. In some cases they can also borrow money by presenting the card at a member bank. This "cash advance" is actually an unsecured loan for which the maximum amount has been prearranged by the bank. This maximum prearranged amount the bank will permit you to borrow is called your credit line.

Bank cards also carry a maximum limit on how much you can charge. This limit is also prearranged. Bank card balances can be paid in full after billing, usually within twenty five days, or the balance rolls over to the next month, just as in a department store account. The finance charge is typically 1 or 1.5 percent a month, 12 or 18 percent a year.

Consumer advocates advise consumers to be aware that with an annual finance charge of 18 percent you are paying almost one-fifth the total purchase price of the goods you have bought during the month just in finance charges alone.

You should also be aware of emerging trends among bank charge plans that can affect your cost of borrowing. Some banks have decided to assess a finance charge on all new purchases from the date of posting if there is a previous balance outstanding. Up until recently, if you paid your bank card balance immediately after receipt of the bill, you could avoid all finance charges. However, one leading bank has just closed a loophole by charging a fifty cent monthly service on all accounts with charge activity when there is no previous balance outstanding.

Since lenders use so many different methods in extending credit to customers, no one set of criteria can be established to determine whether an application for credit should be approved. All types of credit do have some features in common.

Any firm that lends you money for a period of time is, of course, in the business of making money and wants to guarantee its income. It must also operate on the basis of certain financial considerations. One is that it will have to pay overhead—salaries, rent, and many other expenses of doing business. The lender meets these needs by charging interest. The amount of risk involved in extending credit is another major consideration and one that varies greatly. Credit institutions set aside a certain percentage of their income from interest to cover possible losses. The firms that are willing to deal with people who are higher credit risks must set aside a larger amount, which in turn pushes up their interest rates.

Time is also an important factor. A lending institution has to meet its own obligations promptly—salaries, etc. In order to do so, it has to be able to count on getting regular payments from borrowers. This is why lenders often charge late charges. It is compensation for the problems caused by not having money when the lender expected it.

Sometimes a loan contract will also carry penalties for early payment. Up to a point, paying off a loan early is good for the lender because it means that the firm has the use of its money again in a shorter time. However, in making the loan to you, the lender figures to bring in a set amount of money through interest, and early repayment deprives the firm of some of this income and interest plus profit. When the financial disadvantage of losing interest becomes greater than the benefits of having the money back sooner, the lender will charge a penalty.

Collateral usually enters the picture when large amounts of money, long periods of time, or a high degree of risk are involved. In these instances, the chance of a loss for the lender is greatest. Collateral can be something you already own, or it can be something you are buying, like a car or home. If you fail to pay back the loan, you risk losing the collateral.

Credit institutions are usually very reluctant to get involved in foreclosures, repossessions, and forfeitures because they are in the business of lending money, not repossessing people's goods and then disposing of goods. Therefore, loan contracts using collateral are usually written with plenty of leeway for the borrower to catch up on payments before the final step becomes necessary.

CREDIT PROBLEMS

At some point you may become involved in a dispute with a creditor over money owed, purchases made, or services rendered. This could affect your credit record if the dispute is not resolved. The best approach is to deal with the creditor directly because most problems can be solved on this level. Under the Fair Billing Act (Chapter V of the Truth in Lending Act), you have sixty days to register your complaint in writing. The creditor has ninety days from the time he receives your complaint to correct the cause of the problem or send you a letter of clarification. During this time the creditor cannot charge you interest on the disputed amount or make an unfavorable notation of it in your credit record.

If you are not satisfied with the response, you may take your complaint to the appropriate officials in your state. Remember, even if all the decisions go against you, you have the right to include your version of the dispute in your record.

If your application for credit is turned down, again it is best to deal with the creditor first. Within thirty days write and request an explanation of the denial. The creditor must answer within thirty to one hundred days and name the credit bureau or other sources that provided the information used in evaluation of your application. If you are denied credit because of information given by a credit bureau, you have the right to find out what information is in your credit file. Call the credit bureau, and ask to review your file. There will be a fee for this, usually payable in advance.

If you disagree with what you find there, you have the right to ask the bureau to recheck the information. If it is found to be incorrect, the credit bureau must remove it from your file and then notify all creditors who received the incorrect information that the file has been corrected. Complaints can be taken to the same state official who handles credit disputes.

An unfavorable item in your file will not follow you around forever. In most instances it must be removed after seven years; that gives you the opportunity to improve even the worst mistakes and misjudgments.

NEVER MARRIED WOMEN AND CREDIT

Never-married women have had a more difficult time establishing credit than never-married men especially if young and entering the job market for the first time. Credit became easier to obtain as an employment record was established. Now, under the provisions of the Equal Credit Opportunity Act, there *should* be no difficulty at all. Your application for credit must be judged on its merits alone, and a lender cannot turn you down or impose higher terms than he would for a man with the same income and credit history.

MARRIED WOMEN AND CREDIT

Some of the most important provisions in the Equal Credit Opportunity Act deal with married women. Of these, one of the most important is the guarantee of a married woman's right to credit in her own name. Changing circumstances may make you responsible for your own and your family's finances. If you are divorced, separated, or widowed or faced with severe illness or other financial emergencies, you will avoid many problems if you already have the protection of your own credit rating.

When you marry, if you already have established a credit history, you should find it easy to change your charge accounts to your new name (Mary Robinson Smith, not Mrs. John Smith). It should not be necessary to file a new application for credit or provide additional information to a creditor—unless there has been a major change in your personal income or if you wish to establish a joint account with your husband. The National Association of Women, however, advises women that in most cases it is best to have separate accounts from their husbands. In case of a divorce or widowhood, it is a lot easier, from a financial point of view, to have credit already established in your own name. They do feel, however, that some joint charge accounts are beneficial when both husband and wife are bringing in income. This double-income figure allows you a higher credit line. In other words, you're allowed to charge more against a $40,000-a-year income than against a $15,000 one.

Reestablishing separate credit is also possible if you have been married for some time and have used your husband's accounts. If you have your own income, this can qualify you without any references to your husband's financial status. Even income from steady part-time work, which was not counted for credit before, must now be considered as regular income in the evaluation of your credit potential. Even if you are not employed and have no income of your own, you can still establish your own credit by using provisions of the new laws that refer to joint accounts.

As of June 1, 1977, any new joint accounts you and your husband open *must* be maintained in both names (Mary Robinson Smith and John Smith, not Mr. and Mrs. Smith). You also have the right to change any existing accounts you now have in your husband's name, to include both his name and yours.

By doing so, you will establish your own credit history during your marriage. Then, in the event of divorce or widowhood, you will not be faced with the prospect of building a credit record from scratch at a time when you already have more than enough problems. If you or your husband allows your joint credit accounts to develop an unsatisfactory credit record, it will apply to each individual, even though only one may be at fault.

This warning is doubly important to women living in the community property states of Arizona, California, Idaho, Louisiana, Nevada, New Mexico, Texas, or Washington, where all credit transactions are normally considered joint transactions. This means you will have a larger asset base on which to draw for credit, but it also means that if the marriage "community's" credit rating is poor, you will have a more difficult time disassociating yourself from it. Even here, it is possible for you to have separate property and establish a separate credit record, but the laws are complicated and vary from state to state. We suggest you turn to your state commission for women, if you have a specific question or problem.

Another provision of the Equal Credit Opportunity Act of vital importance to married women deals with home mortgages. In the past it has been common for mortgage lenders to look only at the husband's income in calculating how large a mortgage a couple could afford. The wife's income was usually discounted entirely. The new act specifically prohibits this practice and requires that mortgage lenders consider the full combined income of the husband and wife, including income from regular part-time employment. Obviously this means a great increase in home purchasing power for married couples.

The law also forbids lenders to ask about birth control methods and childbearing plans, a practice which some mortgage institutions have used when they were doubtful of the long-range stability of the wife's income.

SEPARATED OR DIVORCED WOMEN AND CREDIT

The new law's requirement that joint accounts be kept in both spouses' names becomes especially important in cases of separation or divorce. You can have your own well-established credit rating to rely on at a time when changes in your life will probably make credit purchases necessary. Lenders are forbidden to withdraw or refuse credit simply because of a change in marital status as long as you yourself are still creditworthy.

Elinor Baggett has a real horror story to relate about paying off a former husband's debts. "After my divorce in 1961 I bought a home in Alabama for fifteen thousand dollars. I was making four hundred fifty dollars a month and had two small children to support. On that amount I had to live, make my house payments, and make monthly payments to my mother for the down payment she had lent me. But worst of all, I had to pay off ten thousand dollars of debt my former husband had incurred in order to reclaim some Florida property my father had left me! I rented out the upstairs bedrooms in order to survive."

Elinor turned her dismal situation into stable financial position when, after she moved to California in 1972, she not only had all her debts paid off, but was able to buy a house for $39,000 that is now worth $125,000. Last year she sold the Alabama and Florida properties and was able to take back the mortgage papers herself. However, even with her remarkable history a loan company did not want to grant her a loan. "I had to show my income tax return several times to substantiate my income, despite the fact that at the time I had properties on which to borrow. I'm not so sure that would have happened to a man." Elinor has since gone on to be half owner of a travel agency.

If your husband has a bad credit rating, it can no longer be used to deny you credit unless you have signed jointly for credit or live in a community property state.

These provisions will help women who become divorced or separated in the future. But the law's greatest change for divorced women affects you no matter how long you have been divorced as long as you derive some or all of your income from alimony or child support. Credit institutions must now give full weight to these sources of income in evaluating your application, provided they are steady and reliable.

It is true they are not always reliable. Therefore, you have to prove to the lender that your alimony and child support are income that you can count on. Such proof might consist of a court order or of the agreement setting the payments and records showing that the payments have been made promptly and on time over a period of years. Under these circumstances, the lender has the right to ask for credit information on your ex-husband because you derive your income from him.

WIDOWS AND CREDIT

It is extremely important for all married women to take advantage of the new law to establish credit in their own names because unfortunately they are going to need it. Women live longer than men and will more than likely face widowhood.

The widow's credit situation has a lot in common with the divorced woman's. In both cases the man, whom lenders believed to be her financial prop, is no longer there, so his credit is no longer available to her. In each instance the woman has to start from scratch to prove her creditworthiness.

The death of a husband no longer means that all joint accounts, such as savings, checking and charge accounts, will be withdrawn from the widow. Creditors cannot terminate accounts because of a change in your marital status unless they have *evidence* that your financial situation has changed for the worse. However, if the account is based solely on your husband's income, you may be asked to reapply to prove you are still willing and able to pay.

The Equal Credit Opportunity Act can protect you from other people's prejudice, but it cannot protect you from your own folly. If you are a poor money manager, if you run up too many debts and don't pay your bills, you will still find yourself being turned down for credit.

If, however, you do experience discrimination based on sex or marital status when applying for credit, your first step is to let your creditor know your feelings. If the situation is not rectified to your satisfaction, write to both the state and federal agencies that have jurisdiction over the credit-granting institution, and send a copy to the prospective creditor.

On the state level, write to your state banking commission or consumer protection agency. On the federal level, write directly to the federal agency that has jurisdiction over the credit-granting institution. (If you are applying in writing, you'll find the name of this agency either on the application or an accompanying notice.) Or you can write to:

Bureau of Consumer Protection
Federal Trade Commission
Washington, D.C. 20560

or:

Office of Saver & Consumer Affairs
Federal Reserve Board
Washington, D.C. 20551

These two agencies can refer your letter to other agencies.

Good money management has as its basis a very simple rule: Buy only what you can afford, and borrow only what you can pay back. As oversimplified as that may sound, it's a safe guide to building and maintaining a credit history of your own. It is, after all, *your* credit history. It is a record of the loans you have assumed and how you have repaid these debts. It is a record that you and you alone write. Just make sure you are receiving all your rights while you are writing this history.

YOUR CREDIT RIGHTS

Under the *Equal Credit Opportunity Act* you have a right to:

- Receive credit in your own name.
- Refuse to answer questions about childbearing.
- Have your income considered on the same basis as a man's on credit applications.
- Have alimony and child support considered as income.
- Find out the reasons for credit denial.

Under the *Fair Credit Reporting Act* you have a right to:

- See your credit bureau file.
- Correct any errors.
- Write a statement telling your side of the story.

Under the *Fair Credit Billing Act* you have the right to:

- Suspend payment until the credit issuer resolves the dispute.
- Have an acknowledgment from a creditor within thirty days.
- Have a creditor resolve a dispute within two billing cycles.

Under the *Truth in Lending Act* you have the right to:

- A full written explanation of the dollar and annual percentage rate you owe on any credit transaction.

If you need more information about women and credit or if you feel you have been denied credit because you are a woman, get in touch with the National Association of Commissions for Women in your state. It will advise you of your rights and send you literature advising you on the necessary procedures. We include a state-by-state listing of names (which vary from state to state), addresses and phone numbers for your convenience.

Federal:	National Association of Commissions for Women 1 DuPont Circle NW, Suite 831 Washington, D.C. 20036 (202) 883-4692
Alabama:	Alabama Women's Commission 9 Office Park Circle, Suite 106 Birmingham, Alabama 35223 (205) 879-1237
Alaska:	Alaska State Commission for Human Rights 2457 Arctic Boulevard, Suite 3 Anchorage, Alaska 99503 (907) 274-4692 State Court Building, Pouch AH Juneau, Alaska 99811 (907) 465-3500
Arizona:	Arizona Women's Commission 1624 W. Adams #305 Phoenix, Arizona 85007 (602) 271-3609
Arkansas:	Governor's Commission on the Status of Women Room 001, State Capitol Building Little Rock, Arkansas 72201 (501) 371-2174
California:	California Commission on the Status of Women 926 J Street, Room 1003 Sacramento, California 95814 (916) 445-3173
Colorado:	Colorado Commission on the Status of Women Room 600 C, 1525 Sherman Street State Services Building Denver, Colorado 80203 (303) 892-2821

Connecticut: Permanent Commission on the Status of Women
                        6 Grand Street
                        Hartford, Connecticut 06115
                        (203) 566-5702

Delaware: Council for Women
                        630 State College Road
                        Dover, Delaware 19901
                        (302) 678-4923

District of   D.C. Commission on the Status of Women
Columbia: Room 204, 14th and E Streets NW
                        District Building
                        Washington, D.C. 20004
                        (202) 629-5238

Florida: Governor's Commission on the Status of Women
                        Office of the Governor, The Capitol
                        Tallahassee, Florida 32304
                        (904) 488-4812

Georgia: Georgia Commission on the Status of Women
                        c/o Office of the Governor, State Capitol
                        Atlanta, Georgia 30334
                        (404) 656-2196

Hawaii: Hawaii State Commission on the Status of Women
                        250 South King Street, Room 500
                        Honolulu, Hawaii 96813
                        (808) 548-4199

Idaho: Idaho Commission on Women's Programs
                        Statehouse
                        Boise, Idaho 83720
                        (208) 384-3533

Illinois: Illinois Commission on the Status of Women
                        1166 Debbie Lane
                        Macomb, Illinois 61455
                        (309) 833-4282

Indiana: Fort Wayne Women's Bureau
                        P.O. Box 554
                        Fort Wayne, Indiana 46801
                        (219) 743-0033

Iowa: Iowa Commission on the Status of Women
                        507 Tenth Street
                        Des Moines, Iowa 50319
                        (515) 247-4461

Kansas: Mayor's Commission on the Status of Women
                        Mayor's Office, City Hall
                        215 East Seventh Street
                        Topeka, Kansas 66612
                        (913) 235-9261

Kentucky: Kentucky Commission for Women
                        212 Washington Street
                        Frankfort, Kentucky 40601
                        (502) 564-6643

Louisiana: Bureau of the Status of Women
                        150 Riverside Mall
                        Baton Rouge, Louisiana 70801
                        (504) 389-6136

Maine: Maine Commission for Women
                        State House
                        Augusta, Maine 04333
                        (207) 289-3418

Maryland: Maryland Commission for Women
                        1100 North Eutaw Street
                        Baltimore, Maryland 21201
                        (301) 383-5608

Massachusetts: Governor's Commission on the Status of Women
                        Room 1105, 100 Cambridge Street
                        Boston, Massachusetts 02202
                        (617) 727-6693

Michigan: Michigan Women's Commission
                        815 Washington Square Building
                        Lansing, Michigan 48933
                        (517) 373-2884

Minnesota: Women's Advisory Committee
                        Department of Human Rights
                        200 Capitol Square Building
                        St. Paul, Minnesota 55101
                        (612) 296-5663

Mississippi: Mississippi Governor's Commission on the
                            Status of Women
                        1315 Camp Street
                        Hattiesburg, Mississippi 39401
                        (601) 583-8623

Missouri: Missouri Commission on the Status of Women
                        c/o Department of Labor and Industrial Relations
                        421 E. Dunklin Street
                        Jefferson City, Missouri 65101
                        (314) 751-4091

Montana: Montana Status of Women Advisory Council
                        Power Block Building Annex, Room 2
                        Helena, Montana 59601
                        (406) 449-2856

Nebraska: Nebraska Commission on the Status of Women
                        619 Terminal Building
                        Lincoln, Nebraska 68508
                        (402) 471-2039

Nevada: Governor's Commission on the Status of People
                        c/o Dr. Felicia Campbell
                        University of Nevada, Department of English
                        Las Vegas, Nevada 89154
                        (702) 739-3533

New Hampshire: Commission on the Status of Women
                        3 Capitol Street, Room 301
                        Concord, New Hampshire 03301
                        (603) 271-3685

New Jersey: New Jersey Department of Community Affairs
                        Division on Women
                        363 West State Street
                        Trenton, New Jersey 08625
                        (609) 292-8840

New Mexico: New Mexico Commission on the Status of
                            Women
                        600 Second Street, NW
                        Albuquerque, New Mexico 87102
                        (505) 842-3141

New York: Women's Division, Executive Chamber
                    State of New York
                    1350 Avenue of the Americas
                    New York, New York 10010
                    (212) 977-5740

North Carolina: North Carolina Council on the Status of Women
                    526 North Wilmington Street
                    Raleigh, North Carolina 27604
                    (919) 829-2455

North Dakota: Governor's Council on Human Resources
                    Commission on the Status of Women
                    Thirteenth Floor, State Capitol
                    Bismarck, North Dakota 58505
                    (701) 224-2970

Ohio: Ohio Women's Advisory Council
                    Women's Services Division
                    Ohio Bureau of Employment Services
                    145 South Front Street
                    Columbus, Ohio 43216
                    (614) 466-4496

Oklahoma: Commission on the Status of Women
                    Governor's Office, State Capitol
                    Oklahoma City, Oklahoma 73105
                    (918) 333-5730

Oregon: Oregon Governor's Commission on the Status of
                        Women
                    P.O. Box 40011
                    Portland, Oregon 97240
                    (503) 242-5573

Pennsylvania: Pennsylvania Commission for Women
                    512 Finance Building
                    Harrisburg, Pennsylvania 17120
                    (717) 787-8128

Rhode Island: Permanent Advisory Commission on Women in
                        Rhode Island
                    235 Promenade Street
                    Providence, Rhode Island 02908
                    (401) 277-2734

South Carolina: South Carolina Commission on the Status of
    Women
P.O. Box 11467
Columbia, South Carolina 29201
(803) 758-3779

South Dakota: South Dakota Commission on the Status of
    Women
State Office Building, Illinois Street
Pierre, South Dakota 57501
(605) 224-3722

Tennessee: Tennessee Commission on the Status of Women
1212 Andrew Jackson Building
Nashville, Tennessee 37219
(615) 741-1013

Texas: Dallas Commission on the Status of Women
c/o Dallas Public Library
1954 Commerce Street
Dallas, Texas 75201
(214) 748-9071, Extension 259

San Antonio Mayor's Commission on the Status
    of Women
235 Yolanda Drive
San Antonio, Texas 78228
(512) 225-5411

Utah: Governor's Commission on the Status of Women
118 State Capitol
Salt Lake City, Utah 84114
(801) 533-6318

Vermont: The Vermont Governor's Commission on the
    Status of Women
Second Floor, Pavilion Office Building
Montpelier, Vermont 05602
(802) 828-2851

Virginia: Virginia Commission on the Status of Women
Fourth Floor, Fourth Street Office Building
Richmond, Virginia 23219
(804) 358-9518

Washington: Washington State Women's Council
313 Insurance Building

Olympia, Washington 98504
(206) 753-2870

West Virginia: West Virginia Commission on the Status of
Women
Box 446
Institute, West Virginia 25112
(304) 768-4657

Wisconsin: Wisconsin Governor's Commission on the
Status of Women
30 Mifflin Street, Room 210
Madison, Wisconsin 53703
(608) 266-1162

Wyoming: Wyoming Commission on the Status of Women
Office of the Labor Commissioner
Barrett Building
Cheyenne, Wyoming 82002
(307) 777-7261

5

Our Banking Institutions

In most cities you'll find at least one bank or savings and loan on the corner. Even if you do not write checks, and that is highly unlikely, you may need to send a money order or cash an out-of-town check on occasion. It is almost impossible to live in modern society and never use a bank, and it is vital that you understand both the differences between banks and the mechanisms of banking.

While the simple proposition that a bank is a bank is a bank may seem to be true, it is not that simple. You may encounter several types of banks, depending on the state where you live and the types of services a bank offers. First of all, the most common bank is the commercial bank. This type of bank offers checking accounts and short-term loans. You may bank at either a national bank or a state bank. Generally you can determine whether a bank is a national bank by the appearance of the letters *N.A.* or the words "National Association" in the title. This type of commercial bank has been chartered by the Controller of the Currency and is regulated by rules and regulations of the federal government. A state bank is one which has been chartered by the state and is governed by state, rather than federal, banking rules. Generally the larger banks are national banks and the smaller banks are chartered by the state.

Savings and loan banks are also chartered by both the state and the federal governments. Their main function is to use the savings deposits of their depositors, or investors, to invest in long-term loans, especially in real estate. They can, by law, pay higher interest on a savings account than a commercial bank can.

Savings and loans are the major source of residential credit in the United States. They are the financial intermediary that receives money from the public for savings and in turn lends the bulk of those savings to homebuilders and buyers. For this, the savings and loan association assumes the loan risk and collects interest from its borrowers. It pays out the major portion of this interest to savers as a return on their deposits.

Savings and loan associations are private institutions, and the responsibility for whatever each association does lies in a board of directors. Each association is either federally chartered or chartered by the state, as is a commercial bank. State associations are chartered under state statutes and are supervised and examined by the state's applicable banking or savings and loan departments. Federal associations are subject to the supervision of the Federal Home Loan Bank Board. Federal associations must, by law, have their savings accounts insured by the FSLIC (Federal Savings & Loan Insurance Corporation). Insurance of accounts is optional for most state-chartered institutions, but the majority provide their customers this protection. In addition to the FSLIC, Massachusetts, Ohio, Maryland, and North Carolina have set up their own insuring organizations. These four state funds which were authorized by their respective state legislatures, have duties and powers set forth by the laws of their states and are answerable to public officials and supervisory authorities.

SAVINGS AND LOAN ORGANIZATIONS

There are two types of savings and loan organizations or associations: mutual and corporate. The more widespread form is the mutual, in which the savings account holders are the owners of the organization and are legally known as shareowners or shareholders. In a mutual savings and loan, you are entitled to one vote for every $100 you have invested at the time an election for members of the board of directors is held. Not all states have mutual savings and loans. Corporate savings and loan companies issue stock just as other corporations do. This form of savings and loan is more prevalent in the states of California, Ohio, and Texas. Many corporate savings and loan companies pay interest instead of dividends. Dividends paid out of profits by savings and loans are not guaranteed, and as such the dividends could be reduced if there was a lack of profit, although this would be a rare occurrence. At a bank the depositor is a creditor, and the interest is legally guaranteed, whether or not the bank makes a profit. If a savings and loan association pays interest instead of a dividend, the interest is guaranteed.

Basically savings accounts are insured by the federal government for amounts up to $40,000. Because of an arrangement for multiple-account insurance, a family of two can have several combinations of accounts that add up to $200,000, and have their money insured. For example, each party has one account insured for $40,000; two people have a joint account insured for $80,000; they can hold special-purpose accounts, etc. These different accounts will add up to the $200,000. A family of three can have a total of $400,000 and so on, fully insured.

In addition to offering mortgages, a savings and loan can offer you several types of savings accounts with higher interest rates than a commercial bank. Most of them can provide you with money market certificates, based on the average return obtainable for six-month U.S. treasury bills. These money market certificates are issued by the savings and loan on a weekly basis, with the interest rate guaranteed for six months. The method of computation of interest varies by institution. It could be compounded daily, weekly, or quarterly. Generally, the certificates must be purchased for a minimum amount which differs according to which savings and loan you consult.

You can have investment certificates which mature on a four to ten year basis and yield higher interest than shorter term certificates.

A savings and loan can also offer you regular passbook accounts as well as certificates of deposit. A certificate of deposit may also be known as a bank bond, guaranteed income bond, or savings certificate. Before you deposit your money in any savings and loan, shop around for the best deal. Interest payments can be figured in so many different ways that the same amount of money you deposit can earn one sum of interest in one institution and many times more interest in another. So you should find out the method of interest calculation before you open your account. You will receive the best return on your money when the interest is compounded daily and paid from day of deposit to day of withdrawal. How long you keep your money in your account naturally will determine what kind of interest you will receive. Any account in which the money remains untouched for a period of ninety days or more receives higher rates than the ordinary passbook account. A passbook account is one in which you can deposit and withdraw money at any time. Interest is paid on your account balance.

A savings and loan, however, may offer a variety of inducements to attract your money. For example, the *Wall Street Journal* stated that in Missouri and Arkansas the supermarkets and savings and loans teamed up on a consumer discount plan. The participating store gave discounts from 1 to 3 percent, but instead of the amount being deducted from its customer's bill, the cash was deposited in the customer's account at a local savings and loan association. To take advantage of this plan, the customer opened a new account with a minimum deposit of $10; the supermarket then transferred the accumulated discounts directly into the savings account.

In Los Angeles, California, a savings and loan established a consumer buying service for the benefit of its customers. It provided a centralized buying service, enabling its customers to purchase, at the best price possible, all kinds of consumer goods and services.

Other savings and loans provide even more unusual benefits. Claire Julini and her husband, Bill, have lived in the same small town since they were married more than sixty years ago. Claire is unable to see, and Bill has a bad heart condition. Because they have dividend checks and other income checks to deposit each week, the savings and loan comes directly to their house to see them. The savings and loan employee drive them either to the savings and loan itself to conduct business or, on occasion, to their commercial bank. This is not something that is a general policy of savings and loans or their personnel, but it is indicative of the courtesy that may be extended to customers by a financial institution to please you, the customer.

A savings and loan can offer you safe-deposit boxes and related services. You can obtain notary services, have documents copied, and purchase government securities as well as invest in certificates of deposit. You can establish a retirement plan—either an Individual Retirement Account (IRA) or Keogh, whichever applies to your personal situation. Some savings and loans even sell life insurance and provide income tax preparation.

The following is a chart which shows how a fixed investment grows. (A fixed investment is one in which the dividend or interest is contractually fixed until maturity.) A certificate of deposit is a fixed investment and is the type of investment found at a savings and loan.

How a Fixed
Investment Grows

This chart shows how given amounts grow when left in your savings account for various periods of time. Figures are projected at 5¼% a year, compounded daily.

HOW SAVINGS GROW	$50	$100	$500	$1,000	$5,000	$10,000
6 mos.	51.34	102.69	513.47	1026.95	5134.75	10269.50
1 year	52.70	105.39	526.95	1053.90	5269.50	10539.00
2 years	55.54	111.07	555.35	1110.71	5553.53	11107.05
3 years	58.53	117.06	585.29	1170.57	5852.86	11705.72
4 years	61.68	123.37	616.83	1233.67	6168.33	12336.66
5 years	65.01	130.02	650.08	1300.16	6500.80	13001.61
10 years	84.52	169.04	845.21	1690.42	8452.09	16904.18
20 years	142.88	285.75	1428.76	2857.51	14287.56	28575.12

THRIFT AND LOANS

If you live in California, Colorado, Hawaii, Indiana, Iowa, Kentucky, Minnesota, Nebraska, Rhode Island, Utah, or West Virginia, you should be aware of institutions known as thrift and loans. Thrift and loans are also known as industrial banks, industrials, industrial loan companies, industrial savings banks, industrial loan and thrift companies, and loan and investment companies.

What is a thrift and loan or an industrial bank? For our purposes, they both are the same type of institution, organized under the industrial banking laws of a state. A thrift and loan is regarded as an institution which extends consumer loans, repayable on an installment basis. Thrift and loans purchase sales contracts from furniture or appliance companies, among others. The laws that govern these types of institutions are often indefinite and sometimes conflicting. (For example, many companies use the words "Morris Plan" in their name, but an increasing number are not affiliated with the original Morris Plan system. One of the very first forms of a thrift and loan was established in Virginia by Arthur J. Morris; hence the name.)

Another difference between a thrift and loan and a bank is that a thrift and loan does not have checking accounts. In states where there are no thrift and loans or industrial banks, a company may operate as a consumer finance company. (You can borrow money, but you cannot invest it.) At a thrift and loan, you can also purchase term investment certificates. A term investment certificate is a time certificate which requires a larger investment and yields a higher return than standard savings accounts. The rates for a term investment certificate will be competitive with all financial institutions, although at any given time one institution may pay higher rates than another, and you must be aware that the amount of interest you receive on a term investment certificate when you invest on one day may not be the interest you receive the next time you invest. This interest rate variance happens in any financial institution.

One of the best reasons for opening a savings account (known as an installment investment certificate—in simpler terms, a current passbook account) at a thrift and loan is that the interest rate is usually higher than a savings and loan or commercial bank offers. Commercial banks are allowed to pay only a statutory (by law) amount on savings. In states like Colorado and California, thrift and loan investments must be protected against losses by a guaranty fund which is not the same as Federal Deposit Insurance. This is not true in other states. According to Richard Leahy, assistant vice-president and assistant director of industry relations at Avco Financial Services, "One of the best ways to earn more interest on your invested money is to purchase a term investment certificate, open a passbook savings account for as little as a dollar at the same time, and then have the interest from the time deposit transferred to the passbook account, so that you will be earning interest on your interest." A woman should shop for the highest interest rates. As not all states have guaranty fund protection for investors, however, she should make certain that her funds will be properly protected.

Harriette Beasley, who was in her sixties, had taken $6,000 she had received from an inheritance and invested it in a thrift and loan. What she did not know was that she should have asked that important question of whether her funds would be protected. As it happened, the thrift and loan closed its doors because it had not complied with all the necessary state laws that governed thrift and loans, and the company was not maintaining the proper insurance protection. Harriette was unable to recover her money. She now says she wishes someone had told her to find out whether her money was protected, rather than find out too late that it was not protected at all.

Thrift and loans finance all kinds of consumer loans as well as second mortgages. The lending rates vary with the conditions of the economy and the prime rate. The procedure of obtaining a loan through a thrift and loan is no different from the procedure at commercial banks or savings and loans, and loan information has become more standardized with the passage of the Equal Credit

Opportunity Act. The thrift and loan still looks at your income versus your expenses and at your capacity to repay the amount of money you want to borrow. In most cases, however, you will probably find a thrift and loan is much more liberal in its lending policy than the savings and loan or bank is, but be prepared to pay more interest.

COMMERCIAL BANKS

A bank comes in two categories: state or nationally chartered. The large bank feels it can offer more services with its convenient branch banking. The smaller bank contradicts this by saying it provides a hometown feeling and that it is more people-oriented. You can shop for the bank you like just as you shop for clothes; you choose a store where the merchandise is quality and the employees are helpful and courteous.

One might call a bank a financial department store because a bank generally provides a variety of services other than just checking. At most banks, you may have your Social Security check, government pension, or even paycheck automatically deposited to your savings or checking account. You can also arrange to have payments for your house or insurance released automatically from your checking account on a monthly basis. If your credit is good, you can obtain overdraft protection as well as check guarantee cards, for either Master Charge or Visa and in some cases, for both. A bank will also sell you traveler's checks and provide or redeem foreign currency for you. If you are over sixty-two, many banks provide free checking accounts. (Remember, you need a Social Security number to open a bank account.)

One of the newest ideas in finance finding its way to commercial banks is an interest-bearing checking account, which means that the money lying idle in your checking account will be earning interest under certain predetermined conditions as stated by your bank. An interest-bearing checking account combines features of both checking and savings accounts: You still write checks, but you also earn interest. You'll receive a direct payment of interest based on an established interest rate and your account balance. The amount of interest you earn will be reflected in your monthly statement. The banks that are doing this often charge for services which were formerly free. One of the most common of these accounts is called the NOW account. This is really a savings account with special withdrawal privileges. As a practical matter it works like a checking account that earns interest. Instead of writing a check, you prepare a negotiable order of withdrawal (NOW). This order looks just like the familiar personal check.

Most banks offer, besides checking and savings accounts: time certificates (high-interest-yield accounts), a full trust department, safe-deposit boxes for valuables, a travel department, Christmas clubs, an auto-leasing department, and a credit department. Also, most banks have a customer service department you use when you are having trouble reconciling your statement or when you are seeking more banking information. According to Pat Mellor, head bookkeeper of the Bank of Newport in Newport Beach, California, "We have just as many men needing assistance with their banking as we do women."

When asked what the most common errors she sees are, Mrs. Mellor responded, "Not balancing statements, errors in addition and subtraction, failure to write down checks, adding deposits twice. People should realize that checks represent money and be as careful with their checks as they would be with their money. Many times we will receive checks written in pencil, unsigned checks, checks with no accompanying deposit slips. Then customers don't understand why we haven't credited their accounts. One customer never wrote down the exact amount of a check. She would round it off to the nearest figure, above or below. Naturally her figures didn't gibe with ours."

Mrs. Mellor does not feel that banks necessarily discriminate against women when granting loans. "If anything, they go overboard to help a woman get a loan. They know many women are now comparison shopping. Also, banks, under the new fair credit laws, have to give a reason for denying a loan. If you are turned down, pin the loan officer down as to why. Loans are still granted on the basis of your financial statement, your ability to pay, and your credit rating." Mrs. Mellor went on to say, "The bank is the right place to obtain a loan, open a checking account, or take advantage of some of the other services, but I'm a firm believer in not keeping more than $100 over what it takes to meet your monthly obligations in a checking account because you are not earning interest on the money."

In conclusion, Mrs. Mellor went on to tell about a woman who had never written a check in her life and didn't know how to. She left everything of that nature up to her husband. "When he died, we had to teach her how to write a check. Let us hope there are not many women out there like that, for they may be in for a shock if something happens to their husbands." Mrs. Mellor knows of what she speaks. She was widowed five years ago and left with three children. "Fortunately I had always handled the money, and I would advise any woman, married or single, to become aware of finances.

"One final comment worth mentioning is that banks do make mistakes in account balances. If you find you are continually facing this problem, and it is the bank's error, you might be more than wise to change banks."

BALANCING YOUR CHECKBOOK

One of the most timeworn clichés husbands use when referring to their wives is: "She never has known how to balance the checkbook," an annoying statement, to be sure, since many husbands are inept when it comes to managing money and many wives handle all the finances. There are some women (as well as men) who don't list working with numbers as one of their talents; if you are one of these, here are some simple procedures for balancing a checkbook and figuring your bank statement.

When you balance your checkbook or reconcile your bank statement, compare your record of your checking account with the bank's record of your account. To balance, both records must show the same additions and subtractions.

The Balancing Procedure

The checkbook balancing procedure has been developed by banks over the years to enable you to know how much money you have in your checking account today, even though you may have made deposits and written checks since the date of the bank statement.

Your checkbook contains a listing of checks you've written and a "running balance" computed by subtracting checks as you write them and adding deposits as they are made. (If you have not kept a running balance, do the necessary arithmetic before you begin balancing your checkbook.)

A *bank statement* is the bank's record of your checking account—up to the statement date. It shows all checks and charges subtracted and deposits added by the bank during this statement cycle (period ending on the date your statement is prepared by the bank). Your statement is issued regularly each month or regularly each quarter.

Canceled checks are enclosed with your statement.

What Balancing Does

- Tells you how much money you have in your checking account.
- Reviews *your record* and the *bank's record* to make sure they both show the same additions and subtractions and balance.
- Shows agreement between *your record* of your account (as shown in your checkbook) and the *bank's record* of your account (as shown on your bank statement).

Reconciling Your Statement and Your Checkbook

- Find the *New Balance* on your bank statement.
  Copy it on the back of the statement.
- Locate the *Deposits* area on your bank statement.
  Compare the deposits listed on your bank statement with deposits you have recorded in your checkbook.
  If you find a deposit recorded in your checkbook that is not listed on your bank statement (not yet certified by bank), write it down on the back of your statement.
  If you find a deposit on the bank statement that you did not record in your checkbook, first verify, by checking your deposit slips, that it's your deposit; then record it in your checkbook.
  Add *New Balance* and *Deposits Not Yet Credited by Bank* to get *Subtotal*.
- Record in your checkbook any deposit of yours listed on the bank statement that you have not already recorded in your checkbook.
  Add this amount to the last balance you have recorded in your checkbook.
  Now all additions to your account during this statement cycle are recorded on both your record and the bank's record.
- Mark off (√) canceled checks in your checkbook. This tells you what checks the bank has already subtracted from your account—what checks the bank has "paid."
  If you find a canceled check that you have not recorded in your checkbook, record it now, and subtract the amount from your checkbook balance.
- Return to the back of the bank statement. List and add up the checks *not* marked off in your checkbook. These are "checks outstanding"—checks the bank had not received and "paid" by the statement date.

Subtract the *Total* of *Checks Not Yet Paid by Bank*—checks outstanding—from the *Subtotal* to get the *Adjusted Bank Balance Statement*.

(Since you have already subtracted these checks from your checkbook, you must also subtract them from the bank statement so that both your record and the bank's record will show the same subtractions.)

- Find the service charge listed at the top of the *Checks and Other Debits* area on your bank statement. If you have not already subtracted it, subtract the service charge from your checkbook balance now. You may have a service charge if you write more than the minimum number of checks allowed by the type of account you maintain, or you may be charged for each check you write. In still other plans you may have free checking as long as you maintain a minimum balance. The amount of monthly service charges can vary from bank to bank and account to account.

  If there are other charges listed that you have not subtracted, subtract them from your checkbook balance now. What you have left will be your *Adjusted Checkbook Balance*.

- Compare your *Adjusted Bank Statement Balance* with your *Adjusted Checkbook Balance*. They should be equal. If you have followed steps 1 through 6, your record should show the same additions, subtractions, and balance as the bank's record.

  When *your record* equals the *bank's record*, you have "balanced your checkbook." This is how much money you have in your checking account today. If you cannot get it balanced, see the teller at your bank.

Once you've balanced your checkbook and have an accurate balance, you have a reference point—a starting point that helps you keep an accurate record of your check writing and deposits, that helps you know how much you have in your account from day to day. You should try to balance your account whenever you receive your statement.

The Bank's Record—Your bank statement is the bank's record of your checking account. It is issued regularly each month (or quarter) and lists all the activity in your account.

As you make deposits, they are posted and added to your account. As the checks you write reach the bank, they are posted and subtracted from your account. Your checks are then canceled and filed. On the statement date—at the end of your statement cycle— your bank statement is prepared and delivered to you along with your canceled checks.

Your Record—As long as you have a checking account, you will receive a bank statement and have the bank's record of your account. But without your own record of your account, there is nothing for the bank statement to balance *with*. For that reason, the record you keep of the activity in your checking account is the most important part of balancing your checkbook; it makes "balancing" possible.

Your record keeping need not be complicated, but it does require consistency: (1) Record each check when you write it and each deposit when it's made; (2) subtract each check or add each deposit immediately; and (3) keep a running balance in your checkbook.

Review and Correction—By bringing both records into agreement promptly when you receive your statement, you have the opportunity to: (1) review the checks you've written during the past month (or quarter); (2) verify the amounts of deposits, checks, and charges; (3) correct any errors in your record of your account; and (4) correct any errors in the bank's record of your account.

Prevent Bounced Checks—Regular checkbook balancing is the only way of being certain of how much money you have in your checking account. And knowing your account balance is the best way to prevent bounced checks.

Bounced checks are costly and embarrassing. The bank charges a fee for each overdraft or returned check. Supermarkets and other business that allow you check-cashing privileges may also charge you a fee for checks returned to them.

Checks are being processed faster than ever. A check you cash today has a good chance of being posted to your account tonight. With computers, a large bank may process more than a million checks in a single day. Planning on "float time"—time to cover your check with a deposit—is risking a bounced check these days.

Responsibility—Your checking account represents a contractual relationship with your bank. Both you and the bank have certain responsibilities with regard to your account. The bank's are determined by law and sound operating procedures. Your responsibilities are based on your legal duty to examine promptly your statements, canceled checks, and other included items and to report errors, suspected forgeries, or alterations on any check or item. You also have the responsibility of writing only checks for which you have money in your account. For your own protection, report lost or stolen checks promptly.

Credit Reference—A properly maintained checking account can become a good credit reference; it can indicate the way you handle your finances. It also establishes the fact that you have a banking relationship.

Sound Money Management—Your checking account can be an effective budgeting tool. By recording deposits and checks, you develop an efficient record of income and expenses. By balancing your checkbook regularly, you have a built-in review of your financial situation: You know where your money is going and where spending adjustments may be needed.

CORRECTING CHECKBOOK ERRORS

If you've gone through the balancing procedure described and your checkbook still won't balance, this checklist may help you locate the error.

☐ *Automatic Transactions.* Make sure you've added to or subtracted from your record all automatic deposits and deductions—and all miscellaneous credits and charges that appear on your statement. Don't forget instant cash deposits.

☐ *Arithmetic.* Check the addition and subtraction in your checkbook and in the balancing procedure. (If the difference between your balance and the bank's can be evenly divided by 2, the error could have been caused by adding—instead of subtracting—a check in your checkbook.)

☐ *Transposing.* Can the difference between your balance and the bank's be evenly divided by 9? If so, there's a good chance the error was caused by transposing numbers—for example, recording a $23 check for $32, or $5.17 as $7.15.

☐ *Recording Errors.* Compare the check numbers and check amounts that you recorded in your checkbook with the check numbers and check amounts on the canceled checks you received. (On each check, the check amount recorded by the computer is encoded on the bottom right corner of the check under your signature. This should also be the same as the check amount you wrote and recorded.)

☐ *Last Month's "Checks Outstanding."* Any checks outstanding from *last* month's balancing that still have not been paid by the bank (that still don't show up on your statement) must be included in *this* month's list of checks outstanding.

☐ *Balance Carry-Forward*. In your checkbook, be sure that you carried forward the same balance from the bottom of one page to the top of the next page.

☐ *Unrecorded Canceled Checks*. Have you recorded—and subtracted from your checkbook balance—all the canceled checks listed on your statement and enclosed with your statement?

☐ *Missing Check* (missing from your checkbook record or from the numerical listing on your statement). Did you forget to record a check you've written? You may have saved a sales receipt that would help jog your memory. Have you destroyed a check? You can visit the statement window at your bank and learn about your canceled checks before they're normally returned to you.

☐ *"Less Cash" Deposit*. When you deposit a check and withdraw part of your deposit in cash (in one transaction using one deposit slip), you have a "less cash" deposit. Be sure you recorded the correct amount that is added to your account. Check the teller's stamped entry on the deposit record page of your checkbook or your receipt (stamped duplicate deposit slip).

☐ *Same Deposits*. Do you and the bank show the same number of deposits and for the same amounts? You should have a receipt or a stamped entry in your checkbook to verify the amount of each deposit.

☐ *Matching Statement Balances*. Be sure the previous balance on this month's statement is the same as the new balance on last month's statement.

☐ *Still Won't Balance?* If you need further help, gather together all your records—checkbook, deposit receipts, statements, and canceled checks—and visit the statement window at your bank.

Receiving "Today's Balance"—Here's an important point to remember: Today's balance, as given to you by your bank, may not necessarily be the true balance of your account. It won't include checks you've written that have not yet reached the bank. You need to make allowance for these checks to prevent overdrawing your account.

If you have not balanced your checkbook in months, the best method is to systematically reconcile your statements to your checkbook, starting with your oldest checks and your oldest statements and balancing month by month until you are up to date.

If you don't have a complete record of deposits and checks written: (1.) Visit the statement window at your bank for help in reaching an accurate balance. Bring your checkbook and your last two bank statements with the enclosed canceled checks. (2.) Once you have balanced your checkbook, keeping your future records current will enable you to know how much money you have in your checking account from day to day. Regular balancing will become easier.

BORROWING MONEY

Now that you understand all the mechanics involved in maintaining a checking and savings account, there is yet a third very important function of banking institutions. Banks and savings and loans are our most important source of borrowing money for purchases for which we do not have cash. These purchases can be anything from a car to a new home.

When you borrow money, you obtain the use of someone else's money in order to increase your purchasing power. For the use of this money, you pay a fee in the form of a finance charge. What goes into this fee is the amount of money you pay to borrow the money plus your lender's cost of overhead to allow you to borrow the money. There are legal limits on how much interest can be charged by private individuals and national banks, but not by financial institutions. If you borrow from a private lender and you are charged higher than your state limit, it is called usury, and you can take legal steps to recover the excess amount you paid. Usury laws can also refer to mortgage ceilings on conventional housing contracts other than FHA or VA loans or to those not made by national banks. National banks are allowed to charge 1 percent above the federal discount rate.

Each time you consider borrowing money, ask yourself whether you can afford to repay the loan without taking money away from other necessary expenditures. If the answer is yes, you should have no fear in borrowing funds to finance a home, a car, an education, or new furniture. You might want to borrow to consolidate a lot of your debts, but remember, over a long period of time, you will pay more in total interest.

There used to be a cartoon about putting all your monthly obligations into one backbreaking load, but it becomes not so funny when this happens to you, and it can, if you are not debt-conscious.

When you find you want to borrow money, you should know what annual percentage rate (APR) you will be charged. Remember, the Consumer Credit Protection Act states that the terms of various credit transactions between lender and consumer be fully disclosed before the transaction is completed. Your lender must identify the cash price, all other charges, the down payment, and the amount you are going to finance. This last amount must be equal to the cash price, plus all other charges, minus your down payment. The total cost of your credit will be expressed in terms of APR. Also, when you are shopping for a loan, state what the loan is to be used for, because different loans command different interest rates. Most short-term loans are based on the prime interest rate—that is, the rate offered by a commercial bank to its best customers. If the loan is for your home, it could be the best rate given on single detached residences. Lenders charge interest on money you borrow to make money. Loan rates will vary only slightly from institution to institution, however. One thing you should especially remember is never to be embarrassed to shop for the best loan terms. Banks, savings and loan associations, thrift and loans, consumer finance companies, and credit unions are merchants. It just so happens their product is money.

6

Budgeting Your Income

A budget, or a spending plan, is an aid to help you spend your money wisely, meet your obligations, and reach your financial goals. Preparing a budget takes planning, and following a budget takes discipline. If you are already on a budget and inflation has not been playing havoc with it, you are indeed lucky. But if you are like most of us, you are wondering what you can do to improve your financial situation.

If you have been working for some time and are already painfully aware of what you have to live on, or if you are a woman at home who handles the money and find your income isn't covering your expenses, you should consider budgeting. You may be able to iron out some money wrinkles by finding the trouble spots in your spending.

The American Bankers Association has set down ten questions that serve as signals to help you spot "money trouble".

1. Do you use credit to buy many of the things you bought last year with cash?
2. Have you taken out loans to consolidate your debts or asked for extensions on existing loans to reduce monthly payments?

3. Your standard of living is constant, but does your checking balance get lower each month?
4. You used to pay most bills in full each month, but now do you pay only the minimum amount due on your charge accounts?
5. Although it rarely happened in the past, do you now receive repeated late notices from your creditors?
6. Lately does the withdrawal column in your savings account passbook have more and larger entries than the deposit column?
7. You've borrowed before on your life insurance, but this time are the chances of paying it back remote?
8. Do you now depend on extra income, such as overtime and dividends, to get you through the month?
9. Do you use your checking account ready reserve fund to pay regular monthly bills?
10. Are you juggling your rent or mortgage money to pay other creditors?

The Family Banker, a money management newsletter published by Continental Bank, Chicago, also has a checklist of early-warning signals which should help identify a mismanagement of income:

□ *Absence of a "peak and valley" credit pattern.* That means you are constantly adding to your level of debt without any reduction of your debt.
□ *Sudden difficulty in meeting your regular payments.* If you have noticed an inability to pay what is owed, there has probably been a decrease in your disposable income—that amount of income left over after meeting outstanding payments. This could be due to inflation, job layoffs, emergency expenditures, or overspending on such things as entertainment.
□ *Abuse of credit cards.*
□ *No predetermined payment plan.* Are you delaying paying your bills?
□ *Witholding information of a financial nature from your creditors.*
□ *Lack of a regular savings program.*
□ *No idea of cost of living.*

After reading the above lists, if you found yourself and your financial situation mentioned even once, the time is *now* to think of getting yourself on a budget you can live with (and within).

WITHOLDING TAX

Before you can figure a budget, you must have funds (usually a paycheck) to budget. One of the first bits of business you are asked to do when you go to work is to fill out your W-4 Form (Employee's Witholding Allowance Certificate) on which you indicate the number of witholding allowances (or exemptions) you want to take. How many deductions you take will in part determine whether or not you will receive money back at tax time or have to pay more.

Cammie Jenkins is thirty-five years old, divorced, and has three children to support. She is anxious to have her paycheck as large as possible in order to meet her expenses. When she filled out her W-4 Form, she claimed an allowance for herself and her three children, plus a special witholding allowance (based on the fact she is divorced), on the advice of the personnel department at the company where she is employed. Claiming this special exemption nets Cammie about $10 extra each paycheck. Cammie realized that though the increase is not much, every little bit helps her toward stretching her household budget.

Carmen Munoz has four children and is married to a doctor who claims no witholding whatsoever. In order to make certain there will not be a huge tax to pay at income tax time, Carmen not only has witholding taken out of her gross earnings, but requests an extra amount of money be taken out each payroll period. Her employer has agreed to withhold an extra amount.

Employers have certain IRS regulations, based on the size of the company, which they must follow regarding money deducted from a paycheck for tax purposes. The employer must make deposits payable to the IRS at a bank (generally the company's bank), with specific amounts earmarked for each employee.

If you are having trouble deciding what to withold from your paycheck, it might be wise for you to talk with someone in your personnel department or to seek advice from your tax consultant.

Julian Block, a New York lawyer and tax editor of the Research Institute, suggested the following regarding witholding tax: "Take a close look at how much witholding tax is being deducted from your paycheck, especially if you discovered that you were entitled to receive a hefty refund or obliged to pay a sizeable sum when you settled with the IRS last April. The hitch could be that your withholding is out of whack and that your employer took out too much or too little from your paychecks, and is still doing so."

The same thing will occur this year unless you revise the amount subtracted from your pay. Overwitholding means that the IRS gets the interest-free use of your money until you receive a refund. You can, of course, stay overwithheld each payday as a way of forcing yourself to save, although the government does not pay you interest. Underwithholding means you have to pay the balance, which is due all at once, and you may have to pay interest plus a penalty fee.

There are some points to keep in mind if you think that you should readjust your W-4 Form. One way is to claim extra exemptions. You are also allowed additional exemptions based on your estimates for child care as well as deductions for alimony payments. Remember, though, that even if you qualify for any of these new exemptions, you need not revise your W-4 unless you want to boost or reduce your take-home pay. You can also increase the amount of money in your paycheck if you qualify for any of the following withholding exemptions over and above those you ordinarily claim for yourself or your spouse, children, and other dependents. You get a "special withholding allowance" if you work for only one employer and are single—or are married and your spouse does not work. There are also additional withholding allowances that cut the amount set aside for the IRS if you are to submit an itemized tax form because you expect to have sizable expenses for medical bills, interest payments, charitable contributions, and the like. Just how many of these allowances you can claim is spelled out in a table on the back of the form. Remember, too, that you must file a new W-4 if the number of exemptions you previously claimed decreases as a result of divorce or loss of a dependent.

Now suppose that you have to cope with the reverse problem: You're having too little taken out. It's just as easy to change your W-4 to claim fewer exemptions than you are allowed, thereby increasing the amount that is withheld from each of your paychecks.

Assume, for example, that you are entitled to five withholding exemptions. Simply claim fewer exemptions or none at all on Line 1 of the form. If you want to go even further, ask your employer to withhold an additional amount. Line 2 is where you indicate this.

The marital-status section of the W-4 has a box labeled "Married, but withold at a single rate." To increase the amount of tax withheld, this box can be checked by married couples when both spouses work or by a married person with more than one employer. You can also use extra withholding to avoid the need to make quarterly payments of estimated taxes, due on income from sources not covered by withholding—for instance, earnings from self-employment, alimony, or profits from the sale of investments. If you feel you need more information on the withholding rules, contact your local IRS office and get a free copy of *Tax Witholding and Declaration of Estimated Tax* (Publication 505).

THE W-2 FORM

At the close of the year, or shortly thereafter, you will receive from your employer a statement of your earnings called a W-2 Form. An employer is required to issue a W-2 Form for each employee by January 31. The W-2 gives the amount earned and the income and Social Security withheld during the year. Other information, sometimes found on a W-2 Form, includes state and local taxes withheld; special payroll deductions (for example, private retirement plan contributions, credit union deductions); additional compensation such as life insurance premiums paid by the employer; and reimbursement for moving or travel. Unemployment insurance may also be deducted from your check.

There are several copies of the W-2 Form. Copy A, the original, is forwarded to the Internal Revenue Service by the employer. Copy B (one of the ones you receive), should be attached to your income tax return to be matched with the original by the IRS. Copy C (also one you receive) should be retained by you (a good place is stapled to your copy of your tax return). Copy D is retained by the employer for his records. In states that have a withholding tax, another copy of the W-2 may be issued to the employee for attachment to the state return. This is designated Copy 2. If required, Copy 1 is forwarded to the state taxing agency by the employer.

Most employees have a specified percentage of their gross wage (the total amount you earn) withheld by their employer for the FICA (Social Security payroll deduction). FICA is the Federal Insurance Contributions Act. In 1979 FICA applied to the first $22,900 of earnings of each employee. For persons earning $22,900 or less, all the earnings are subject to FICA deductions (see Social Security chapter). Many government, both federal and local, and railroad employees have their own retirement plans, and thus do not pay FICA. The maximum income limits apply to each individual, not to the combined incomes of a working husband and wife.

WRITING A BUDGET

To be workable, your budget should be tailored to your and your family's needs and income. You may find it easier to keep within your budget if you use a financial record book, available at any

stationery store. The first step in making a budget is to establish
goals: education for the children, buying a car, making a down
payment on a home, reducing debts, starting a savings plan, or just
being able to meet monthly obligations and expenses. List your
goals, to enable you better to keep them in mind.

The next step is to estimate your income for a specific planning
period—one year, three years, five years. Usually budgets for one
year or two years are more realistic and easier to plan. Write down
all the funds you expect to receive during this period. Start with
fixed amounts you receive regularly, such as wages, salary, Social
Security benefits, pensions, allowances, alimony, child support, and
any other income. Then put down, if applicable, the variable income you anticipate, such as income from stocks and bonds, interest
from savings accounts, rents, and any other monies. When your
earnings are irregular, base your estimate on your previous income
and current prospects. Be honest with yourself.

CHART A

Estimated Income for_____

Item	Amount
Wage or salary of— Husband_____	$_____
Wife_____	_____
Net profit from business, farm, or profession_____	_____
Interest, dividends_____	_____
Other_____	_____
Total_____	$_____

Estimating Expenses

Once you have figured your current income, estimate your current expenses. If you do not keep records, you can use checkbook
stubs, receipts, and old bills.

If you are totally new at figuring money, keep a record of current
expenses for two or three months before you attempt to set up a
budget. Use these records to help you decide whether you can
continue your present spending pattern or whether you need to
make some changes. If you have been satisfied with this pattern in

the past, continue to use it as your spending plan. If you are not satisfied, look at your spending critically. Unless you study your records, you may be unaware of overspending and poor buying habits. Be realistic in revising your new plan; resolve to cut out shopping sprees and overuse of credit. Keep your estimate of expenses. Try to plan any large expenses to see how realistically you are appraising your financial situation so they occur at intervals throughout the year—buying a washer and dryer, then six months later the new refrigerator—so that these purchases do not burden your income and destroy your budget.

In evaluating your living expenses, consider that the total monthly housing costs should not exceed one week's net income, monthly installment payments should not exceed 20 percent of your monthly income, and new credit payments should not exceed one-half of your income.

The following table, devised by the federal government, is one way of keeping track of expenses.

CHART B
Plan for Family Spending

Income, set-asides, and expenses	Amount per month
Total income _____	$_____
Set-asides:	
Emergencies and future goals _____	$_____
Seasonal expenses _____	_____
Debt payments _____	_____
Regular monthly expenses:	
Rent or mortgage payment _____ $_____	
Utilities _____ _____	
Installment payments _____ _____	
Other _____ _____	
Total _____	_____
Day-to-day expenses:	
Food and beverages _____ $_____	
Household operation and maintenance _____ _____	
Furnishings and equipment _____ _____	
Clothing _____ _____	
Personal _____ _____	
Transportation _____ _____	
Medical care _____ _____	
Recreation and education _____ _____	
Gifts and contributions _____ _____	
Total _____	
Total set-asides and expenses _____	$_____

Sample Budgets

Penny, a single woman, has take-home pay, after contributions to her medical and life insurance, Social Security and taxes, of approximately $700. She budgets her money in this way:

	Percentage	Amount
Apartment rent	30	$210
Clothes	8	56
Laundry, hairdresser, incidentals	2	14
Car and related expenses	20	140
Utilities	7	14
Installment payments on furniture	8	56
Food	15	105
Savings	4	28
Recreation	4	28
Contingencies	2	14

Neva and John have a combined take-home income of $1,900 per month. They have four school-age children. This is how they budget after all deductions:

	Percentage	Amount
House payments including taxes and insurance	18	$342
Food, including necessities such as postage stamps, barber	30	570
Medical	7	133
Clothing	4	76
Life insurance	4	76
Automobile, including insurance, installment payments	11	209
Church	10	190
Recreation and entertainment, saving for vacation	5	95
Utilities	6	114
Savings	5	95

If your income is quite low, you will need to plan carefully to take care of your immediate needs and pay your current bills. It may be unrealistic to include long-term goals. To help you figure this form we will discuss some of the items listed, in detail.

Set-Asides

The best way to have money available for emergencies and major expenses is to set aside money regularly. The secret is to earmark the money for savings *before* you spend your income. By setting aside a planned amount every month, even if it is a small amount, you establish good money habits and a base for credit. Remember you will be receiving interest on your money while you are saving it. (See chapter on banking institutions.)

Remember large expenses often seem to occur all at once: taxes, school clothing and supplies, insurance, Christmas gifts, household emergencies (if one appliance breaks down, they all seem to break down). It's a nice feeling to be somewhat prepared for these emergencies.

Debt Payments

If you have debts or past-due bills, you will want to plan your budget so you can clear them up. Work out a systematic plan to repay your debts. Begin immediately to earmark at least a small amount for debt repayment every payday. Enter the debt payment on your spending plan. You will want to clear up any past debts before you incur any new ones and to insure a good credit rating in the future.

Regular Monthly Expenses

On your plan enter the expenses you expect to have each month. These will probably include rent or mortgage payments, insurance, utility bills, telephone, car payments and expenses, etc.

Day-to-Day Expenses

You are now ready to plan your day-to-day expenses—those that vary from week to week or month to month. Because these are the most flexible entries in your budget, they are the easiest to cut when you need to economize. Use your records to estimate how much to spend on food, clothing, and other budget categories. You may decide to try to cut down on some expenditures (like clothing—that's always the first to go).

Comparing Expenses and Income

Add the figures in your spending plan. Now compare the total with your estimate of income for the planning period. If the two-figures balance, fine. If your expenses exceed your income, reevaluate your plan. Adjust the budget. Can you possibly postpone or drop some items? Can you reduce expenses? If they're not at all close, you will have to make some difficult decisions, such as moving to a cheaper home or buying a more economical car. Can you save some precious food money by shopping for weekend specials? You might want to send for the United States Department of Agriculture food plan booklets. In general, to reduce monthly obligations, don't buy it if you can't afford it.

If you are unable to balance your budget by cutting (even drastically), you may need to increase your income. It may mean taking a second job for you or your husband (if you are married). If you are a wife who has not worked, it may mean you will have to seek full- or part-time employment. More and more wives are having to work out of necessity than for self-fulfillment (the term that was so popular a few years back). Also, you may need to review your goals. That new car purchase may have to wait until next year, or moving to a bigger place might have to be postponed a while longer.

USING A BUDGET

When you have gone to all the trouble of making out a budget, use it! You would be surprised how many people sit down with sharpened pencil and a clean sheet of paper, make out a very neat budget, then put it in the desk drawer and never look at it again. When asked if they are on a budget, they reply, "Sure, it took me two days to set it up." That's all very well and good, but if a budget isn't used, it might as well never have been set up.

Be sure you keep records; they can clearly tell you your financial story. Make the records simple. You don't need a detailed account of every single penny, but you do need to know where your money is going.

EVALUATING YOUR BUDGET PLAN

At the end of six months, compare what you spent with what you had planned to spend. If your spending was different from your planning, find out why. That answer will help you find ways either to stay within your budget or to make a new one.

A budget is something you sometimes have to rework until it fits. Do not expect to have a perfect budget the first time you set one up. As circumstances change, you will need to adjust the budget, possibly to make out a new one, but at least if you are without funds at the end of the month, you can see why in black and white and possibly do something about it. If you are a hopeless case when it comes to figuring money or if you are in the enviable position of having some money to invest, you might want to consult a certified financial planner (CFP).

As we said in the first chapter, a CFP can be found in the Yellow Pages under "Financial Consultants." Make sure she/he has a CFP degree—that is, she/he is, in fact certified. You can check this out by writing the International Association of Financial Planners, 2150 Parklake Drive NE, Suite 260, Atlanta, Georgia 30345. You can ask a lawyer or an accountant to recomment a CFP. A financial planner will help you set up a budget you can live with.

Judith Goldberg, a CFP in California, told us that women (especially) don't look at the "what ifs" in life: what if you are widowed; what if you are divorced; what if the rate of inflation keeps going up? "When I set a woman up on a budget, I go over with her what she is spending now and ask her what her objectives are this year, in five years, in twenty years. Women must start thinking finance and *must* learn to look to themselves for their financial futures. On salary women usually have fringe benefits, but even so, I check to see if they are vulnerable to disaster (medical calamities, disability, being widowed or divorced). In almost every case I have to tell a woman to cut what she is spending if she wants to prepare for her future in a mature way.

"I charge an hourly fee to set up a budget. I will go over a case and give an estimate of my charges for setting up the budget beforehand. Different CFPs, however, charge different ways and varying amounts, but for a woman who can make no rhyme or reason out of her financial situation, it can be cheaper in the long run to have some help. A woman should be very sure she is dealing with someone reputable even if she has to take the time to check out the CFP. A responsible CFP won't mind this a bit."

This is all very interesting, but it's too late for you? You are head over heels in debt? Relax! There's a way to start fresh, thanks to the United States government, of all institutions. During the Depression days of 1938, the U.S. government added an amendment—Chapter 13—to the U.S. Bankruptcy Act, officially called the Wage Earner's Plan. Its purpose is to bring immediate relief to people who are losing the financial battle but aren't ready to sell out their dignity and lose their possessions in bankruptcy. This law was designed to help the wage earner. You qualify as a wage earner if you derive more than one-half of your income from wages, salary, or commission. Income from Social Security and retirement, having been earned, is also considered wages.

Normally the process of setting up a Wage Earner's Plan begins in an attorney's office. The attorney reviews all debts, net income, the amount of money needed for living expenses, the amount of money actually available for creditors. If, in the attorney's opinion, a Wage Earner's Plan will solve the problem, the attorney files a petition with the court. After the plan is filed, the court sets a hearing date at which time the plan is presented. The court usually confirms the Wage Earner's Plan and appoints a trustee who will be responsible to receive and pay out funds until the plan is completed.

The protection of this law is valuable. Creditors are issued a restraining order which stops all collections and legal action, such as wage attachments and unauthorized repossessions. Chapter 13 stops all service charges, late charges, and, in most cases, interest charges. The trustee is a representative of the court and administers the Wage Earner's Plan while it is in effect. She/He maintains complete records while receiving and paying out funds to the creditors.

When you apply for a Wage Earner's Plan, you will incur some court costs, the expense of the trustee, and an attorney's fee, which will be set by the court. These costs need not be advanced but may be added to the total of your other debts and paid from the payments you make to the trustee. Chapter 13 makes it possible for a debt-pressed person to pay bills in a dignified, honorable way and also to learn some rules of self management that will help in the future.

The Wage Earner's Plan was of great benefit to Marion Estes. When her husband left her and disappeared, he left her with a raft of bills that were in both their names. Therefore, she was held responsible for paying them. Since they had not been financially sound with two salaries, Marion knew she wouldn't be able to meet all their bills on one. A neighbor told her about Chapter 13. Marion applied for it and was put on the plan. "It took quite a while; but I did get my obligations cleared up, and I learned how to stay on a budget. I had always let my husband handle the money, and he had gotten us in a real mess. If I hadn't heard about this plan, I don't know what I would have done. I will never again let anyone do my financial thinking for me."

The subject of money, and the hows and whys of handling it, is of interest to almost everyone. In the ten years that Judith Rhoades has written a financial column, she has had more questions on budgets and budgeting than any other subject. We include a sampling of these questions and the answers, in the hopes you will derive some benefit from them.

Question: My fiancé and I are having an argument about money and how, after we are married, we should divide and budget it. We're both in our early thirties; we plan to keep our jobs after we're married. I would like to keep my money in savings and pay the bills with my husband-to-be's paycheck. He thinks this is unfair. H. T., Rockford, Illinois.

Answer: Money is one of the main causes of disagreement in marriages, so you should certainly settle on what your arrangements will be prior to your marriage, rather than continue to argue about it after you are married. You might find a compromise in a common checking account, in which you put all your earnings (except for a certain figure which you each agree upon) to pay all household expenses, groceries, medical bills, etc. Then each of you could keep a specified amount—for example, $100 apiece—in your own checking account to buy clothes, lunches, and so forth. Three checking accounts can give you added expense each month, so you might consider the possibility of placing your private money in a savings account with withdrawal privileges. In that way you'll at least be earning some return on what money you each plan to set aside.

Question: I earn around $1,700 a month. I wonder how much money I should allocate to pay rent. Is there any set figure or percentage that I can use as a guideline? B. G., New Orleans, Louisiana.

Answer: Yes, there is. Approximately 25 to 35 percent (in some states, such as New York and California, this figure would be higher) of your monthly income has usually been the standard guideline. That figure is before taxes. So, if your gross salary is $1,700, you could afford monthly rent payments of $425 to $595 per month. I would advise you to spend less, however, if you can. The cost of food and clothing has spiraled in the last year and shows no sign of declining. If you are considering the purchase of a house, your combined monthly payments, which include property taxes and insurance, as well as the mortgage, should not exceed 25 to 33 percent of your net monthly income.

Question: How can we as a family really do something about inflation? The demands against my paycheck seem to grow every week. U. B., Daly City, California.

Answer: It is difficult to understand why each week your paycheck stays the same while it buys less and less, even though you continue to shop at the same grocery store and buy the same products. But then again, the concept of inflation is also difficult to comprehend. Perhaps a family conference to discuss this problem would be in order. What you are attempting to do is to maintain your standard of living at the same time your buying power is shrinking. There are several things that you might consider to help you do that. One is to lower your cost of food as much as possible. For example, buy powdered milk instead of homogenized; it tastes the same as whole milk when it is substituted in cooking, and mixing it with regular milk on a one-to-one ratio will also help lower the cost of the milk you drink. Cut down on major purchases; if you need new furniture or appliances, go the secondhand route, and most of the time you'll be able to find exceptional bargains. Instead of shopping at a department store, purchase from a catalogue order store. You can buy good clothing from sample or outlet stores if you have any in your vicinity. Otherwise, try to buy just at sale time, usually January and August.

Question: Are there certain months of the year that feature bargains, and if so, what months and what bargains? W. R., Kansas City, Missouri.

Answer: Yes, there are, and here is a list:

January—appliances, blankets, sheets and towels, radios, toys and stereo equipment.
February—sports clothes, furniture, lamps and rugs.
March—washers and dryers, storm windows, ski equipment.
April—dresses and clothes dryers.
May—pocketbooks, tires, television sets.
June—frozen foods, furniture, and lumber.
July—air conditioners, freezers, and refrigerators, fuel oil.
August—new cars, coats, furs, window curtains and drapes.

September—lawnmowers, dishes and glasses, car batteries, bicycles.

October—school clothes and supplies, silverware, fishing equipment.

November—used cars, water heaters, fabrics.

December—men's and women's shoes, blankets and quilts, used cars.

Question: My husband has money withheld weekly from his paycheck by his employer for a stock purchase plan. This money is forwarded to a brokerage house, which keeps it two months before investing it. He receives no interest for this two-month period. Is this legal? I wrote to the brokerage house, but I have yet to receive an answer. D. D., Boyertown, Pennsylvania.

Answer: No brokerage house pays interest on money in an account for a period as short as two months. Yes, it is legal and is a common practice. You might have your husband ask his employer to maintain a special passbook savings account in order for you to receive interest on your money until it is invested. Perhaps all employees who have money withheld could have their money pooled and put into a savings account. Then any interest received during that interim period could be applied toward your stock investment.

Question: I have just gone to work for a company that has a credit union. Just exactly what is a credit union? B. W., Detroit, Michigan.

Answer: A credit union is a group of people who agree to save their money together and make loans to each other from the savings pool at a low interest rate. Your credit union is organized by the employees of the company. Credit unions could also be formed by a labor union, a fraternal order, residents of a closely knit community, or even a church. The members of your credit union elect officers and committee persons and set policies at annual meetings. The effectiveness of a credit union lies in how much you want to use it. The basic features of a credit union are savings plans, life insurance, and low-cost loans. Another benefit of a good credit union is that it can provide financial counseling for its members. While credit unions do not provide deposit insurance, there are methods that will protect you against loss if your company should fail. The value of a credit union over a savings and loan or a bank is that because it is both a nonprofit organization and exempt from income tax, it must generate only enough income to meet its usually modest expenses. Hence, it pays rather high interest on savings (yet does not charge high rates for loans). I think you will find your credit union a most beneficial place in which to save part of your income.

Income and budgets are the most fundamental and important items in a woman's financial picture. Responsible use of both of them is a prudent way toward becoming a financially secure woman.

7

Your Social Security

The subject of Social Security can boggle the mind. It is steeped in a jargon all its own, and since each woman's circumstances varies widely, it is next to impossible to spell out specifics which apply to *you*. But you need to be aware that if you work, and/or your husband works, and wages are being deducted from your paychecks for social security, you will be eligible to collect Social Security benefits.

Often women do not think to check with Social Security when faced with a death a divorce, or retirement or when there is a disability. In some of these instances the women are not eligible for benefits, but in many cases they are and don't even know it. Train yourself to think Social Security—after all, it's your money. Almost any woman who works earns Social Security protection not only for herself but also for her family. For example, if you are single now and have no dependents, the Social Security credits you earn count toward monthly benefits for any family you may have in the future. If you have children who are retarded or disabled, monthly checks are also available to them. If you are widowed, you may be eligible to receive a lump sum for burial expenses. These are just a sampling of the "Social Security facts" you should know. What follows is a breakdown of the most pertinent Social Security information.

Giving out Social Security cards is just one service of the Social Security office. You can also apply for benefits there, or you can discuss any matters you are confused about. Social Security is a complex, confusing subject. Don't be intimidated; keep asking questions until the answers make sense to you. To find the address of the office nearest you, look in the telephone directory under Social Security Administration or ask at your post office.

WHAT SOCIAL SECURITY IS

The basic idea of Social Security is simple: During working years, employees, their employers, and self-employed people pay Social Security contributions (payments). This money is used to pay both the monthly Social Security benefits to people eligible for them and the administrative costs of the program. When today's workers' earnings are substantially reduced or stop altogether because of retirement, death, or disability, benefits will be paid to them from the contributions of people in covered (paid into) employment and self-employment at that time. Social Security benefits are intended to replace part of the earnings the family has lost. These contributions also provide the money for Medicare hospital insurance, which helps pay the hospital bills of workers and their dependents after they reach sixty-five. People who have been entitled to Social Security checks for two consecutive years or more also have the protection of Medicare hospital insurance.

Basically, if you're employed, you and your employer each pay an equal share of Social Security contributions. The contributions are deducted from your salary, and your employer pays an equal amount. If you are self-employed, you pay the total contributions. If you are employed, your employer is required to give you a form showing the amount of your earnings that count for Social Security. Your employer does this at the end of each year or when you stop working. These receipts, usually W-2 Forms, can help you if there is an error in the amount of earnings reported on your Social Security record. You should keep a record of any self-employment income you have reported.

APPLYING FOR A SOCIAL SECURITY CARD

You need a Social Security number if your place of employment is covered by the Social Security law. With very few exceptions, which we will discuss later, most places are. Show your card to your employer when you start to work or when you change jobs so that your wages will be properly recorded and credited to your Social Security earnings record.

Your Social Security number is also used for income tax purposes. You may be asked to give your number to anyone who pays you dividends, interest, or other income that must be reported to the Internal Revenue Service. If you do not have a Social Security card or number, you can get an application for one from any Social Security office. Try to apply for a card at least six weeks before you'll need it.

You need only one Social Security card during your lifetime. If you lose your card, you can get a duplicate. If you change your name, it is imperative you go to the Social Security office and let them know. They will issue you a new card, but it will have the same number.

YOUR SOCIAL SECURITY BENEFITS

Chances are when you think about Social Security, you think mostly about older people and retirement and Medicare. But that's not the whole Social Security story by a long shot. Social Security can mean a lot more. It can mean monthly cash benefits to disabled workers and their families; it can mean monthly checks to widowed mothers or fathers and their children.

Social Security can mean that the financial burden caused by the death of the wage earner will be greatly eased, that the family can stay together, that the children can complete their education, that disabled children, including those who are severely mentally retarded, can receive a lifetime income. It can also mean that a disabled worker and his or her family can be sure of an income that will continue as long as the worker is disabled. A disabled person may also receive rehabilitation to help him or her return to productive work. Social Security can assure you of some kind of income when you or your husband retire and can protect you from being financially destroyed because of medical expenses.

Before you or your family can get monthly cash benefits, you (or your husband) must have credit for a certain period of work under Social Security. The exact amount of work credit depends on your age.

Social Security credit is measured in quarters of coverage. In 1979 employees and self-employed people received one quarter of coverage for each $260 of covered (paid into) annual earnings. No more than four quarters of coverage can be credited for a year. The $260 measure will increase automatically in the future to keep pace with the average wages.

More than nine out of ten jobs in paid employment and self-employment in the United States are covered by Social Security. This means that Social Security plans cover approximately 87 out of every 100 people in the United States work force. For those people who come under the Social Security umbrella, the coverage is compulsory. Individuals who are not covered under Social Security include some government employees, farm and domestic workers who are not regularly employed, self-employed persons whose earnings do not exceed $400 per year, and railroad workers who are covered under their own plan. Social insurance, which is another name for Social Security, covers old-age, survivor's, and disability benefits, hospital insurance, unemployment insurance, workmen's compensation, and sickness insurance. If you stop working under Social Security before you've earned enough credits, you cannot get benefits at a later date. But the credit you've already earned will stay on your record, and you can add to it later if you return to work. Having enough credit means only that you or your family can get checks. The amount of your check depends on your average earnings over a period of years. Once you have worked for ten years, you can be certain that you will be fully insured for life. The amount you will be paid, of course, depends on your average earnings covered by Social Security. The following table shows how much credit is needed for retirement and survivors' benefits.

Work credit for retirement benefits		Work credit for survivors and disability benefits		
If you reach 62 in	Years you need	Born after 1929, die, or become disabled at	Born before 1930, die or become disabled before 62 in	Years you need
1975	6	28 or younger		1½
1976	6¼	30		2
1977	6½	32		2½
1978	6¾	34		3
1979	7	36		3½
1981	7½	38		4
1983	8	40		4½
1987	9	42		5
1991 or later	10	44		5½
		46	1975	6
		48	1977	6½
		50	1979	7
		52	1981	7½
		54	1983	8
		56	1985	8½
		58	1987	9
		60	1989	9½
		62 or older	1991 or later	10

Special rules

Although almost all jobs in the United States are covered by Social Security, there are special rules which apply to some.

You should check with a Social Security office about these special rules if you work in or about someone's home doing housecleaning, gardening, or babysitting; if you are a student and also are employed by your school or college; if you own, operate, or work on a farm; if you are a member of a religious order; if you have a job where you get cash tips; or if you are an employee of a state or local government or a nonprofit or international organization. Special rules also apply to those who work or are self-employed outside the United States.

Leaflets containing information of special interest to self-employed people, farmers, farm landlords, people who receive cash tips, and others are available at any Social Security office. State and local government employees should direct their questions to their state Social Security Administrator.

Family Payments

Social Security is valuable financial protection for a family. Benefits may be payable not only to a worker but to family members. This steady monthly income does much to ease the financial burden caused by the death or disability of the worker. Dependents and survivors eligible for benefits include:

— Unmarried children under the age of eighteen or over eighteen, up to twenty-two if they are full-time students
— Unmarried sons or daughters eighteen or over who were disabled before they reached twenty-two and who continue to be disabled
— A wife or widow at any age if she is caring for a child that is under eighteen or disabled and the child is entitled to payments
— A wife sixty-two or a widow sixty or older, or a disabled widow fifty or over.
— A widowed father if he is caring for a child that is under eighteen or disabled and the child is entitled to payments
— A husband sixty-two or over, or a widower sixty or over, or a disabled widower fifty or over
— Surviving dependent parents sixty-two or over
— A worker's grandchildren if the natural parents are disabled or dead and if the grandchildren are living with and supported by the grandparent.

The following benefit information is of special interest to women:
The benefits that could be paid to a widow may, under certain conditions, be paid to a surviving divorced woman.
In a ruling which became effective in January 1979, the length of

time a woman had to be married to her ex-husband to collect benefits from his work record was decreased from twenty years to ten
years. You can also receive benefits when your ex-husband starts
collecting retirement or disability if you are sixty-two or older and
were married at least twenty years.

In addition to monthly benefits, a lump-sum benefit of $225 may
be paid to the worker's widow or widower if he or she was living in
the same house at the time of the worker's death. This lump-sum
payment can be used to help pay the worker's burial expenses.

As a widow without children you are entitled to widow's benefits
if you are sixty years or older. These benefits are based on how long
your husband worked and how much he contributed. Though the
above is welcome news for widows, generally the part of the Social
Security benefits law covering widows leaves many of them unpro-
tected. For example, a woman may be fifty-five years of age, widowed, never have worked, have no children, be left bereft and
penniless, yet not be entitled to Social Security benefits. Perhaps
one day we shall see the administration more capable of fulfilling its
duties toward widows in this category. Widows' benefits range from
71½ percent of their deceased husbands' benefit amount at age sixty
to 100 percent at age 65. If you wait until you are sixty-five, you will
receive the exact amount your husband would have been receiving
if he had retired rather than died.

Your widow's benefits will cease when you no longer have a child
under eighteen or a child who is disabled in your care. Your benefits
may also stop if you remarry before the age of sixty. As long as your
children are eligible for payments, however, they will continue to
receive them even if you do remarry.

You can apply for survivor's benefits at any Social Security office.
You should apply for benefits as soon as possible after the decedent's
death since it will take some time to process your claim. Your benefits could be withheld for several weeks or months after filing, depending on how long your Social Security office takes to process a claim.

You will probably need the following documents in order to provide proof of your claim:

- Your Social Security number
- Your decedent's Social Security number
- Proof of your marriage if you are a widow
- Birth certificates of your children if you are applying for their
  benefits
- Proof of your age

- Income tax forms or returns of the decedent in the year of death
- Proof of support if you're applying for benefits as a dependent of the decedent.

You may be asked to provide a death certificate, proof of your relationship, disability, or school attendance, depending on the kind of survivor's benefit you're applying for.

Because of polio at an early age, Edith Moyer has been confined to a wheelchair since she was a teenager. Her older sister, Nelia, had been her sole support for the last twelve years. When Nelia died, Edith was left without any funds whatsoever. When she went to the Social Security office, she found out she was eligible not only for survivor's benefits but for benefits as a disabled person as well.

Don't put off applying for Social Security because you do not have all the necessary documents. The people at your Social Security office can give you suggestions on where to obtain missing documents or what documents may be substituted for the ones requested.

Social Security and Disability

If you have a disability that will keep you from working for a year or more, you may be eligible for Social Security benefits. Monthly benefits can be paid to: disabled workers under sixty-five and their families; unmarried persons disabled before age twenty-two who continue to be disabled (these benefits are payable when a parent—or in certain cases a grandparent—receives Social Security retirement or disability benefits or when an insured parent dies); disabled widows, disabled widowers, and (under certain circumstances) disabled surviving divorced wives of workers who were insured at death (these benefits are payable as early as age fifty).

If a worker dies after a long period of severe disability but did not apply for benefits, his or her survivors may apply within three months after the death of the worker. Disability benefits are payable on the basis of credit for work under Social Security. Disabled dependents and survivors get benefits based on the earnings of the worker.

Generally, to have disability protection for yourself and your family, you need Social Security credits for at least five years out of the ten-year period ending when your disability begins. Workers disabled at forty-three years or older need credit for more than five years of work. If you become disabled before age thirty-one, the requirement ranges down with age to as little as one and one-half years. There are special provisions for people who meet the Social Security definition of being blind. Again, check with your Social Security office.

If you are a worker or a person disabled in childhood, you are considered "disabled" under Social Security if you have a physical or mental impairment which prevents you from doing any substantial gainful work, is expected to last (or has lasted) for at least twelve months, or is expected to result in death. If you have an impairment that prevents you from doing your usual work, then your age, education, and work experience also may be considered in deciding whether you are able to engage in any other type of work. If you can't do your regular work but can do other substantial gainful work, generally you will not be considered disabled. Vocational factors such as age, education, and work experience cannot be considered in deciding whether a widow or widower is disabled.

A disabled worker and family members or a disabled widow or widower generally cannot begin to collect benefits until the sixth full month of disability. A person disabled in childhood may be eligible for benefits as soon as a parent begins getting retirement or disability benefits or dies after having worked long enough under the law to make payments possible.

It is important to apply to your Social Security office soon after the disability starts because back payments are limited to the twelve months preceding the date of application. You can shorten the time it takes to complete your application if you have the right information ready when you apply. Check with your Social Security office to find out just what information and documents are required.

Social Security and Retirement

When can you retire and receive Social Security benefits? It's difficult to give a single answer to this question because each person's situation is different. Social Security retirement benefits can be paid as early as age sixty-two. But if your benefits start before sixty-five, the amount of your checks will be reduced to take account of the longer period you will be getting them.

The amount of the reduction depends on the number of months you receive benefits before you become sixty-five. The reduction amounts to 20 percent at sixty-two, 13⅓ percent at sixty-three, and 6⅔ percent at sixty-four.

There may be other factors involved in your decision about retiring. A company pension, for instance, would influence your decision.

So would your ability to continue working and your own financial situation among others. The important thing is that it is your choice.

Once you decide when you will retire, remember to apply for your Social Security retirement checks two or three months before you plan to stop working. This way your benefits will be ready to start when your income from work stops.

There is another factor to consider. If you work past sixty-five, your monthly benefit will be increased by one percent for each year (1/12 percent for each month) that you don't get a benefit because of your work. For people who reach sixty-five in 1982 or later, the credit will be 3 percent for each year (¼ percent for each month).

What documents do you need? First, you need your Social Security card or a record of the number. Next, you need proof of your date of birth. You can submit an official record of your birth or baptism recorded early in life. If this is not possible, submit the best evidence you have available. The best is often the oldest. If you're not sure what is best, just call any Social Security office. The people there can tell you what kinds of documents are acceptable.

Other records that might be acceptable include school, church, state or federal census, insurance policies, marriage, passports, employment, military service, children's birth certificates, union, immigration, and naturalization. This is not an exclusive list, and there are other records which may prove acceptable.

You should bring in your latest W-2 (wage and tax statement) Form or, if you're self-employed, a copy of your latest self-employment tax return since the most recent reports may not be in the records. You need these so that you'll get the highest possible benefit as early as possible.

If your husband or wife is also going to apply for benefits, he or she will need pretty much the same documents. It would also be a good idea to have your marriage certificate available, although this is not always needed. If either of you were married before, you will need information about the duration of the previous marriages.

If you have eligible unmarried children, you should bring their birth certificates along, together with a record of their Social Security numbers if available. In some situations, other documents may be needed, but those listed here will be enough in most cases.

If you have applied two or three months before your retirement month, your checks will start the month you retire. If you apply closer to that month or after, your checks will start six to eight weeks after you apply. You will receive your checks monthly, once you are on the Social Security benefit rolls. Your checks will increase automatically to keep pace with increases in the cost of living. Each year living costs are compared to those of the previous year. If the cost of living has increased by 3 percent or more from one year to the next, benefit rates will be increased by the same percentage the following July.

Additional Retirement Considerations

A working wife who has earned her own Social Security credits also has certain options at retirement. For example, suppose your husband continues to work past the age of retirement and is earning too much money to receive benefits. Or suppose he is younger than you are. You may go ahead and retire on your own record. Then, when he does retire, you may take your payments if they would be higher than your husband's.

As the law now stands, if you are between the ages of sixty-five and seventy-two and work while receiving Social Security payments, you can earn up to $4,000 without losing any of your benefits. If you are under sixty-five, the amount is $3,240. Beginning in 1982, if you are a beneficiary over seventy years of age, there is no limit put on your earnings. Today you must be over seventy-two to enjoy that privilege.

MEDICARE

What is Medicare? Medicare is a government health insurance program under Social Security which assures hospital and medical insurance protection to people sixty-five and over or to those under sixty-five if they are disabled.

Medicare is really two kinds of insurance: hospital and medical. The hospital part of Medicare helps pay for in-patient hospital care and certain follow-up care after departure from the hospital. The medical insurance part of Medicare helps pay for doctor's services, outpatient hospital services, and other related medical items and/or services not covered under hospital insurance.

Medicare medical insurance has a seven-month initial enrollment. Be sure to apply for medical insurance two to three months before the month you become eligible, which is age sixty-five, so that you will have full Medicare protection when you turn sixty-five. You have a three-month grace period after turning sixty-five in which you may apply. If you turn down medical insurance and then decide you want it after your seven-month initial enrollment period ends, you can sign up during a general enrollment period—January 1 through March 31 of each year. If you enroll during a general enrollment period, however, your protection won't start until the following July, and your premium will be 10 percent higher for each twelve-month period you could have been enrolled but were not.

If you are entitled to monthly Social Security benefits, either those of your husband's or your own, you will have Medicare hospital insurance protection automatically at age sixty-five. If you are not entitled to benefits, you will need some credit for work under Social Security to have hospital insurance without paying a monthly premium. If you want to obtain Medicare insurance and are not entitled to it by your work record, you may enroll for it and pay monthly premiums. Remember that the benefits payable to your husband may be reduced when you retire or become disabled by the amount of any pension or annuity he receives based on his work in noncovered public employment (a job not covered by Social Security). The offset will be discontinued, however, after December 1982.

If you are at least fifty years old and become disabled while you have young children in your care, you may also be eligible for Medicare even though you haven't filed a claim based on disability. You may collect Medicare only if you are disabled for two years or longer.

Medicare medical insurance will not cover diagnostic treatments, routine physical checkups, prescription medicine and drugs, eyeglasses, examinations to fit them, hearing aids or an examination to determine if you need them, dentures or routine dental care, homemaker services, home nursing care, orthopedic shoes, personal comfort items, and the first three pints of blood you receive in each calendar year.

You can obtain Medicare facility information with regard to hospital facilities available that meet Medicare standards by inquiring at your Social Security office. As we stated before, if you are receiving Social Security benefits, you are covered for Medicare after age sixty-five. If not, you can enroll for Medicare insurance and pay a monthly premium. You do this by contacting your local Social Security office.

If you decide to cancel your Medicare insurance, your coverage and premium payments will stop at the end of the calendar quarter following the quarter that your written cancellation notice is received by the Social Security Administration. You can reenroll in medical insurance only once after canceling your protection.

8

How, What, and Why
to Insure

Insurance has traditionally been a man's game. Men have sold it, and men have purchased it. But now that more and more women are becoming heads of households and many wives handle the family finances, insurance should also become a woman's game.

Insurance, or the lack of it, affects almost every aspect of your life: your home, your car, your health, your life. When you purchase insurance, you are really buying protection—protection against being financially depleted because of illness, death, accident or loss.

You as a woman today have definite ideas about what you wish to accomplish and have some worthwhile things to protect. Whether you are a homemaker or a businesswoman or both, you have financial responsibilities and obligations and, as such, have the right to protect your interests and plan for your future.

In the past women (and many men) have been apprehensive and confused when it came to insurance. Insurance has generally been considered a technical subject steeped in a jargon of its own. Some insurance companies and agents have tended to go out of their way to make it more complicated than it needed to be. Fortunately these companies are beginning to realize that women are a burgeoning, untapped market and are starting to consider their needs in regard to personal insurance. (Personal insurance is insurance that is sold for personal benefit or protection of human beings, as opposed to mortgage insurance or title insurance, which is sold for the protection of things.)

Insurance companies are starting to hire more women as agents and are writing pamphlets that approach insurance in a more realistic manner. Even so, insurance can still be a complicated subject that gives rise to many questions that you as a woman need answered: What types of insurance are available, and exactly what do they do? What types of insurance do you really need? What do some of the insurance words and phrases mean in plain language? Most important, when it comes to insurance, where do you begin?

The first thing you should do when considering purchasing insurance is to find a reputable agent or agents. An insurance agent is a person licensed by your state to sell you insurance. She/He can be licensed to sell insurance through one company or several companies. An agent's job is to sell you a policy and to service that policy.

You can find an insurance agent that is reputable through your local National Association of Life Underwriters (NALU), which is listed in your phone book, or by referral of someone you trust, or by calling one of the large insurance companies and asking it to have an agent contact you. Companies with good reputations pride themselves on the integrity of their agents. When you choose an agent, there are certain points to keep in mind:

- Select an agent who is willing to come to your home or your office (even if you don't really want her/him to). An agent who can't be bothered calling on you doesn't deserve your business.
- Make sure the company your agent represents has a good service department and a local claims office.
- Though there are many fine male insurance agents, you may be more comfortable dealing with a female agent. She generally will not talk down to you, and she is more apt to identify with your particular problem.
- Remember, a good agent will *not* try to oversell you and *will* take it upon her/himself to go over your file and tell you when it is time to update your insurance.

After finding a reputable agent you feel comfortable with, she/he should sit down with you and go over your whole financial picture: your needs, your possessions and assets, your liabilities, your obligations, your dependents, and your strong and weak financial points.

The agent should then help you select insurance that is right for you.

You will often deal with more than one agent, as agents usually specialize either in life and disability or in casualty—not both. Life and disability basically includes life, medical, and health insurance. Casualty, for the most part, includes homeowners and automobile insurance. The first agent you select will often recommend another agent to supplement your insurance needs. You may want to choose an insurance broker who handles all lines of insurance.

Insurance brokers' and agents' fees are paid through commissions, which are included in the premium cost of your policy. If you alady have some insurance, you can arrange to have your existing policies examined by a reputable agent or an insurance consultant. The duty of a consultant is to analyze your policies and tell you where you are underinsured and where you are overinsured. A consultant cannot sell you anything. Most insurance companies offer this service.

The types of policy or policies women require vary with each individual. Financial planners and insurance experts, however, tend to agree that the basic insurance policies a woman should be covered by are: life, disability, medical, auto, and personal property (homeowners).

LIFE INSURANCE

Life insurance is insurance which protects your loved ones in the event of your death and can help secure your and your family's future.

Equating life insurance with the phrase "for men only" is not only a dated but an absolutely false concept. Ask yourself realistically, "In my lifetime am I ever going to need life insurance?" Ownership of some type of life insurance simply means acceptance of responsibility. Men have no corner on the responsibility market.

In 1973 women earned 30 percent of the family income. By 1980 half of all wives will be working. Currently there are some 26 million children under eighteen whose mothers are working. The latest statistics show that women buy 20 percent of all insurance policies sold. Women under age thirty account for 57 percent of these sales. These statistics indicate that more and more women are buying insurance.

Any woman who is included in the following list needs life insurance:

- If she is a single woman, who may or may not choose to marry, she needs to secure her future.
- If she is the sole support of her family, her protection needs duplicate a man's. Who will support her family if she dies?
- If her earnings supplement or match her husband's, her share of the family expenses is of great insurable value.
- If she is a wife and mother, her family will need the means to pay for all the services she performs in case of her death. Her contribution to the life of the family, if it could be measured in dollars, has been estimated at $12,000 a year.

What Life Insurance Covers

- It pays for your final expenses, leftover debts, and estate taxes.
- It replaces some, or all, of your family income.
- It guarantees you a fixed amount of money at a certain age or guarantees money will be paid to your beneficiary upon your death.
- It guarantees you an income when you retire.
- It builds up a fund that you can draw on as income, for loans and emergencies, or to finance an education, while it protects your dependents.

Types of Life Insurance

Basically there are three kinds of life insurance: term, whole life (permanent), and endowment.

Term insurance is insurance that covers you for a certain period—a term. You can insure yourself for any specific time span (one year, ten years, twenty years). When that period has elapsed, you may renew your insurance. Each time you renew your policy, it costs more simply because you are older and (by insurance company figures) closer to death. As you approach the age of sixty-five, term insurance becomes rather expensive because the mortality rate is higher for each progressive year.

Term insurance for young healthy persons is quite inexpensive. Most term policies include a provision which allows you to convert to whole life insurance at a later date without taking a qualifying physical. If you are employed, you may be covered by group insurance. This is term insurance paid for, at least partially, by the employer. It may terminate when you leave, or you may have the option to convert it to permanent insurance.

Term insurance was very important to Leona Perry. She had been married for almost sixteen of her thirty-eight years when her divorce was final. She was left with three children, ages fifteen, seven, and two. Her lawyer made certain that as part of her divorce settlement her ex-husband had to maintain a life insurance policy on himself until each child turned eighteen. This insured support until the children were older and Leona did not have to alter their lifestyle as much as she would have if she had been forced to pay for the insurance herself.

Whole life insurance (permanent) is insurance that protects you for your whole life but the premiums of which remain the same amount and never increase. The cost of whole life insurance is higher than term insurance when you're young, but the premium will not go up as the years go by. The insurance company arrives at the premium cost by averaging the costs, using a standard rate (by age) which you then pay. One very important result of paying this average premium is the cash value that accumulates during the life of your policy. This can be used to your advantage by letting you cash in your policy or letting you borrow against it. Ask you agent to explain this process as it varies greatly, depending on the amount of premiums paid and the duration of policy.

Whole life insurance comes in two forms: straight life and limited payment life. Straight life means that the policy premiums are paid in equal amounts each year and continue for life until you either cash in your policy or select one of the settlement options available. This form of insurance policy accumulates the least cash value.

Limited payment means that the policy is paid up in a certain number of years, say, ten or twenty, or at age sixty-five; after that you don't pay anymore, but you continue to be covered. Naturally the premiums on limited payment life insurance are going to be higher than the premiums for straight life, but the cash value is also higher.

Whole life insurance is also referred to as permanent insurance because as long as you pay the premium, your policy will remain in force—*PERMANENTLY!*

Endowment insurance is somewhat like an insured savings plan. You receive a certain amount of money within a certain time—e.g., $10,000 after twenty years. If you die before the twenty years are up, $10,000 goes to whomever you have named in the policy. If you don't die, you receive the money for yourself as an endowment. The premiums are higher than the other two kinds of insurance, but the policy builds up cash value the most rapidly. However, it offers less insurance protection per premium dollar.

There are other policy names you may hear or read about, such as family income plan, family plan, participating, non-participating, etc. These all are variations of the three basic life insurance policies— term, whole life, or endowment.

One life insurance variation you may be interested in if you are a businesswoman is key person insurance. If you are a partner in a business, key person insurance can be of value. For example, if your partner should die, this type of insurance would provide you with sufficient money to pay for your partner's interest in the company without having any hardship placed on you or your partner's beneficiaries. You can also obtain key person insurance on yourself so that your debts would be paid in the event of your death. You may also wish to purchase stock redemption insurance, to enable surviving stockholders of a corporation to buy back the corporation's stock from the deceased stockholder's heirs.

Cash Value

The cash value of a whole life insurance policy is frequently misunderstood because it calls for some technical considerations. When a policy is designed for the whole of your life, the insurance company (in effect) adds up the total cost of your insurance over your expected lifetime. The company then works out an average cost or level premium. As a result of the averaging, the premium in the early years is somewhat larger than the protection actually costs. In the later years the same premium is considerably smaller than it should be, considering that the risk of death has risen sharply.

Your premium "overpayment" in the early years goes into the insurance company's reserves, which must then be accumulated with interest and held for you until payment to your beneficiary or until the time you cash in your policy. You, the policyholder, have the right to a share of the company's reserves if you should wish to give up your protection by surrendering your policy. The measure of your share is called cash value.

CASH VALUE

You can use this cash value in various ways. One way is as retirement income. Using the cash value of your policy for income at retirement is very popular. When you retire, you're not getting as much income as before, and you don't usually have the same financial responsibilities—kids are on their own and so on. So you simply draw out the cash value of your policy as income or in a lump sum. Most people do keep some of their death protection, though. There are special life insurance policies designed specifically to build up cash values rapidly for retirement while they protect your family as long as they needed it; these are called retirement income policies.

There are other ways to use the cash value of your policy:

— You can use the cash value as collateral to borrow from the life insurance company in a financial emergency.
— You can, at a later date, turn in your policy and take the cash value as a lump sum (or in monthly payments), according to your needs.
— If you want to continue your life insurance coverage after retirement but don't want to pay more premiums, you may use the cash value to buy prepaid insurance, either for a specified period of time or for life.

There are numerous variations on the theme of cash value. Your agent should go over them with you and spell out these options. Also, your policy will have a cash value chart that you may use as a guide.

Figuring the Cost of Life Insurance

The price of any life insurance policy is affected by four main factors: the company's cost of doing business, the rate of return on the company's investments, the mortality rate that the company expects among its policyholders, and the specific features contained in your policy.

You can compare the prices of policies at various insurance companies if they are for the same plan and the same amount and contain the same features. Ask the agent who offers the policy to explain all the details about premiums, benefits, and cash values or ask her/him to bring along a copy of the rating book put out by A. M. Best.

Best's ratings book is published each year, independently of any and all insurance companies. This volume has information covering the policies, rates, values, and dividends of the life insurance companies which write the majority of life insurance coverage in the United States (98 percent of the legal reserve life insurance in force). It also contains data on selected fraternal organizations plus business figures and sample rates value and settlement options for 400 companies.

Life insurance premiums are based on mortality rates, which are consistently lower for women than men, at all ages. Premiums reflect this difference; hence, they are lower for women than men. Women live longer than men, however, and can expect to pay premiums for a longer period of time.

Although there are various types of insurance available, and many variables in figuring costs, statistics show that 73 percent of women buying policies have purchased whole life insurance with an average annual premium of $181.

Ginny Patterson lives in Dallas, Texas. She is thirty-five years old and an executive secretary. Her total net income from all sources is $11,800 annually. This money goes to support her three small children. She owns her own home and has monthly household expenses. Her ex-husband lives in Wyoming and at the present time is unable to provide any support whatsoever, except that he does carry medical insurance on their children. Ginny knew she needed some type of life insurance in case something happened to her. The insurance agent she went to see advised her to buy $50,000 worth of term insurance, at a cost of $120 per year, and approximately $29,000 in whole life insurance at a cost of $600 per year. This would also provide a potential retirement-income supplement. For the $720 per year in premiums, which Ginny could buy in monthly, quarterly, or semi-annual payments if she so desired, it would provide survivors benefits of $79,000 to her children. In the event she did die before her children were of an age to support themselves, she knew this money, coupled with Social Security benefits, would go a long way to help support them.

What should you do if you want to purchase life insurance but don't have much money? There are four possibilities you may wish to consider:

- Purchasing term life insurance. This would give you the most protection for your insurance dollar on a temporary basis.
- Purchasing a policy providing term which can be converted to whole life at a later date (regardless of your health), in a single contract. This type of policy is less expensive than buying them separately. You can stretch your insurance dollars through such combinations.
- Purchasing modified or graded life insurance. This is a whole life policy, the premiums of which are smaller than usual in the

early years and gradually increase to a level premium in three to five years. After that premiums go up and thereafter remain the same. This is especially useful if you are just starting out in the business world and planning a career since the premiums are geared to income growth.

- Purchasing a policy that contains a guaranteed insurability option. This guarantees you the right to buy additional life insurance protection at several points in time, usually up to age forty. With it you can purchase specified amounts of insurance at each of these points regardless of your physical condition.

Points to Consider Regarding Life Insurance

— In life insurance there are no bargains. If you are receiving one, be wary and carefully read the small print. As a rule of thumb, in insurance, the big print giveth and the small print taketh away.

— You should review your life insurance every year, and any time there is a change in your situation—new baby, change of income, change of marital status, etc.—notify your agent of this change.

— It is especially important for married women to go over the family's insurance policies to know just what they contain.

— Purchase a life insurance policy that includes a premium waiver, if at all possible. A premium waiver means that in the event of your illness or disability the insurance company will pay the premium for you. A conscientious agent will endeavor to sell you a life insurance policy with the premium waiver benefit. It will make the plan self-completing in the event of disability.

— Life insurance varies primarily only in five areas: the face value of the policy, the amount of the premium, the policy period, how the cash value accumulates, and what the policy is designed to do.

DISABILITY INSURANCE

Disability insurance is insurance to replace income lost from illness or injury.

Life insurance agents, who are also licensed to sell medical and disability insurance, believe that medical and disability insurance should be the first types of policies a woman buys. To be coldly realistic about it, if you are under the age of sixty-five, you are more likely to become ill or disabled than to die. Statistics prove that you will use disability and medical insurance more than any other types of insurance.

If you are head of your household, disability insurance is a must and the most important insurance you can have. When you cannot work, who will provide the money to feed your children or pay your bills? If you are a nonworking wife and have small children, does your husband have the necessary assets to compensate housekeepers, baby-sitters, etc. in case of your illness? You may want to look into obtaining disability insurance on yourself. If you are a working woman, you should protect your earning power, which could be lost through accident or illness. You will want to insure yourself an income in case disability puts a stop to your paycheck.

Tanya Morgan, who is an OB-gynecologist in a beach resort city told us about her disability insurance. Last year she had a Caesarean section baby and had all sorts of postoperative complications, forcing her to leave her job. In one year her insurance paid back every penny she had ever paid into the premiums plus more than the premiums for the next twenty-five years!

Many employers offer disability insurance, and this is by far the least expensive way to obtain it. If your employer does not offer it or if you are in business for yourself, buying disability insurance is up to you. Remember the *less* money you are earning, the *more* you need to limit your liability.

In buying disability insurance, be careful. Make sure what you are buying will give you want you want. Look for a policy that tells you exactly what it will and will not do. Make certain there is a clause that allows for a rehabilitation period and related expenses that will adequately take care of you. Also, see that your disability insurance is renewable. Once you have the policy, the company cannot forgo renewing it if you become disabled. It is also important to see that your disability insurance is noncancelable, so that if you do become ill, the insurance company will not disallow your illness.

In recent years there has been a great deal of abuse and misuse of disability insurance claims according to insurance companies. Many agents feel that the disability portion of the insurance industry will change drastically in the future, with premiums increasingly substantial.

At present two-thirds of all claim benefits are on a long-term basis, which means that the person who filed the claim will have income until retirement age or until she goes back to work. The other third of the claims are on a short-term benefit basis, which generally means that the income will cease after a maximum period of two years.

The cost of disability insurance premiums will vary from company to company, depending on the type of coverage you are seeking and whether you are paying the premium as a private individual or an employee of a company.

If you work now or have ever worked, you may be entitled to medical and disability benefits under the federal Social Security system and your state's workers' compensation program. These benefits can form a base on which to add the disability coverage limits you desire. They will, however, rarely satisfy completely your needs for health and disability insurance.

HEALTH INSURANCE

Health insurance is insurance that will pay all or part of your medical expenses when you are ill or injured.

Health insurance experts say that if you are a woman—whether married, single, divorced, working, unemployed, professional, or blue-collar—there is a better than even chance that you have too little health insurance or the wrong kind. With medical costs skyrocketing, health insurance has become a necessity. The U.S. Department of Labor estimates that in the past ten years costs for doctors have risen 112 percent, medical care 180 percent, and hospital rooms more than 200 percent.

One of the insurance agents we talked with told us a story about one of her clients, Fran Mason. Fran was divorced, in her mid-thirties, had a five-year-old son, and was concerned about her estate plan. In a review of her information, it was discovered that Fran had no medical insurance. Our agent friend told us she worked diligently to convince Fran that she needed that medical insurance. After three months of conscientious prodding, Fran purchased a sizable policy. One month after the policy was in force, Fran underwent a mastectomy. Without the medical insurance it would have been financially catastrophic for her.

Currently most companies that have twenty or more employees offer some type of group health insurance. This is, by far, the least expensive way to obtain medical insurance. When you are job hunting, it is imperative that you consider the health benefits various companies offer. Remember, though, the company benefits almost always terminate thirty days after you leave that company.

If your place of employment does not offer health benefits, you will want to obtain a policy on your own. If you are a married woman, chances are you are covered under your husband's group policy. You can check this out by calling the employee benefits department where he is employed.

Louise Zach and her husband live in a small town in Connecticut. Their twelve-year-old daughter, Carol, became very ill and was admitted to the Yale Medical Center. Twelve thousand dollars and three months later, it was discovered Carol had a viral infection that totally destroyed her thyroid. Louise stated that if it hadn't been for her husband's company medical insurance policy, the family would not have survived financially.

The Health Insurance Institute claims that a reasonably good basic plan (not covering long-term illness) now costs $900 and up a year for a family of four and at least $400 for a single participant. Insurance companies offer more types of policies and prices of medical coverage than almost any other insurance. For a prospective buyer, sorting them out can be a problem. Primarily there are three kinds of health insurance plans available: Blue Cross and Blue Shield, health maintenance organizations, and commercial insurance companies.

Blue Cross and Blue Shield are the largest single health expense plans in the nation. Blue Cross offers primarily hospitalization coverage, whereas Blue Shield provides surgical and general medical insurance. Often these nonprofit associations cooperate in issuing joint plans for compenhensive medical care. To receive medical treatment, you go to any doctor's office or any hospital (except an independent association) and show proof of membership in the plan.

Using the Kaiser Foundation Health Plan in California as a model, the federal government in 1973 provided millions of dollars toward the establishment of privately operated health maintenance organizations (HMOs). The purpose of an HMO is to offer efficient and effective care rather than reimbursement for that care, as do typical health insurance policies. Individuals become members of HMOs by enrolling and paying a fee that entitles them to full use of health care services provided by that HMO. As a prepaid health care delivery system HMO bases its economic survival on the value of preventive care—that is, it costs less money to prevent disease than to cure it. These associations are composed of doctors and medical personnel who own their own facilities and provide medical care at a comparatively reasonable cost.

Most major commercial insurance companies offer individual health plans, but they are the most expensive type of plans owing to the number of claims. Of the top fifty companies, only six broke even on health insurance in the last year. If you are going to be changing jobs, going to school, in business for yourself, or working for a company that does not offer group insurance, you will need to purchase an individual health plan. It may cost you more and may give you less than some group insurance. However, no matter where you relocate or what your employment is, the policy will always cover you, and your rates will not increase.

Commercial insurance companies sometimes offer group rates to companies with fewer than ten people or through businesses with four or less key people. Some of them offer group insurance to organizations such as college alumni associations or service groups. If at all possible, find a group plan to join.

A life insurance agent can advise you on health plans, group or private. Ask your agent to explain the health insurance deductible clauses that are available to you because they can greatly affect your premium.

A good health plan should fit your needs, cover both accident and illness, pay attention to preventive care, have a short waiting period before it takes effect, and pay back in benefits the maximum for every premium dollar. Be sure to read and reread the fine print of all health policies.

AUTOMOBILE INSURANCE

Automobile insurance is insurance to protect you, your car, and your passengers when you are involved in an accident, and it limits your liability if you cause that accident.

Probably one of the largest single purchases you will ever make is your car, so it is important to know what you have to deal with in purchasing insurance on that car. Each state has minimum coverage requirements to meet when you insure your car. Several states require insurance before the car can be registered or the driver receives a driver's license. Although costs of car insurance have risen, a startling 60 percent during the past 10 years, coverage for your automobile is essential.

Automobile Coverage

Automobile coverage is divided into five basic categories; comprehensive, collision, uninsured motorist, liability, and medical payments.

Comprehensive coverage encompasses almost any kind of loss or damage to your car or its contents. It may include damage caused by theft, fire, vandalism, falling objects, or collision with animals. Although comprehensive coverage is fairly expensive, it may be worth paying the additional charge to have it as part of your policy. If your car includes special equipment, such as a CB radio, tape deck, or car phone, be sure those items are specifically listed on your policy.

Collision insurance is designed to cover the cost of repairs to your own car as a result of an accident. If your car is more than five years old and has a market value of less than $1,000, doing without collision insurance may be an avenue to save you money. The way to determine if this would be advantageous for you is to weigh the value of your car against what it would cost you to purchase collision coverage. If collision coverage would cost you more than the replacement value of your car, you will probably want to forgo this particular coverage.

There are more than 25 million uninsured motorists in the United States. *Uninsured motorist coverage* will protect you and your passengers in case you are involved in an accident and the other driver has no insurance. Many states have made this coverage mandatory. It might be wise to consider *under*insured motorist coverage also. This means that your insurance company would step in and cover any medical or damage costs which would not be covered by the other party's insurance.

Our friends Gertrude and Mark James bought a brand-new station wagon. For the family vacation last summer they went to visit relatives in the Midwest. On the way back they were sideswiped by another car—an accident which was impossible for Mark to avoid. The man who hit the wagon had no insurance, but just a few months prior, the James' insurance agent had suggested that they add an uninsured motorist coverage, which they did. The station wagon was completely destroyed, and the insurance company paid for a brand-new one so they could return home. If they had not had the coverage, they would have been out a brand-new car.

Liability coverage assumes the responsibility for injuries to others, or damage to their car, caused by you. This kind of insurance is a must, because it protects you or anyone driving your car if there is an accident which injures or kills someone in the other car or causes damage to the other person's car.

Medical payments coverage is designed to protect you and your family (whether you are injured as a passenger in another car, driving your own car, or struck by a car) by paying the medical bills. It will also cover medical or funeral expenses for anyone hurt or killed getting in, getting out of, or riding in your automobile.

Ways to Save on Auto Insurance Premium Costs

—Compare various insurance companies to see what is the best buy for the type of policy you need. Before you renew your insurance, check to see that you have the most competitive rate. If you are insuring only one car, it may be less expensive for you to insure that car through an automobile club.

—If you have been living in one area and move to another, be certain to check with your agent to find out if there is an increase or a decrease in the insurance rates, since rates are based on locale.

—You might consider increasing the deductible on your policy, which will result in your premium being lower. Deductible is the amount you must pay before the insurance company pays any money toward car damage or loss. By increasing the deductible, you can save anywhere from 25 percent to 50 percent on your collision insurance.

—Remember, if you are insuring more than one car, the insurance will be less for the second car if only adults drive the vehicle.

Agents who sell casualty insurance deal with automobile insurance. They can usually be found in the Yellow Pages under "Casualty Insurance" or "Auto Insurance."

Rosa Cicotti is an insurance agent for the Automobile Club. "A very common occurrence I see is when a husband does not tell an ex-wife that he has taken her off his insurance when they are divorced. She often does not realize this until she is involved in an accident. Then she finds she is not covered for the accident, and to add insult to injury, she now has an accident on her record, and whether or not it was her fault, she will pay more for a new policy since this accident puts her in a higher risk group. If a woman has a change in marital status, she should add insurance coverage to the list of items she needs to check on.

HOMEOWNER'S AND RENTER'S INSURANCE

A homeowner's insurance policy protects your home and its contents against fire, theft, or other types of damage. It also limits your liability if someone is injured on your property. Renter's insurance protects only the contents.

As a homeowner you should consider protecting your investment. Many states will not allow an escrow to close if the new owner does not have adequate homeowner protection. The minimum amount of coverage suggested by insurance companies is 80 percent of replacement value of your home and its contents, not including the land.

For purposes of a homeowner's policy, how do you figure in dollars and cents how much your home is worth? Unless you are active in the real estate market or spend your time studying home values, you will probably need the services of an appraiser. If you personally don't know someone who can help you in this area, check the Yellow Pages of your telephone directory for a name. This appraisal will determine only the market value of your home and the exact square footage. Then call a local contractor, and find out how much it would cost per square foot to rebuild your home. Take the square footage of your house, the builder's construction figure that you were quoted to reconstruct, and multiply the two numbers together. That will give you the replacement value of your home, not including land. Then you should insure your home and its contents for a minimum of 80 percent of that replacement figure.

You can insure anything that belongs to you and has a determinable value except land. Insurance companies insure only property that, if damaged, will cause you a financial loss. In determining what you need to insure, make an itemized list of your personal property for each room in your home. Many agents who sell homeowner's and renter's insurance have booklets with printed inventory lists which make this a much easier task.

In addition to your personal property inventory, it might be wise to take snapshots from various corners of your rooms which show placement of your furniture and accessories, for use in case of theft, when you might have to prove the existence of your special paperweight collection, for example.

If you are only renting your home, the minimum policy for contents generally issued is between $5,000 and $6,000. The cost of the insurance is based on the area where you live. The incidence of theft is more prevalent than that of fire, so if you live in an area which has a high crime rate, naturally your rates will correspondingly be higher. Renter's insurance is very inexpensive, but it is the area which has the greatest number of claims caused by burglary.

If you are a homeowner, whatever basic homeowner's insurance you carry, there should be provisions covering the contents also. Most policies will contain a contents coverage for certain items but are also limiting on what the policy will or will not cover. Common among policies is to limit cash to $100 and not to include jewelry, watches, furs, fine arts, china, silver, crystal, antiques, Persian rugs, guns, coin and stamp collections, golfing equipment, and musical instruments.

How sad it would be if some of your favorite possessions were stolen and your homeowner's or renter's policy had limitations which did not cover your new engagement ring.

Kay Sanchez had been living in her own home for about three years. She was squirreling away money in her dresser drawer to buy a ring she wanted and had accumulated approximately $194. There was a fire in her bedroom which completely destroyed the contents. She had no insurance. Even though keeping a lot of money around is not the wisest thing to do, if Kay had had a scheduled homeowner's policy, she would have been automatically reimbursed for some of the money lost. To eliminate this problem, list specific items to be insured for a specific value on or off the premises separately. (This is called scheduling.)

When you schedule your special antiques or the oil painting you inherited from Aunt Betsy, it will probably be done by a coinsurance policy on the items listed. Coinsurance is similar to a deductible form of insurance; you tell the insurance company you will pay for a certain percentage of the loss.

Remember, special coverage means that your policy is more comprehensive and covers all your possessions with the exception of listed items. Broad coverage covers *only* what is listed in the policy.

The homeowner's policy is a package policy which contains a number of types of coverage under the same policy—home, personal property, and personal liability. A good homeowner's policy should contain features covering the following areas:

1. Dwelling. This provides coverage for loss or damage from virtually any peril, including fire, windstorm, vandalism, aircraft, and

auto, and water damage resulting from broken pipes. Among the prominent exclusions are earthquake and flood (both of these available at extra cost), rain damage, landslide, termites, and dry rot. Losses will be adjusted on a depreciated basis instead of replacement cost if the amount of insurance is less than 80 percent of the current replacement value.

2. Appurtenant private structures. Same coverages as above are applicable for detached buildings, garages and swimming pools, etc.

3. Personal property on premises. This supplies coverage for fire, its allied perils, windstorm, vandalism, and theft, $100 on money, stamps, coin collections. Coverage for jewelry and fur items not scheduled on the policy is limited to $500 total for any one loss. Coverage on jewelry, furs, or fine arts above the $500 limit is available. For any of these items over $500, you must carry coinsurance.

4. Personal property away from premises. (not owned, leased, or rented residences). Coverage is the same as above. Loss from an unattended automobile is insured to a limit of $1,000 and requires evidence of forcible entry into the auto.

5. Additional Living Expenses. This provides reimbursement for necessary additional expenses incurred if the dwelling is untenable because of damage by any of the perils covered under the policy.

6. Comprehensive personal liability. This protects you and members of your household for bodily injury or property damage liability sustained by others because of your negligence on or off the premises.

7. Medical payments. This provides for reimbursement of medical expenses incurred for injuries in connection with the above coverage. Medical payments do not apply to the benefit of household members.

8. Physical damage to property of others. This provides coverage for damage to property of others caused by members of your family on or off your premises, regardless of legal liability, for property in your custody or control.

9. Deductible clause. This applies to all property losses, including fire and theft.

There are ways in which to lower the cost of your homeowner's insurance: Pay the premiums on more than a one-year basis if it is available. Increase your deductible. If you are purchasing a house, buy one that has been constructed with fire-resistant materials. Put fire extinguishers throughout your home, and purchase a package policy rather than a separate policy for each peril (i.e., fire, theft, flood damage, etc.).

Fortunately, or unfortunately, depending on your point of view, insurance has become ingrained in the American way of life. With auto repairs and medical costs spiraling, incidents of burglary on the rise, people suing at the slightest provocation, and even the cost of dying becoming prohibitive, insurance is a necessity.

The subject of insurance could fill an entire book, not just a chapter. We have touched briefly on insurance basics and terms, but only you know your personal insurance needs and your unique financial situation.

If you are on a limited budget, you should plan to include insurance premiums in you future. If you are ready at this time to purchase insurance, you will want to take into account the following:

- If your death would create any financial hardship on your loved ones, you should be covered by life insurance.
- If you operate a car, you should be covered by automobile insurance.
- If you own or rent a home, you should be covered by personal property (homeowner's) insurance.
- If you work for a living, you should be covered by medical and disability insurance.

When dealing with insurance, you will want to: select an agent or agents who not only are reputable but are sincerely concerned with your needs, take advantage of some of the simplified insurance booklets now available through many insurance companies; read over carefully any insurance documents before you sign them; take out your existing policies and reread them (use the glossary as your guide for any words you do not understand). Remember, when it comes to insurance, question anything you do not fully understand until the concept becomes clear in your mind.

After all, your life, your health, your car, and your home are of the utmost importance and value to you.

9

Purchasing a Home

Out of the 900 women who have been graduated since 1972 from an eastern college, only 120 have married. The divorce rate nationwide is one out of three marriages, and in California, it is rapidly approaching one out of two marriages. There are 12 million widows in the United States; 6 million of them are under fifty-five, and 1 out of 4 is under forty-five. Women living outside a husband/wife household represent 48 percent of the female population. Women currently make up 41 percent of the nation's work force.

These startling statistics clearly indicate that a large segment of the population is women alone, women who have their own incomes. As more and more doors are opening for you as a woman, what about the door to your own home?

Is purchasing your own home a sound investment? Will you be discriminated against when applying for a loan? Are there new laws available to protect your rights? Can you purchase a home jointly with a friend? How do you know how much house you can afford? Can you consider alimony, child support, unemployment, and/or Social Security benefits an income? After you find your dream home, what then? What problems do women encounter as homeowners? All these questions contribute to the housing dilemma—to buy or not to buy? Women interviewed throughout the country shed some interesting light on these questions.

Barbie Kneckt is twenty-four years old and has a degree in architecture. She purchased a Victorian house in the East Bay area, northeast of San Francisco, California. "Financially I was lucky that I could even consider the possibility of buying a house. I had inherited money from my grandmother, not a great fortune, but enough that I could raise a down payment and convince a lender that I was worth lending the balance to. The idea of buying a house split into units was very appealing since rent helps defray the monthly mortgage payment, and there are income tax deductions for rental property, even though that income cannot be included for loan purposes. Buying the house was fun at times, always worrisome, and certainly exciting."

According to the Federal Bank Board, which compiles statistics on homes purchased, there are no breakdown figures available on just how many home buyers have been women, single or otherwise. The real estate forecasts, however, project that in the next three years one out of every ten home buyers will be a woman.

Statistics show that although single-family dwellings still make up the majority of real estate sales, condominiums are growing in popularity, especially among single women. One reason may be such attractive features as: very little, if any, upkeep; security; appliances already installed; and no landscaping costs.

PROS AND CONS OF HOME BUYING

Before you decide to buy or not to buy, you will want to consider the advantages of being a homeowner.

The main advantage is the most obvious one—*equity*. In most cases, all monies you put into a home, unlike rent, will be returned to you, plus a profit. Even the added expenses a homeowner has that a renter does not have (taxes, insurance, maintenance and remodeling costs) will be recovered upon resale. By owning your own home, you are making an investment. You also have a future source of money available through refinancing.

Other advantages of being a homeowner are: (1) having the freedom to remodel, decorate, and landscape your home to suit your tastes; (2) obtaining a certain amount of privacy that renters don't always enjoy; (3) tax write-offs resulting from interest and upkeep; (4) pride of ownership; and (5) not having to move unless *you* wish to.

One possible disadvantage or drawback to being a homeowner can be the added monthly expenses—taxes, insurance, and upkeep costs—that a renter does not have. Even though you will probably recoup these monies upon resale, your monthly outlay is often more than it was as a renter.

The main drawback of owning a home, according to the women interviewed, is the maintenance and upkeep problems that confront them. "You can no longer call the landlord when the plumbing needs fixing or the walls need painting," one woman said. Many of the women felt they did not have the time or the inclination to do household repairs. They did not feel they wanted to depend on friends or relatives, yet they were tired of having to pay top dollar to get repairs and upkeep done. Some of their suggestions were: Find a neighborhood teenager or a retired gentleman who does handiwork part time; take advantage of the home maintenance classes that many of the junior colleges and four-year colleges now offer; avail yourself of books on home maintenance, such as *The Reader's Digest Complete Do-It-Yourself Manual*.

Anita Parker bought a town house in a suburban development in New York State. She told us that living costs were so high in her area she bought a condominium, which cost much less than the single-family home she originally wanted. "Actually I think I prefer this type of living now because I have little or no maintenance outside. The only feature I don't particularly enjoy is the fact that people hibernate all winter long, and it's difficult to meet any of your neighbors."

HOW MUCH HOUSE CAN YOU AFFORD?

Once you decide that owning your own home may be to your advantage, how do you go about figuring how much house you can afford? People shopping for a house often overestimate what they can afford to pay. They find the house of their dreams, only to be terribly disappointed when their application for a mortgage is turned down. "Too often," according to one savings and loan president, "people are found in lending institutions asking for help in bailing out of housing situations that are not affordable on their income."

The way to avoid this is to visit a bank or savings and loan and find out how much you can afford to borrow *before* you go house hunting.

This is known as prequalifying. The bank or savings and loan will evaluate your job stability, credit history, income, and debts and give you a general estimate of the size mortgage you can expect. In making this determination, it will apply two rules: (1) Mortgage payments and property taxes shouldn't take more than 25 percent of your annual gross income; (2) your combined payments for mortgage, property taxes, homeowner's insurance, and other long-term debts should not exceed 30 to 33 percent of your annual income. Depending on where you live, the state of the mortgage market, and other variables, lenders may go a little higher or lower than those figures, so be sure you check with them personally before you go out and buy.

As a general rule a bank or savings and loan tends to be more conservative than a real estate agent in figuring how much house you can afford. To qualify for a loan, your gross income must be approximately three to four times your anticipated monthly payment. This is a rule of thumb and can vary, depending on your outstanding debts, the number of your dependents, and other financial obligations. You can now, under the new credit laws, buy a house with an unrelated person, using your combined incomes as a base.

Say, for example, that you and a friend are going to buy a house together, that your combined annual gross income is $24,000, and that you have no outstanding obligations except your car payments and credit card bills (and food and utilities, of course). Divide that figure by 4, and you have a conservative estimate that your yearly housing costs should not exceed $6,000—divided by 12, equals $500 each month. That $500 should not only include the monthly loan payment (both principal and interest) but also take into consideration property taxes, homeowner's insurance, and condominium association fee, if applicable. These costs are referred to as fixed monthly costs—costs that recur every month at the same time and for approximately the same amount.

The second step is to ascertain how many dollars you can comfortably come up with for the down payment. Say you have $15,000 in the bank, or perhaps you and a partner can gather that much together. Keep some money aside for furnishing or remodeling expenses and for closing costs (see mortgages chapter).

Do some calculating and recalculating. Don't be put off by the numbers. Work with an actual example of a house currently on the market in your area. For instance, the house costs $60,000. You can find out from a real estate agent an estimate of the yearly property tax (e.g., $600, or $50 a month). A call to your insurance agent discloses that good coverage can be had for around $145 a year for a house of the same price in a neighborhood comparable to the one you're interested in. With this information, you already know what a portion of your fixed monthly costs will be—$62 a month for taxes and insurance.

If you're seeking a conventional loan on, for example, a $60,000 house, you, the buyer, must come up with anywhere from a 20 to 30 percent down payment, and the lender finances the remainder of the selling price of the house. If you pay a down payment figure of $12,000, you will be asking for a $48,000 loan. A typical interest rate is between 9 and 10 percent per year. You can buy an amortization book (available at most stationery stores for about $3), which will break down monthly payments according to interest rates, or you can ask your real estate agent for these figures. You may learn that to pay off such a loan, over the usual thirty-year period, will cost you about $404 per month. Combined with taxes and insurance, your total payment is $466 a month—well within the $500 limit you have budgeted for your monthly housing costs.

The best way to figure your projected monthly housing expenses is with the aid of an accountant. For instance, your tax savings can range from several hundred to several thousand dollars annually. During the first few years of your loan, your payments will be mostly interest with about 10 percent applying to the principal. The interest, however, is tax-deductible, so depending on your tax bracket, you could get one-third to one-half or more of that interest back as a tax refund. If you initially figure your housing expenses as $300 a month, you might find that you can reduce that by $100 a month when tax deductions and equity buildup are figured in. If you were paying the same $300 in rent, you would be losing those advantages and the long-term appreciation as well.

How much money will be required for a down payment? Down payments vary from situation to situation. You should figure that anywhere from 5 to 25 percent of the purchase price will be necessary for the down payment. If you do not have this amount available, you may want to check into a second mortgage—the money you lack between the amount required down and the amount the lending agency will lend on the purchase price. Real estate agents often have a list of people who will finance second mortgages. The seller sometimes will take back a second mortgage. That means he will lend you money and still maintain a small interest in the house he sold you. (We will discuss principal mortgage loans in the next chapter.)

If you are obtaining the down payment from a friend or relative, your loan source may sign a gift letter, saying the money does not have to be repaid. The money cannot then be considered a debt by the lending institution.

WHAT'S AVAILABLE AND HOW TO FIND IT

With the ever-changing real estate market, how do you go about finding what is currently available?

A place to start might be the real estate sections of your newspaper—the Thursday and Sunday editions offer the largest selections. Real estate ads are grouped by geographic area and listed by neighborhood, under the headings of various real estate companies. You may find ads in which the description and price of the property match your requirements. Be cautious—numerous superlatives are used to describe property in classifieds. Note the areas that sound attractive and the names of brokers serving that area.

You can also drive through an area, spot For Sale signs, and note the names of the brokers handling the properties. Most brokers belong to a multiple listing service and cooperate with other brokers; your broker can arrange to show you almost any property but those listed exclusively with one company.

When you meet a real estate agent, mention the area you are interested in, the physical features you require in the property, your price range, and other factors such as schools, shopping, transportation, etc.

Real estate companies, brokers, agents, and salespeople are usually licensed by the state where you reside and are required to conduct business in accordance with legal and ethical standards.

New tracts of houses or condominium projects are normally listed in the newspaper's real estate section or in real estate magazines. Often there are real estate agents on the premises of the projects.

Prices of homes vary widely. However, on a national level, the median price is $44,000.

When deciding what type of house you wish to purchase, you might want to consider the various pros and cons of the different types of housing available, such as condominiums, new houses, or older houses.

CONDOMINIUMS

If you are thinking of purchasing a condominium dwelling, don't be afraid to ask questions. Condominiums come in many forms, from towering inner-city structures to suburban townhouses with luscious green expanses. You may even be considering a unit which was formerly an apartment rental. Condominiums were created under a special real estate law in the state where you reside. The documents will differ from one development to another because they must describe the characteristics of the development they represent, not a condominium in general. If you are looking at an unfinished project, make certain that the developer has enough capital to complete it properly.

You should check to be sure there is sufficient liability coverage for the entire development and that the policy names the board of directors and each unit owner individually as co-owner of the insurance policy. Before you sign any documents, find out on what basis your ownership, assessments, and voting rights are being determined. You could be considered a part owner of the entire project or total owner of one unit with assessments for maintenance, gardening, repairs, etc. Read a copy of the bylaws, operating budget, management agreement, and regulatory agreement (if any mortgage in the project is HUD-FHA-insured). A sales contract normally states that you have read all these documents.

You would also be wise to check whether the condo plan you are shown is the entire development or if the developer plans to enlarge the project with additional land and more units at a later date, the physical boundaries to your potential home, and what degree transient occupancy is allowed. Be sure to ask about the return of down payments in case your purchase arrangements fall through, and ask about resale rights. Most states will not allow buildings to be occupied until all necessary building codes have been met, but if you live in a state where this is not a requirement, you should verify the building quality with your state real estate commission or other appropriate state agency. Make certain you are purchasing a condo, not a planned unit development because each is a different type of purchase arrangement with regard to what you own. A planned unit development (PUD) is five or more lots with attached or detached houses. A PUD has areas owned in common, such as pools and tennis courts, which are reserved for some or all of the owners of the lots. As owner of a unit you pay a monthly association fee to cover the costs of maintaining those common areas.

When you purchase a condominium, you own the apartment unit where it is situated plus a shared interest in the common area. You pay a monthly fee into an association to cover gardening, repairs, and maintenance. Taxes may be assessed and paid separately or through the association.

A NEW HOUSE

The reliability of the builder is an important consideration in choosing a new house. Arrange to talk with people who are living in single-family residences or condominiums constructed by the builder you are considering. When looking at a new or model home, consider these points:

1. Don't be overwhelmed by the appearance of a glittering model home. Pin down exactly which features are extras displayed in the models.
2. Be sure that the contract is complete and that there is a written agreement on all details of the transactions. Don't assume an item is included and later discover you've misunderstood.
3. If the community is to have new street paving, water and sewer lines, and sidewalks, make sure you know whether you or the builder will assume the costs. Find out about charges for water and trash collection.
4. Check the lot site in advance. Is it the size and setting you want for your house? After the bulldozer has arrived, it may be too late.
5. Don't take anyone else's word about the zoning uses permitted for the area in which you plan to buy a house. The neighborhood may be strictly residential or zoned for certain commercial uses. This information could affect future or current property values. The city, county, or township clerk's office can tell you where to inquire about zoning.
6. The contract with the builder should set forth the total sales price. If possible, try to locate a lender who will allow you to take advantage of lower interest rates which may apply at the time of closing. When you are quoted a rate, make certain the lender will stand by it. In any event avoid an arrangement which would allow the lender to increase the mortgage interest rate if market conditions changed between the date of mortgage commitment and the closing date.

7. Be sure your contract with the builder definitely stipulates the completion date of your new house.

8. Don't be afraid to check construction progress regularly while the house is being built. If you do not like the workmanship or if a feature has been sloppily completed, insist that it be redone.

9. Any extra features that are to be included in the finished house should be described in writing.

10. The day before you take title to the house (closing day), make a thorough inspection trip. Check all equipment, windows, doors. This is your last chance to request changes.

11. Insist on these papers when you take possession: (a) warranties from all manufacturers for equipment in the house; (b) certificate of occupancy and certificates from the health department clearing plumbing and sewer installations. It would also be best to obtain all applicable certificates of code compliance.

AN OLDER HOUSE

Statistics show that two out of every three buyers select a used house. The one person out of three who buys a new house is likely to purchase one that has already been built rather than building his own. This is a choice each home buyer must make. Usually one of the biggest advantages an older house offers is more space for the money. In addition, the lot may have been planted with trees and shrubs by previous owners and therefore present relatively few landscaping costs. In an established neighborhood taxes are usually stable.

Don't fail to weigh the possibility of shorter commuting times and distances from older neighborhoods to schools, offices, and other frequent destinations. Future road construction also could affect the value of a house, so you may wish to check plans for construction with local authorities. Many older houses are located in neighborhoods that have started to deteriorate. That will make your purchase price lower, but you may lose money unless the trend reverses itself. Before purchasing a house in an older neighborhood, be sure to check on any future plans for neighborhood improvement, urban renewal, or land appropriation for new highways or other projects which might make the older house a good investment.

Many older houses have ample bedroom and closet space, and this is an important factor when choosing a house. Observe how the floor space has been used by the builder. You may prefer a house containing fewer rooms that are spacious and livable to a house with a larger number of small, cell-like rooms. Once you have found a house you like, evaluate it carefully. You are buying the property "as is" and you must literally live *in* as well as *with* your mistakes.

Sometimes, however, in an older house, what first appeared to be a bargain may turn out to be a headache. A thorough inspection may reveal hidden defects and obvious remodeling needs. Few people make a full-time business of checking house construction; however, if you have doubts about the soundness of the house you have selected, hire an expert who will not only appraise the property but discover any deficiencies as well. In many cities there are reputable inspection firms that will examine the building and give you a detailed report. The $50 or $100 fee may be well spent; some buyers have faced the expense of replacing basic equipment within the first year of ownership. If you have doubts about the wiring, plumbing, or heating plant, the owner may permit you to have it checked. You must be prepared to pay for this inspection.

The age of a house should not necessarily limit your choice. While older houses may require more care and repair work, many have received excellent attention from previous owners and will compare favorably with new structures. If you must call in experts, first check their reputations, and beware of unscrupulous operators who may justify their fee by exaggerating flaws, which they may want to repair at inflated costs. If it appears that repairs and improvements are needed, be sure to secure estimates in advance of the cost of the work and find out who will pay for it—you or the seller.

Older houses deserve special attention in nine areas before a prospecitve buyer signs on the dotted line. So check them carefully:

1. Termite infestation and wood rot. The importance of a check by a termite specialist cannot be overemphasized, particularly in those coastal areas of the country that have a history of infestation.

2. Sagging structure. Look carefully at the squareness of exterior walls.

3. Inadequate wiring. Be sure that there is sufficient amperage and enough electrical outlets. Request inspection by the local government for code compliance to make sure the wiring is not dilapidated, exposed, and dangerous.

4. Run-down heating plant. Check the general condition of the heating system. What kinds of repairs are needed, and how long will the system last?

5. Inadequate insulation. Ask if the attic and the space between interior and exterior walls has been filled with an insulating material. What material was used, and how was it installed?

6. Faulty plumbing. Choose a home that is connected to a public sewer system in preference to one served by a septic tank or a cesspool. Check with the plumber who last serviced the house to determine the condition of the plumbing. Test the water pressure.

7. Hot-water heater. Check the type and capacity of the tank to determine if there will be sufficient hot water for family needs. Look for any signs of rust or leaks. Obtain any guarantee held by the present owner if it is still in effect.

8. Roof and gutters. What kind of roofing material was used, and how old is it? Check inside the attic for water stains and discolorations. Ask the owner for a roofing guarantee if one exists.

9. Wet basements. A basement that looks dry in summer may be four inches under water in the spring. Are there signs of water penetration around the foundation walls? Examine the condition of the outside paint and the paint and wallpaper inside the house. Be sure all windows and doors operate and are in good repair. If there is a fireplace, it should have a workable damper. Inspect floor and wall tile and fixtures in the bathroom. Determine if the attic has sufficient storage area.

Remember, there is no perfect house. Just be sure you know in advance the shortcomings of the house you are buying. Don't wait to be shocked after you move in. If you do decide to purchase an older house, you will have to determine how much remodeling you want or the house needs.

This brings up the subject of home improvement loans. In general, larger loan amounts will give you longer repayment periods and sometimes lower interest rates. Virtually all institutional lenders, such as banks, savings and loans, credit unions, and finance companies, offer home improvement loans. Depending on the lender and the size of the loan, you may be required to give a deed of trust on your home to secure the loan. If that is the case, your lender may want a title report and property appraisal (these will be at your cost). You will have to submit a personal financial statement or, if you are self-employed, your business profit and loss statements and income tax returns for several previous years. You can often finance through your contractor. No matter where you obtain your loan, read carefully what you are signing before you sign; if you do, the story could be a happy one.

Trisha Jordan relates her story:

"After my separation from my husband, I moved to a small country town five hundred miles away from where I lived when I was married. I fell in love with the town on my first visit there and decided this was where I wanted to live. I purchased a one hundred-year-old house, which was literally falling on its side. But it was on a beautiful large lot with walnut trees and blackberries, and I thought it would be a healthy place for my young son and me to live. I asked several people for the names of contractors who might rebuild my old farmhouse, and five people gave me the same name, so that was the contractor I settled on. Dan was marvelous, although he had difficulty picturing what I wanted. So with the assistance of graph paper, I redesigned the living space, removing walls, turning a bathroom into a den, and a bedroom into a master bathroom. There was no kitchen in the house, so I designed that also. I really found I had a knack for remodeling, and the finished product was just great. I hope someday to have the opportunity to do it again. I wouldn't have missed the experience for anything. However, when I had to sell it, I just barely broke even since the house cost me twenty thousand dollars to remodel on top of the original twenty-seven-thousand-dollar purchase price.

On any project which involves new construction, first check with your city or county planning and building inspection departments to see what kinds of restrictions you might encounter. If you are an artistic person, can envision what you want your finished project to look like, and have a talented contractor, you can probably bypass an architect. Otherwise, you will need an architect to take over the entire project; he will hire a contractor and supervise the work. An architect's fee is usually calculated by the hour or for a percentage of the project's cost.

If you live in an area where you must comply with many city and local ordinances, you might need the services of a building designer. His fee is usually by the hour or for a fixed fee. If you live in a small town or rural area, a local contractor can probably fill all the necessary functions. Should you decide you want to do most of the work yourself, you can become an owner-builder and hire licensed contractors to do jobs which you are not equipped to do—electrical wiring or plumbing, for example. If the remodeling takes more skill and time than you have, you should probably get a contractor. The best way to get a good contractor is through the recommendations of satisfied customers. If you do not know anyone who can recommend a contractor, you can visit your local lumber company, and it will probably supply you with a number of names. Get in touch with these people, and ask for references. You can then call these references and even look at his/her work if you think it necessary. When you sign a contract, sign one that is for a total price, not a contract that is open-ended on which you can wind up paying much more than you originally thought you had bargained for. For your own protection you should consider asking your contractor to obtain additional bonding for your project, especially if it's a costly one. The bond protects you against the contractor's failure to perform the work as specified or to pay suppliers or subcontractors. The contractor buys the bond, typically for the full amount of the contract, and adds the bonding fee to the price of your remodeling job.

DISCRIMINATION

After finding a home you wish to purchase, are you apt to face discrimination while applying for a loan? Lenora Oppenheim, a loan officer at a major savings and loan, feels that this is true, but it is changing: "Lending institutions are realizing that women are becoming financially independent and are a new source of revenue; since financial institutions are in the business of making money, they are not going to turn their backs on a revenue source."

Ms. Oppenheim's position is that women are still too often denied true equality in lending, and this can be hidden in subtle forms, which can range from poor service to a particularly long period of waiting for loan approval. She advises that if you have been subjected to this type of discrimination, take your business elsewhere or report the lending institution to:

Bureau of Consumer Protection
Federal Trade Commission
Washington, D.C. 20560

or:

Office of Saver and Consumer Affairs
Federal Reserve Board
Washington, D.C. 20551

You should also be aware of the Federal Equal Opportunity Credit Act, which became effective on October 28, 1975. This act and its regulations prohibit discrimination based on sex or marital status in both mortgage and consumer credit transactions. (See the chapter on credit.)

PREPARING YOURSELF FOR FUTURE HOME BUYING

This discussion of becoming a homeowner is all well and good, you say, but you have been on your job only a short time and are bringing home $600 per month. You haven't been able to save a penny toward a down payment. How do all these facts apply to you?

Now is not too soon to begin planning for your home of the future. The following suggestions are made to help you obtain that goal: (1) Establish credit in your own name; (2) open a savings account where you think you may be applying for a mortgage loan in the future; (3) sign up for a payroll deduction where you work to help you save for a down payment; (4) familiarize yourself with terms and forms you will be asked to complete such as a financial statement; (5) look at open houses to acquaint yourself with the real estate market and property values in the areas you think you may want to live; (6) take a financial awareness class at a local college; (7) explore the possibility of pooling your resources and buying property with a friend; and (8) begin acquiring furnishings so you will not be burdened with a tremendous financial layout for necessities, on top of other new home expenditures.

FACTS TO KEEP IN MIND

Whether you are planning to buy a home now or in the future, you should keep in mind certain facts when purchasing a home. The additional costs involved in buying furnishings, and paying for necessary remodeling or repairs can be sizable. You must have access to other money, not just what you have allotted for the down payment. In that way, you will be prepared for any contingency that might arise. You must also consider the possibility of loss of income, because of accident or illness.

A certified financial planner told us that "in any year, the occurrence of a foreclosure is five to seven times more likely because of lack of income than of death. You should provide yourself with disability income coverage. Before you sign, read the policy carefully to make certain the provisions of the policy are applicable to your situation." She also advises the homeowner to buy insurance that provides an automatic increase each year to keep pace with the rising value in property.

To summarize:

1. Find a reputable real estate agent.
2. Learn property values.
3. Make certain your credit is adequate through prequalifying.
4. Know the new laws and your rights when you apply for a loan.
5. Don't figure your finances so closely that you are without an emergency cushion.
6. Don't sign any document until you have read it thoroughly.
7. Don't forget to add taxes and insurances when calculating your monthly outlay.
8. Consider settling for less than your dream house on your first purchase. Look at it as an investment toward that dream home.
9. When looking at model homes, remember you will be getting the barebones house, not the professionally decorated one.
10. Prepare a list of reasonable features you feel you must have in a house and take it with you when house hunting.
11. When purchasing an old house, check the age of the house, the condition of the plumbing, major appliances (especially the water heater), the roof, and the storm drainage system.
12. Don't be afraid to ask questions, and continue asking until you receive an answer that satisfies you.

The general consensus of women interviewed who have purchased their own homes is definitely positive. Not one of the women expressed regret in having purchased a home of her own. They all were in agreement that pride of ownership and the security that comes from the building of equity more than compensate for any problems they have encountered.

To quote homeowner Barbi Knecht, "The physical tangible problems and results of owning a home are challenging and more readily comprehensible than the mental and emotional ones. There is a certain stability and tranquillity that I feel in not arranging my life according to one-year lease terms. Even with the annoyances, such as having repairmen ask to speak to my husband, looking all over town for a particular water faucet part, and receiving junk mail addressed to

Mr. and Mrs. Knecht, buying a house was probably one of the financially wisest and most emotionally satisfying things I have ever done."

After the advantages and disadvantages of being a homeowner are weighed, the answer to a woman's dilemma to buy or not to buy a home has to be a resouding YES! The phenomenal rise in the number of women who are buying or considering buying their own homes may necessitate an old cliché's being changed to read, "A woman's home is her castle."

10

Mortgages, Costs and Conditions

Now that you have found the castle your budget figures have told you you can afford, you will enter into the settlement or closing phase of home buying. This is a process whereby the title (ownership) of your new home is transferred to you by the seller.

In some states all the closing aspects of buying a home are completed through escrow accounts, and in others they are completed with the service of a lawyer.

If you live in a state where lawyers are used in the purchase and sale of a house, you will want to find out what the legal fees are for reading documents and issuing opinions. If you feel the charges are not justified, seek another lawyer. You should ask your potential lawyer what charges aside from the cost of reading documents and giving advice he will be making. There may be a charge for appearing at the closing (also referred to as settlement). This is a meeting between you, the seller, your lawyer, and other interested parties to make sure documents are signed and funds distributed. Determine if his firm will also be representing the seller at the same settlement. If the answer to the last question is affirmative, you might want to seek other counsel, for there may be a conflict of interest.

If you live in a state that has escrow procedures, your signed sales documents will be delivered to an escrow company, which is usually chosen by the real estate agent. The function of an escrow is similar to that of a third party that looks out for the interests of both buyer and seller. The escrow company holds the papers on your prospective new house until all the conditions of the sales transaction are met.

When you initially open an escrow account, there are conditions which the seller wants you as buyer to meet, and there are conditions which you want the seller to meet. For example, if you purchase an older house, you will want the seller to offer a warrant that the property has a clear title (there are no liens against it). The escrow company will check the deed to the property to be certain what the seller warrants is true. Another condition may be the length of period of your escrow account. It can be as few as ten days or as long as six months, whatever number of days both buyer and seller agree upon. Remember, the shorter the time, the less time you have in which to obtain your loan. The escrow account will not be closed or the sale consummated until every provision of the sales agreement is adhered to, including loan approval. Once you have your loan, the money is paid to the escrow company. At that time the company will disburse the proceeds, the deed will go to you, and the escrow account is closed.

FINANCING

As a general rule, new home financing is available through the housing development lender; if you are considering a new home, you should check with the agent on the premises. If you are purchasing a previously owned property, your real estate agent may have some helpful ideas about where you can obtain a loan. In some instances, you might be able to assume the seller's mortgage if it is made part of the sales agreement and if it is advantageous for you to do so. You may wish to seek out a lending institution of your own, in which case you should try to use the bank or savings and loan where you have an account.

When you do go to a lending institution, it will in turn send an appraiser to look at the property. Its appraised worth plus your credit rating will determine the amount of money a lender will lend on that particular piece of property. As a rule, buyers of a resale home will receive a loan of only 80 percent of the appraised value.

There are several questions you should ask your lender, such as: "Am I required to carry life or disability insurance, and must I obtain it from a particular company? . . . Is there a late payment charge, and if so, how much? . . . If I am late, how late can I be before a charge is imposed? . . . Is there a prepayment penalty? How Much? For how long is it enforced? . . . Will you release me from personal liability if my loan is assumed by someone else when I sell the house? . . . Will a new buyer be allowed to assume a loan, or will you require full payment of the loan? . . . If I have a financial emergency, will the terms of my loan allow me to borrow additional funds? . . . Will I have to have a special impound account to cover taxes or insurance? If so, how much of a deposit will I need?"

Buying a home may well be the biggest decision in your life. Selecting an institution or an individual to finance your home is one of the most important decisions you will make after selecting that home. You can obtain a mortgage loan from a commercial bank, a savings bank, a savings and loan association, an insurance company, or even Grandma Mathilda (if you have one). It's more likely you'll obtain a loan through one of the former entities rather than Grandma, so all we'll say regarding her is that if you do use a relative or friend to finance your home, you should not leave any details of your loan to an oral agreement. *Get everything in writing.*

It is wise to find out as much as you can about the terms and payment plans of as many different lending sources as possible. Then you can decide on the source that best suits your needs. As you consider the different institutions, compare annual percentage rates, their methods of making payments, the length of time given to repay the loan, and how a large cash down payment will affect your loan payments and interest rates.

A mortgage is a loan contract. If the home you want to buy already has a mortgage on it, you may be able to assume that old mortgage. Usually, you will need to obtain new financing (a new mortgage).

A lender agrees to provide the money you need to buy a specific home or piece of property. You, in turn, promise to repay the money on the basis of terms set forth in the agreement. Under the federal Truth in Lending Law, the contract should state the amount of the loan, the annual percentage rate, which includes the mortgage interest rate, the premium paid for insuring, the mortgage and "discount points" (a point is a one-time charge equal to 1 percent of the loan), the size of the payment, and the frequency of payments. Certain other charges collected by the lender from the mortgagor—

such as penalties and prepayment privileges and any special conditions agreed on by the lender and you—must also be included.

Cynthia Wellankamp was buying a used house when the bank she was going to get her loan from said she would have to obtain a new loan rather than assume the old one. She hired an attorney to represent her in a lawsuit against the bank. The sum of money involved was $16.48 a month. In 1978 the case went all the way to the Supreme Court of California, and the court ruled that the bank was fraudulent to claim it had the right to interfere in the sale of the house. The bank had no right to new profits on an old loan unless it was somehow harmed. This landmark decision in California guarantees the purchaser the right to assume a previous mortgage.

Since you are the borrower, you pledge your home as security. It remains pledged until the loan is paid off. If you fail to meet the terms of the contract, your lender has the right to foreclose—that is, obtain possession of the property. To exercise his right of foreclosure, however, a lender must follow certain legal formalities.

For the past forty years, the real estate market has relied on the long-term fixed-rate, fully amortized mortgage as the sole instrument for financing single-family housing. In an amortized loan, you are required to make fixed periodic payments, usually monthly, that include the interest (and, in some instances, taxes and insurance). This payment also reduces the principal (total amount) of the mortgage debt after each payment.

Through the early years of repayment, a large share of each payment is the interest. As you keep paying, a smaller share of each payment is for interest and a larger share is applied as repayment of the principal. It works this way because as your payments reduce the amount you owe on the principal, the interest charges are also reduced. Your monthly payment remains the same throughout the life of the loan.

You build up equity, or investment capital, in your home as the outstanding principal is reduced. When the last payment on an amortized loan is made, the loan will be completely paid. All amounts due for principal and interest will have been repaid in full.

Various types of mortgage plans are available: the conventional loan, the VA (Veterans Administration) loan, and the FHA (Federal Housing Administration)-insured loan. If you live in a rural area, the Farmers Home Administration loan may be available to you.

VA-guaranteed loans are made to eligible veterans by private lenders. You can apply for a VA home mortgage loan at a bank, savings and loan association, or mortgage firm. VA direct home loans are also made by the Veterans Administration to eligible veterans in areas where there is a shortage of credit for housing. If you are a veteran, check with the Veterans Administration in your area for information on home financing benefits available to you. Your local bank or savings and loan (or other institution which provides home loans) may also be able to tell you what you are entitled to under the law as a veteran.

FHA loans are made by private lenders and insured by the Federal Housing Administration. This type of loan is insured up to certain limits. Generally the lender you use does not require as large a down payment as would be necessary for a conventional loan without the FHA insurance. The FHA does not actually make loans. It agrees to insure the private lender against loss in case you, the borrower, fail to repay the loan in full.

The Farmers Home Administration, not to be confused with the FHA, makes housing loans to rural families. These loans are available to farm families and to other families in rural areas and small communities (10,000 population or less) not associated with an urban area. Low- and moderate-income urban residents who work in the rural area may qualify for assistance. There are special provisions for interest subsidies which apply to low-income families. For a rural housing loan you should apply at your local county office of the Farmers Home Administration. Your county supervisor will get the necessary information from you and submit it to the proper officials.

As a general comment, government loans take longer to obtain, and your seller may not be willing to wait for you to obtain one.

Conventional loans are made strictly between you and a private commercial lender. The home you are buying and your credit are security. There is no other backing. The amount of your down payment and the length of your repayment period are agreed on by you and your lender.

At the lending institution, ask to talk with the mortgage loan officer. State your desire to buy a home and how much money you wish to borrow. If the lender wants your business, she/he will suggest that you file an application.

You will be asked to file information on the type of loan you wish, the property you want to buy, and your financial situation. The lender will supply any loan documents needed and assist you in preparing them. Your application will then be submitted for a thorough review. If you want an FHA-insured home loan, your application will be sent to the FHA office servicing your area.

You will need to indicate the location and selling price of the property. You will be asked where you work, how long you have worked there, how much you earn, the size of your family, the cost of your present housing, how many debts you have, what installment contracts you are carrying, and how much you have in the bank. There may be questions in addition to these.

Within a few days to a few weeks you will be notified whether or not your application has been approved. If the lender has approved your loan, the closing of the loan will be arranged with you at that time. If your loan is not approved, you will have to seek out another lender and go through the same procedure again.

When money is scarce, a lender may charge a discount or points to make a loan. Charging points is a way for the lender to make up the difference between the legal ceiling on interest rates and the yield he can get elsewhere in the market. Thus, the cost of financing a home may be higher because of discount points.

During the last ten years inflation and the wild swings in interest rates have led to much discussion among economists, bankers, and others interested in the mortgage market. As part of the plan to help alleviate the inflation and wild swing problems, new forms of mortgages are being considered and, in some cases, implemented throughout the country.

One such mortgage is the Flexible Loan Insurance Program (FLIP). FLIP is a private mortgage plan (no government ties) that enables the borrower to pay lower monthly payments during the first years of owning a home. It permits the purchaser to buy when ordinary financing would make it impossible to qualify. Qualifying for a mortgage loan under FLIP involves the same standards used in a conventional loan. (The government has instituted a similar type of loan, but so far there is too much red tape involved to make it practical to apply for one.) Another mortgage alternative now available is the variable interest rate mortgage loan (VIRM). It is similar to the traditional fixed rate loan, except that once the loan is established, the interest rate on the loan can fluctuate in response to the Federal Home Loan Bank Cost of Money Index.

What Is a Cost of Money Index?

This index reflects the cost of money that banks and savings and loans pay for their funds when they borrow from the Federal Home Loan Bank. The index also takes into consideration the amount of interest consumers receive on their savings accounts and eliminates any influence from the cost of corporations or businesses borrowing, depositing, or withdrawing deposits. As a result, the Cost of Money

Index is relatively stable, and its movement is in response to real upward and downward trends in consumer rates.

The Cost of Money Index has historically moved slowly. This can mean that if in the future total incomes continue to rise more rapidly, your mortgage payments will reflect a smaller percentage of your total income.

There are numerous regulations regarding VIRM, and the number and complexity often differ from state to state and between state-chartered and federally chartered institutions. As a rule, the interest rate and payment adjustments are figured only semi-annually, and as a rule, the amount of fluctuation is regulated. State or federal regulations often set a minimum of one-tenth of 1 percent and a maximum of one-fourth of 1 percent. In other words, the interest rate will not change unless the index justifies an adjustment of at least one-tenth of 1 percent. And in any six-month period it cannot be increased (or decreased) more than one-fourth of 1 percent. Also, there may be provisions requiring a thirty-day written notice of any change or special prepayment of assumption provisions. Thus, the interest rate on your home loan, and therefore your monthly house payments, can vary depending on the changes in the money market.

The VIRM mortgage does offer several advantages. One is that many institutions waive all prepayment charges automatically for ninety days following the date of notification of an increase in the interest rate or whenever the increased rate exceeds the initial rate at which your loan was made. Another allows you to extend the maturity of your loan when your interest increases, rather than increase the payment, as long as the term of the loan does not exceed forty years. Most important, the variable interest mortgage loan is guaranteed assumable to a qualified buyer at an initial rate equal to the rate in effect for the seller at the time of the sale. Also, because many lenders will advance more money under the variable type of mortgage, it should be easier for you, the homeowner, to resell your home.

Another mortgage device you should be aware of, currently available in Ohio, is a reverse annuity mortgage. (It is really the opposite of obtaining a mortgage, but to discuss it fits in well with this chapter.) A reverse annuity is a marvelous boon to you if you are retired or a widowed woman who owns her own home. It allows you to use the equity in your own home while still living there. With this type of mortgage, the lender would pay you a fixed annuity, based on a percentage of the present value of your property. You as the annuitant would not be required to repay the loan until you died, at which time your estate would repay the loan through probate. No cash payment of interest would be involved because the increase in your loan balance (the amount of your annuity) each month would include the amount of cash you received plus interest on the outstanding balance. At the time of writing this book, only the state of Ohio was offering the reverse annuity mortgage through the Broadview Savings and Loan in Cleveland. Perhaps if people throughout the country exerted pressure on the mortgage financing institutions in their state, the plan would become available in other states.

SECOND MORTGAGES

When purchasing a home, you may find you need a certain amount of cash to make up the difference between your down payment and the amount of mortgage money you have been lent. Instead of giving up in despair, you can obtain a second mortgage. A second mortgage is a loan specifically secured by the equity you are putting into your new home. It is a smaller amount of money. In case you default on your loan, your primary mortgage would be paid off before your second would. Usually your real estate agent will know someone who will lend you the money for a second mortgage, or the previous owners might even take back a second. (The owners will lend you the amount of money you need). There are also mortgage companies that you can turn to if necessary. (Remember to include the repayment of this loan when figuring your monthly expenses in how much house you can afford. You may find you'll have to lower your price range.)

TITLE INSURANCE

One thing that you'll want to know when you purchase real estate is that you'll have clear title to the property. What this means is that you should find out if someone has placed a lien on the property you want to buy or is selling property that is not rightfully his to sell.

Jim Leitner builds homes for a living. He built a beautiful home that Vi Strickland bought. However, Jim Leitner moved out of the country before he paid the contractor who did the final outdoor landscaping. The contractor put a lien on the house, which meant that until the bill was paid or other arrangements made with the contractor, Vi was liable for the unpaid bill.

If she had had title insurance, this would not have happened because a title search is an integral part of the insurance policy. A title insurance policy would have eliminated the problem. If Vi had bought the house and the lien had not shown up during the title search, or if a lien had been put on after Vi bought the house, title insurance would have paid to remove the lien. Title insurance helps you know as much as possible about a particular piece of property. ("Torrens" may be the word used instead of title evidence in some states—Minnesota and Illinois, to name two—to designate any form of title.) Most lending institutions today require their borrowers to purchase some form of title insurance as a condition of receiving a loan.

When title insurance is purchased, the premiums paid cover the cost of the search, examination of the property, and issuance of the policy itself.

Exactly What Is Title Insurance?

According to Michael Bilyk, a national sales manager for the Chicago Title Insurance Company, "title insurance is an insured statement of the condition of title (your claim to the property). It is a record of ownership or various rights in connection with a particular piece of land. Title insurance protects you for any damage you may suffer if you relied on the seller's telling you that the house had no liens against it."

Although certain lenders may require title insurance, it is usually a voluntary program, but it does give you as a property buyer some assurance that the seller has clear title and that the property is mortgaged as the borrower represents it. In some states and in rural areas a lawyer will provide a legal opinion, or a county recorder will provide an abstract (a collection of what is in the public record regarding the property).

How Much Does Title Insurance Cost?

The price varies. The title insurance policy premium is based on the value of the property you are buying. It is a one-time charge, and the policy is good for the entire time you own your property.

What Will a Title Search Tell Me?

The search will show you who has owned the property prior to you (called chain of title). It will show any easements on your property; an easement is property that your city or town may take for its own use. Perhaps the power company in your city has the right to build a power plant where your swimming pool is. The title search will also let you know if there are any back taxes owing on the property. Even if an error occurs in the title search and you are told the title is clear when it isn't, title insurance will protect you and can reimburse you for the total amount of the sale plus damages.

How Long Does It Take for a Title Search to Be Completed?

The length of time involved in a title search depends on how many documents must be checked or how accessible the material is. Some county recorders' offices or title insurance companies have all the necessary information on microfilm, making the task much easier.

When Does a Title Search Take Place?

In states that have an escrow system a title search takes place after the opening of the escrow. In states where a lawyer is used this may be determined by your lawyer or the lending institution.

Who Pays for Title Insurance?

In some states title insurance is paid for by the seller; in others, by the buyer. The fees are collected at the close of your escrow or at the closing to transfer the property of the seller to the buyer, depending on the state where you live.

How to Hold Title to Your Property

How you hold title to your property is really up to you. Property can be held in single name, joint tenancy, tenants in common, as community property, or as tenants by the entirety. Community property states are different from noncommunity property states. This is an important legal question, so we suggest that when you purchase your home, if you do not know how you want the title to read, ask your lawyer.

All the procedures you are involved in have laws which protect you while you are going through the settlement phase of your home buying transaction. The federal Real Estate Settlement Procedures Act (RESPA) was established to protect homeowners and potential property owners.

During escrow you will hear the words "closing costs." Closing costs are the charges for service from the escrow company, mortgage insurance, or a bill submitted by your lawyer for reading your sales agreement.

Although we have provided a brief account of what happens during the settlement period of home purchase, we obviously cannot cover every facet in the space allotted. When you apply for a mortgage, you may or may not have your choice of all the many variations of loans we have discussed. Also, there are constantly new methods of financing and new rates of interest being charged on that financing. But whatever type of a loan you obtain, we hope this chapter has helped prepare you for what you will encounter when you want to finance that "new" castle.

11

Purchasing a Car

Probably the largest, most important purchase you will make besides your home is your car. Not only does a car represent a sizable investment, but in many cases you are also totally dependent on it for getting to and from work, recreation, appointments, and household errands. Your car can become your friend or your enemy. Knowing the best way to go about purchasing a car and what you can do to help keep it in running condition can save you time and money.

Owning and operating a car are more expensive than you may think, according to Runzheimer and Company, a firm specializing in living costs. When you figure finance charges, depreciation, insurance, license, taxes, maintenance, gasoline, oil, tires, and other expenses, the cost of operating a new or used car ranges from $45.96 per week for a compact car to $83.31 for a full-size luxury car.

In deciding whether you will purchase a new or used car, you must consider which is most practical for you. A new car is going to cost more to purchase, but its advantages include the latest mechanical features, up-to-date styling, perfect condition, and the protection of the manufacturer's and dealer's warranties. But, again, this all comes at a price. A new car may depreciate 27 or 30 percent in value during the first year, and not necessarily because of the type of wear it receives; it depreciates just because it is now secondhand, no longer "new." Hence, a good used car, already depreciated, can and often does represent very real dollar value.

Once the decision is made on whether to buy used or new, the majority of women car buyers prefer compact cars because they are cheaper to operate, take less gas, are easier to maneuver and park.

While large cars are roomier and more comfortable, have more speed and power, the cost of fuel and maintenance is correspondingly higher.

The largest car manufacturers offer a range of models—from the "top of the line" car, which is usually a fairly large car, to the "bottom of the line," which is usually a fairly compact one. Their "middle of the line" cars are often a good compromise between compactness and capacity.

Once the decision has been made to buy a car, women may face some unique problems. Pat Kelly, a new car salesperson for a major dealer, thinks they do. One problem she feels is unique to women is lack of credit. "Buying a new car is a great way to establish credit, but how do you buy a new car without a credit rating or a trade-in? One suggestion I would make is, if a woman has time on the job (which helps establish her stability), she should save or borrow twenty percent of the cost of the car in order to make a down payment. Most dealers, when offered a sizable down payment, and a customer with a good employment record, will usually sell you a car and help you obtain financing. Dealers and lending institutions are realizing there is a large market of career women out there that has virtually been ignored. We will begin to see more car advertising directed toward these women and more banks and other lending institutions taking another look at the buying power of women."

Another suggestion she makes is: "If a woman is in a business situation (uses her car in business) or if she owns her own business, she may want to look into leasing a car. That way she can write off her car expenses from her income taxes, and she does not have to come up with a down payment."

Ms. Kelly advises women to do a little homework before buying anything. "They should at least know the average price for a car [in 1978 it was $7,000]. Lending institutions and credit unions have books that list the invoice price of various makes of cars with standard features. To find out what standard features are, pick up brochures at car dealers. They list not only the standard features but all the optional ones available and sometimes their prices as well. But remember every optional feature will add to the cost of the car. For example, power equipment adds at least an additional one thousand dollars to the price, and your selected model may not need it; also, there is a lot that can go wrong with it. Yet many salespeople will try to convince a woman that power steering and brakes are easier for her to handle."

When actually getting down to the serious business of buying the car, Ms. Kelly recommends, "If you are trading in your old car, don't just be interested in what the salesperson will give you for your car; ask how much he/she is prepared to discount the new car. You will save more money on taxes that way. Don't be intimidated by the salesperson. Tell him/her at the outset that you want to deal in hard figures. What is his car really worth? What is your car really worth? Be prepared to bargain, but if you have done your homework, you should have some figure in mind of what the price of that particular model should be. A salesperson deserves to earn a commission, but he/she shouldn't earn a whole year's salary on your transaction; drive a hard bargain. Check the guarantee the auto manufacturer offers and the warranty the dealer offers. A good warranty will not have any contingencies that limit its effect; it will cover all internal working parts. In one actual case a warranty was invalid unless a certain brand of motor oil was used."

Ms. Kelly feels there should be an emotional factor involved with buying a car. "After all, you're going to be spending a lot of time together, so you might want to read up on different ratings given various makes of cars in magazines like *Motor Trend*. It's easier to fall in love with a car that will be good to you."

Before you can actually purchase a car, you must select a car dealer. Here you really need to proceed with caution, according to Ms. Kelly. "There are basically two types of dealers. There is the straight sell dealer—you deal directly with the salesperson, who carries you through the whole transaction: selecting the car; signing the contract. Then there are what are referred to in the trade as the liners or the turnovers. They are usually big-volume dealers of the type you are apt to see advertise on Saturday afternoon movies on television. They will tell you anything and everything while trying to sell you a car, then turn you over to a closer, a high-pressure salesman who has you sign what you think you have agreed to." She feels it is best to stick to a dealer with a good reputation, even if you don't get quite the "deal" you would get elsewhere. (Ms. Kelly adds that having been a car salesperson for several years, she feels it is a marvelous career for a woman, with more and more dealers realizing that women like to deal with other women in business. "I strongly recommend a woman look into being a car salesperson.")

SELECTING A DEALER

When you do select a dealer (a car dealer is the one who has an agency that sells the car; the salesperson makes you the deal on that car), keep in mind the reputation of the service department. You will probably be dealing more with it than the salesperson. You'll want to make sure it is conveniently located and has loaner cars available. Other services that should be offered are a warranty on the car in writing and guaranteed repair of any mechanical problems or troubles for a specific number of miles or length of time. An ethical dealer will not take advantage of you with trick contracts and concealed costs. A good dealer will have competent salespeople who will be helpful, consider your price range, find a car that fits those needs and offer a good warranty. Do not sign any sales contract for a car (new or used) without reading it over carefully and checking the figures. If you do not fully understand it, ask for a copy (*before* you sign it) and take it to someone you have confidence in to read it over.

THE WARRANTY

New car warranties differ from manufacturer to manufacturer. The most common warranty is for twelve months or 12,000 miles, whichever comes first. From time to time some manufacturers go further than this in an effort to lure additional buyers. In addition to the length of the warranty, examine its provisions very carefully to determine what is actually covered and what is not. If you are unclear about any provisions of the warranty, have them explained before you buy the car.

Basically written warranties provided by a manufacturer are of two types: *full* and *limited*. What's the difference?

The label "*full*" on a warranty means: A defective product will be fixed (or replaced) free, including removal and reinstallation if necessary; it will be fixed within a reasonable time after you complain; you will not have to do anything unreasonable to get warranty service (such as ship the car to the factory), the warranty is good for anyone who owns the product during the warranty period; if the product can't be fixed (or hasn't been after a reasonable number of tries), you get your choice of a new one or your money back.

A warranty is limited if it gives you anything less than what a full warranty gives. For example, a limited warranty may cover only certain parts of a product; cover only parts, not labor; cover only the first purchaser; or allow only a pro rata refund or credit based on how long you used the product.

A product can carry more than one written warranty—that is, it can have a full warranty on part of the product and a limited warranty on the rest. Most car warranties are limited, not full.

In case you are offered an "extended warranty," at an additional cost, you should be aware that this is not a warranty at all; it is a service contract. A warranty comes with a product at no additional charge; a service contract gives extra protection for an extra fee. Be certain you understand the provisions of the extended warranty, or service contract, as noted above. There is sometimes a stipulation that you use a certain brand of lubricant when you have your car serviced. There may also be exclusions, meaning things that the service contract doesn't cover.

You have the right to examine warranties when you are shopping for a car. Under the Magnuson-Moss Warranty Act, warranties must be available for you to read before you buy, so you can comparison shop for the best warranty. The Warranty Act also tries to make it easier for you to force manufacturers to keep their warranty promises. For free copies of a fact sheet about the law, write to the Federal Trade Commission, Warranties, Washington, D.C. 20580.

Make sure you read the requirements of all warranties. Normally you are required to have certain services performed in accordance with a prescribed schedule or to use certain recommended products when periodic services are performed. Later, after you've bought your car, remember to recheck these requirements and to follow them. If you plan a long trip and may miss the prescribed service schedule, discuss the possibility with your dealer before you make the trip, to assure that your warranty is not voided. You can expect the dealer to honor your warranty only if you, too, follow its requirements.

FINANCING A NEW CAR

When purchasing a new car, you will usually be asked to put down 20 percent if you do not have a trade-in. Many lenders still use the old formula for figuring how much to lend. They assume you will be paying 20 percent down and that your monthly car payments *plus* any other installment debts you have would not amount to more than 20 percent of your take-home pay.

Some lenders, however, go by your income and your credit history. If they are good, you may be able to borrow the full purchase price of your new car. The vast majority of car loans are made through banks, but all banks do not charge the same interest rates at the same time.

Under the Truth in Lending Act, all lending institutions are supposed to compute interest rates in the same way—in terms of the annual percentage rate (APR—that is, how much you are being charged to use their money). Unfortunately many banks don't quote you the APR and instead confuse you with words, such as "discount rate," "add-on rate," and "deferred payment." You should insist that the lending institution you are dealing with quotes you the APR. The law will back you up.

Ask each prospective lender what the total finance charges will be over the life of your loan and what they cover. These can vary widely. Compare the figures plus your monthly payment figures, and try to get the best deal for your money.

There are other sources that will lend you money for purchasing a car. Car dealers will often arrange a loan for you through a bond or through a sales finance company. Never accept a dealer's offer without finding out the APR and finance charges you will be paying. Sometimes a dealer will tack on an extra percentage point or two to make a little extra profit. Also, the first interest rate quoted isn't always a final offer. Make it clear that you are going to shop around. In some cases a dealer may be able to get you a loan when you couldn't borrow on you own because of questionable credit, but don't forget that he has placed your loan with someone else who will foreclose if you don't make your payments.

Another excellent source of credit for a car purchaser is the credit union where you work. This can be the best and cheapest way to obtain a loan for your car. Credit unions generally charge (1979 figure) between 10 and 12 percent on the total loan, while members who have money in shares are charged approximately 3 percent less.

A small loan company should be your last choice—the interest rates can be from 20 to 30 percent and up.

Another possibility to consider when you are looking for loan sources is borrowing against the cash value of your insurance policy (if you have a whole life or endowment, not term). Often the interest rate is as low as 6 percent and less. Check with your insurance agent on the pros and cons of doing this.

Savings and loans offer passbook loans that will provide you with 95 to 100 percent of the amount you have in your account, usually at about 7 percent. Your account will continue to earn interest, but you cannot withdraw an amount equal to what you have borrowed. If you choose this kind of loan and repay in monthly payments, at the end of three or four years you'll have the car and your full savings account restored at a relatively small interest rate.

Be wary of balloon payments. These involve a small amount down, regular monthly payments, then a very large final (balloon) payment.

In figuring what interest rates various institutions will charge, according to the American Safety Foundation, the breakdown will generally be as follows:

Credit unions—lowest
Car dealers—higher
Bank financing—higher
Finance company—highest

AVOIDING NEW CAR PROBLEMS

You're about to become a new car owner. Remember that at the moment you take possession of your new car and until the warranty expires, required warranty services for the vehicle become the *joint* responsiblity of the dealer and the manufacturer. Many owners complain that when serious new car problems arise, neither the dealer nor the manufacturer willingly accepts any costly customer obligation that can be shifted to the other. Responsibility must be clear, and *you* can make it clear by following the guidance below.

It's essential to follow this procedure, whether you're buying a car right off the lot or taking possession of a car you've ordered and waited months to receive.

Make sure the car you are buying is exactly:
— What you ordered, all options and equipment included.
— What its window sticker says it is. Check every accessory, piece of listed equipment, and service listed on the sticker. According to federal law, the window sticker must remain with the car until it is delivered to you, the ultimate customer.

— What the receipted bill of sale says you bought. Compare your
bill of sale against both the window sticker and the car itself.

If the car, the window sticker, and the bill of sale do not
agree, track down the reason. If you asked for changes in the vehicle's equipment, the changes may have been made correctly,
but the window sticker wasn't changed. In this case have the cor-
rection written in, and get the dealer or another company official
to initial and date it. If something was added to or left off the car
without your authorization, be sure the extra item is removed or
the missing item installed—and be sure you're being charged
correctly and that the bill of sale is accurate. Whatever the
problem, insist on a correction before you sign anything. For
your future protection the car, the window sticker, and the bill
of sale *must* match. Keep *both* the window sticker and the bill
of sale so that you'll have an exact record of what you paid for
and what the dealer accepted payment for.

Be patient. Wait for "dealer prep."

New cars require checking and varying degrees of service before
they are delivered to a new car purchaser. This service is called
dealer preparation or make ready, and generally there is a charge
for this service. It involves such services as cleaning, checking
fluid levels, checking functional systems, adjustment of ill-fitting
doors and hoods, installation of wheel covers, and corrections of
imperfections in the paint. Make sure that dealer prep is completed by the dealer and that this service is noted on the bill of
sale and marked "Paid in Full" whether or not it is also listed on
the window sticker. If there is no charge for dealer preparation,
have your dealer sign a bill of sale notation, "Dealer Preparation
Completed—No Charge."

Give the dealer time to complete necessary dealer preparation,
and insist that he does so. Never accept the offer to have the work
done later, "after you've lived with it for a while." Your bill of sale
notation about dealer preparation is your proof that any problems
which should have been remedied by dealer prep are clearly the
dealer's responsibility if they crop up a few days later (one example: loss of coolant because of failure to tighten hose clamps).

Inspect the car, inside and out, and road test this specific car.

This is your last crack at road testing. Make sure any problems
are taken care of before you take possession. Squeaky brakes,
rattles, anything—your road test should be thorough enough to

bring such problems to your attention. Have the problems corrected, or don't buy the car.

This is your last chance to inspect the car's appearance also—check carefully for stains or paint flaws that need cleaning or correcting. As you inspect the car, remember that if the specific car you are buying has a lot of scratches or paint imperfections, a repainting by the dealer may not be as good as the paint job done by the factory.

The time to road test your car is before you accept the final papers. Car buyers often find that when they take a new car home, load it up with family, and drive it on the road surfaces they normally use, their new car is radically different from the vehicle they briefly tested on a city street the day before. Try to get the dealer to agree to a thorough road test of your car before you accept it. You'll want to determine whether it handles and performs as well as the demonstrator you tested earlier. And a little money spend driving your new car through a car wash to see if it leaks may avoid problems and frustrations later.

While you're road testing, take time to make sure that the car's odometer is working properly. There have been scattered reports of dealers' disconnecting odometers on their demonstrators, then reconnecting the odometers at time of sale. The federal odometer law is intended to protect car buyers from the deceptive practice of concealing a car's true mileage by disconnecting or turning back the odometer. While violations of the odometer law are more likely with used cars, the law is also designed to protect new car buyers. So when test driving cars, keep your eye on the odometer. In your preliminary road tests—way back at the start of your search—a nonfunctioning odometer on a demonstrator could have raised questions in your mind about the dealer's integrity. At this point, now that you're about to buy, you should be equally suspicious of any car without a functioning odometer.

Just prior to purchasing your new car, be sure you receive an odometer disclosure statement—as required by federal law—*and compare this statement with the mileage registered on the odometer of the car you're about to buy*. The disclosure statement must contain the following information and must be signed by the person transferring ownership to you:

- Odometer reading at time of transfer
- Date of transfer
- Seller's (transferrer's) name, address, and signature

- Make, body type, year, model, vehicle identification number (and last plate number of the vehicle if it has previously been titled and registered)
- A statement certifying that the seller is complying with the Motor Vehicle Information and Cost Savings Act of 1972 and is aware of his civil liability under its provisions
- If the seller has reason to believe that the mileage reading is incorrect, the disclosure statement must indicate that the actual mileage traveled is unknown.

The odometer law prohibits:

- Disconnecting or resetting the odometer with intent to change the mileage reading
- Operating a vehicle with a nonfunctional odometer (with intent to defraud)
- Advertising, selling, using, or installing a device which causes an odometer to register incorrectly
- Knowingly falsifying the written odometer statement
- Removing the notice attached to the left doorframe at the time of odometer service (applicable only when an odometer is serviced, repaired, or replaced, and cannot be adjusted to reflect the true mileage).

BUYING A USED CAR

A used car is cheaper than a new car: A one-year-old car is generally around 20 percent cheaper, and a two-year-old car may sell from 40 to 50 percent less than its original price. But a used car can end up costing you more money than a new car if you purchase one that is mechanically unsound.

A used car can have suspension, steering, engine, or brake problems. Unfortunately however a used car seldom gets a thorough inspection before purchase. Many car buyers treat the transaction too casually and purchase many avoidable problems along with their used car. The first rule in buying a good used car, after having determined your requirements on size, economy, performance, and equipment, is to inspect it as thoroughly as you would a new house. You might want to take along someone you can trust who is more experienced or trained in the workings of a car. Perhaps you will need to pay a mechanic whom you trust or who has been recommended to you. Have him test the car thoroughly inside and out. Try to get as much information about the car as possible, like seeing a record of repairs and service or even talking to the previous owner.

In shopping for a good used car, be *cautious and suspicious*. Remember, the previous owner has some reason for getting rid of it. The reason may be that the car is practically worn out and requires major, costly repairs to make it both safe and dependable. Also, remember that you seldom get more than you pay for, as far as a used car purchase is concerned, and you can often get less if you're not careful. So, if you think you're getting a good used car at a "dirt-cheap" price, you may be buying somebody's expensive troubles instead.

Remember also that all cars require service from time to time, and the older the car, the better the chances that it will soon require major repairs. Thus, before you decide to buy a specific used car, think about where you will have it serviced and whether you will have trouble getting adequate service. In this connection:

- For some makes of cars, adequate service can be provided only by an authorized factory dealership specializing in that make. It's time-consuming and sometimes expensive, in terms of time lost from work and travel expenses, when the nearest service facility having the required parts is a great distance away.
- As used cars become older, some repair parts become scarcer. This is especially true of makes and models produced in limited quantities. At times, the only source for some parts may be a junkyard.

Along with the information in this section on buying a used car, the Hertz Corporation has kindly furnished the following checklist for handy use when you are shopping for a used car:

Exterior

☐ Check all around for rust and corrosion, which can reduce the car's value and its useful life.

☐ Look for paint spray on hinges, chrome, and rubber moldings and in wheel wells. Avoid extensively repainted cars; that could be a sign of major problems.

☐ Check the tread depth.

☐ Check the chrome for "dings" and dents which suggest rough use or perhaps an accident.

☐ Check the front end for sagging that indicates wear.

Interior

- [ ] Lift the hood, and check for frayed wiring and cleanliness of the engine, and look at the insulation on the interior of the hood. Is there any sign of fire?
- [ ] Inside the car, look for signs of wear, and check the fit of the carpeting.
- [ ] Inspect brake pedals and accelerator. Does the wear on them suggest higher mileage than the odometer indicates?
- [ ] Look under the dash and in the glove compartment for water stains that indicate leaks or that the car has been in a flood.
- [ ] Raise the trunk, and check the condition of the spare tire. Also, look for water stains and signs of major repairs such as a new weld.

Now You're Ready for a Test Drive

- [ ] Allow enough time to include a variety of conditions, such as hills, bumpy roads, superhighways, etc.
- [ ] Accelerate hard in safe driving area. Failure to respond may indicate an engine that needs an overhaul.
- [ ] With the engine running at idle, check the exhaust—black smoke may indicate a badly worn engine.
- [ ] Test the starter repeatedly. It should not whine, nor should the carburetor flood.
- [ ] Check the steering wheel. It should not turn more than a few inches before the wheels start to move. Moans and squeaks with power steering could suggest trouble.

Other Tests You Can Run

- [ ] Push down hard and release quickly on each front fender and on the rear on both sides. Car should bounce just once each time if shock absorbers are good. Continued bouncing indicates worn shock absorbers.
- [ ] Park the car over a clean area of concrete (or over sheets of wrapping paper), and let it idle for five minutes. Drive the car off area, and inspect for leaks of engine oil (black), transmission fluid (red), or gasoline (brown).
- [ ] Wet all four tires; then drive a short distance in a straight line on pavement or concrete. If the tracks show four lines instead of two, the frame may be bent or the rear suspension may be out of alignment.

Check Out Comparable Prices

Before you finally decide on the used car of your choice, compare prices on the same model elsewhere. Take into account the equipment, options, and whether the car comes with a dealer warranty. Financing for a used car is harder to obtain than for a new car. Most banks won't write loans on cars more than four years old; on cars that are more than two years old, the length of the loan is usually restricted, and the interest will be higher. Your best bet is probably your credit union or a savings and loan you have an account with.

When you are comparing prices, you should check out the *Kelly Blue Book* (in some states the blue book is red!), which lists prices for cars. Usually a credit union or lending institution will have one. This is especially true if you are buying the car from a private party or dealer; you will want to know if the asking price is within reason.

Prices of used cars vary greatly, but there are no fantastic bargains in used cars. A car that is in poor condition or has many miles on it will sell below the blue book. A top condition car that has been cared for, has fewer miles on it, or has optional equipment will sell above the blue book. The figures in the blue book will at least give you some frame of reference.

What to Buy

Generally your best buy in a used car is one that is only two or three years old. Look for the year and model you like, and when you find one, check the odometer to see how far it has been driven. If cars only a few years old have been given reasonable care by their previous owners, they still have a lot of driving life left in them. Because of their mechanical condition, they should also be safer than older vehicles. Such cars, though, are still fairly expensive and may cost more than you can afford. So, if you find several cars within *your price range*, consider the one with the least mileage on the odometer and best general overall condition.

Odometer Law

A federal law passed in 1972 makes it illegal for anyone to do anything that would cause a vehicle's odometer to show the wrong mileage. No person, not even the vehicle owner, is permitted to turn back or disconnect the odometer (except to perform necessary repairs). The federal law also requires that anyone selling a vehicle or transferring ownership in some other way must provide the buyer with a signed statement indicating the mileage registered on the odometer at the time of the transfer. If the seller knows the registered mileage to be incorrect because the odometer has been broken or previously tampered with, he must include a statement to that effect on the mileage disclosure form. When purchasing a vehicle, be certain you receive a mileage disclosure statement before the transfer of title.

Anyone who illegally tampers with an odometer or who fails to provide the required mileage disclosure statement may be sued in a private civil action by the person wronged by the violation. If the suit is successful, the person will recover $1,500 or three times the amount of actual damages, whichever is greater.

A vehicle may look good and the odometer may read only 15,000 or 20,000 miles when, in fact, it has been driven 80,000 or 90,000 miles. The best way to protect yourself from being victimized by a fraudulent representation of a vehicle's mileage is to examine closely the condition of the vehicle, contact a prior owner to inquire about the mileage when he sold the vehicle, ask to see the mileage form given to your seller by the prior owner, and make sure you receive a mileage disclosure statement. You will probably be able to make a good assessment of the reliability of the odometer's mileage on the basis of the information you receive.

Used Car Warranties

With a used car you may not get a warranty, especially if you buy it from a private party or from an organization that has no facilities to service the cars it sells (e.g., a repossessed car purchased from a finance company). Even when provided, warranties differ from one dealer to another. You may get a complete warranty for parts and labor for periods up to thirty days, a ninety day warranty on parts only with the buyer paying for the labor, or a fifty-fifty warranty for a certain period, with the buyer paying half the cost for parts and labor.

Make sure you understand the warranty before you purchase the car, and make it work for you. If you suspect something is wrong with your used car and it's still under warranty, don't wait. Take it back right away. Do this over and over until you're sure the dealer has corrected your problems, and don't accept an excuse like "The shop is full and we have a lot of appointments this week; bring your car back next week." Next week may be too late—your warranty may have expired, and the dealer or his service manager may not honor any promise made orally. If possible, obtain a written description of any work done during the warranty period so that you will have a record if the same problem recurs after the warranty expires.

Where to Buy

For your driving safety as well as satisfaction with your purchase, where you buy your used car is just as important as what you buy. Sources of used cars include used car dealers, new car dealers, private owners, car rental agencies or companies that buy new cars every year and sell their older cars, and banks or loan companies that have repossessed cars.

A used car dealer who sells only used cars usually has many cars from which to pick, but some of these dealers don't have a service facility (garage) to repair the cars if something goes wrong. If you need maintenance, you may have to take it to some other service facility for required work. Before you buy a car from such a source, make sure there is some place where you can get it repaired, particularly if you get a used car guarantee. Some used car dealers who don't have their own service facilities make arrangements with a garage to repair the cars they have sold and guaranteed.

A new car dealer who also sells used cars taken in on trade will have a service facility for necessary repairs. Normally such dealers keep the best of the used cars they take in on trade and dispose of the others through a wholesale used car outlet.

You can often buy a good used car at a lower price by watching the classified ads in your newspaper and buying from a private owner, but you won't get a warranty. Be careful if you buy a car from a private owner that you don't know. Inspect it carefully; better still, take it to your local mechanic or a diagnostic station to have it inspected before you make the purchase final. Also, make sure you get a clear title—sometimes car buyers get stuck with a car that has been stolen or one that is about to be repossessed by a bank or finance company because the owner didn't pay the loan payments.

You might also be able to buy a repossessed car from a bank or finance company through the newspaper ads. Such institutions often sell repossessed cars for the outstanding balance due on them. Again, inspect the car carefully before purchase; *if the previous owner was lax in making payments, he may also have neglected to perform required maintenance service*.

You might also be able to pick up a good used car from a car rental agency. Many of these agencies buy new cars every year and sell their older cars after using them for only one year. Some big companies that have fleets of company cars do the same thing. Remember, though, that cars bought from rental agencies or fleets will generally have accumulated a lot of mileage in a short time; however, in most operations of this size such vehicles receive better scheduled maintenance.

AVOIDING USED-CAR PROBLEMS

There are a few basic rules that apply especially to the used car buyer. A used car buyer may often have to buy a car "as is"; that means the seller guarantees nothing. Thus, if you want to avoid a great many problems when buying a used car, follow these rules:

1. Don't buy at night, in the rain, or under any conditions that could keep you from seeing everything and examining everything about the car, inside and out. A muddy car lot or a cold rain or a day when you don't have time to be thorough are conditions that invite you not to crawl under the car to inspect it thoroughly. Yet, if the frame is rusted out, if the steering or suspension parts are dangerously worn, or if there is brake fluid leaking down over curb-bruised tires, you might buy these problems and worse by picking the wrong time and place to buy. Rain can make dents, patches, and repaints shine like new. You should check for rusted-out doors, flooring, and tailgates, so don't pick a rainy day to buy a used car. Likewise, don't pick one at night. If you're too cold, too wet, or too busy to try every accessory, examine the whole car, and take it for a thorough test drive, you're just asking to be "taken."

2. Don't buy the car at all if you're refused a test drive with you at the wheel or if you're refused a request to let your own mechanic check the car at his place of business. If any and all promises for brake and clutch adjustments, tune-ups, parts replacement, etc. are not written down and signed by the *person in charge before* you buy, or if you're refused a final test drive or final outside inspection *after* the seller has completed all promised prepurchase repairs or adjustments you may leave the car on the lot.

Remember: Some vehicles on a used car lot may have unrepaired safety defects—defects for which the cars were recalled by the manufacturer, but which the prior owners neglected to return for repair. By calling the National Highway Traffic Safety Administration, Office of Consumer Services, (202) 426-0670, giving the make, model, year, and vehicle identification number (VIN) of the car in question, you can obtain a report of all defect-recalls for that make/model.

Be Careful of Tricks

Some used car dealers and even some private owners use various methods to make a car look better than it actually is. Some of these are:

— Painting tires to make them look new. Always examine the tread for tread wear and the sidewalls for cracks, signs of tread separation, and bubbles.
— Steam cleaning the engine and painting the valve covers and air cleaner to make them look new.
— Installing new rugs or mats to cover rusted-out parts of the floor.
— Spraying black paint on the hoses to make them look new.
— Removing a good battery and replacing it with a battery that won't last very long. Be especially wary of this in the summer when cars are easier to start. Look for cracks in the battery. Check to see if there is a date stamped on the battery; this may tell you how old the battery is.
— Removing an erratically worn tire from the front and placing it in the trunk to mask a front-end problem. Always check the tire in the trunk.
— Putting a cheap repaint job on the car to hide body rust.
— Making makeshift repairs to the muffler and tailpipe. Examine these for signs that holes or rusted-out portions have been repaired with muffler patches or repair tape.

The point has already been made that you will rarely have anyone to blame but yourself for the problems you fail to note when you buy your used car.

— Be PATIENT. Don't be in a hurry to buy the first used car that looks good.
— Be CURIOUS AND OBSERVANT. Inspect the car thoroughly, and test drive it to discover any mechanical faults, operational characteristics, or unsatisfactory features that may make you regret buying the car.
— Be SUSPICIOUS. If you can get the previous owner's name, call

him to verify the condition of the vehicle and its mileage
when he got rid of it.
— Be CHOOSY AND UNCOMPROMISING in your demand for signed
promises and claims if you expect to hold the seller responsible for later, unsolvable problems.

In a word, CAUTION before you buy is the best advice that can be
given. Remember, buying a good used car requires COMMON SENSE.

LEASING A CAR

If you own a business or use your car in your job (for other than
commuting), you may want to lease a car and deduct the cost from
your income tax.

There are several kinds of auto leases: closed end and open end.

A closed-end lease is the less complicated—you contract to lease a
car for a fixed period (usually two to four years) at a fixed price per
month. When the lease expires, you have no further obligation.

An open-end lease appears cheaper because it usually costs less
per month. However, when you sign the original lease, you agree to
a "buy-back" price that goes into effect at the end of your lease. You
then have the option to buy back the car at a buy-back price, or you
or the dealer may sell it for what you can get for it. If you receive
more than the buy-back price, you keep the balance, but if you
receive less, you must make up the difference. You are never sure
what the final cost of your open-end lease until it's over.

Some business people who deduct car expenses on their tax returns believe that leasing simplifies the deduction procedure. It is
easier to list one figure for car leasing then a lot of separate figures
for depreciation, repairs, interest, etc.

The main point to remember when purchasing a car is: Do your
homework before you go to buy. While we can't guarantee that the
advice given in this chapter will result in your making a marvelous
deal on a car, it will help you avoid some of the more common
mistakes.

AVOIDING UNNECESSARY AUTO COSTS

After purchasing a car, you will want to take proper care of it, to
avoid costly repairs. Yet in trying to care for a car, many women are
taken advantage of by gas station attendants or mechanics. They are
often told they need costly repairs or service on their cars when they

don't. Convinced they know nothing about cars, many women rely solely on others to care for their cars, and have holes in their pocketbooks to prove it. Knowing how to find a reputable mechanic when you are in need of car repair, and learning basic facts about your car can save you money.

Often car repairs and upkeep are not as complicated as you might imagine. Taking care of some of them yourself can be one way to cut costs. Finding out what to do in case of "auto emergency" can even be of financial benefit. Instead of panicking and being completely dependent on a mechanic do diagnose the problem, having some idea of what to do, and what might be wrong may keep you from being taken advantage of. There are classes and materials available that can help you get started on learning to care for your car.

Many colleges and night schools are giving classes in basic auto repair, geared especially to women. Also the Chrysler Corporation has a free program entitled *Women on Wheels* (WOW). The WOW program is a series of four, two-hour classes explaining how a car works—from engine to brakes—and how to keep it working. The courses are offered at various times during the year by 1200 Chrysler, Plymouth, and Dodge dealers throughout the country. Classes are open to any woman driver, regardless of make of car. To find out if these classes are available near you, write:

WOW
P.O. Box 7749A
Detroit, Michigan 48207

The Shell Oil Company puts out a series of extremely helpful booklets regarding "do it yourself car repair." They are available free of charge at participating Shell service stations, or you might want to write to the Shell Oil Co., P.O. Box 61609, Houston, Texas 77208, to find out how to obtain the complete set.

Finding a Reputable Mechanic

When you do need professional car care, how can you find a reputable mechanic? This is not easy, and unfortunately even our suggestions are not going to guarantee that you will not be taken advantage of. One suggestion is that it is a good idea to frequent the same gas station and let the attendants and owner get to know you and your car. Also check with some of your friends to see if they have found a mechanic they feel is reliable and fairly reasonable—if there is any such thing as reasonable car repair expenses.

One of the most frequent consumer complaints concerns automotive repair ripoff. In many states new laws have been passed which now give you certain legal rights when dealing with a repair dealer. You can check with your state Attorney-general's office to see if your state has the new laws. These laws state that dealers must be registered and must display a notice of the consumer's rights. If your state has these laws, whenever you have repair work done, you are entitled to:

— A written estimate for repair work *before* any work can be done.
— The repair dealer may not exceed the written estimate without your consent. You are not required to pay more for the repair than stated on the estimate.
— A detailed invoice of work done and parts supplied.
— Return of the replaced parts if you request them at the time a work order is placed.

Another way you can find a reputable car mechanic is through the National Institute for Automotive Service Excellence (NIASE). The NIASE certified auto mechanics have to pass tests in eight fields of diagnosis and repair; engine, automatic transmission, manual transmission and rear axle, front end, heating and air conditioning, electrical systems, engine tune-up and brakes before they can be certified. There is a book that lists auto repair shops all over the country that employ certified mechanics. You can obtain this book by sending a stamped, self-addressed envelope and $1.95 to:

Where to Find Certified Mechanics for Your Car
NIASE — Suite 515
1825 K St. N.W.
Washington, D.C. 20006

The NIASE certifies only the competence of *mechanics*. In order for an *auto repair shop* to be listed, it must employ at least one certified mechanic and meet certain criteria:

— Recommend only those services necessary for vehicle safety, performance, comfort and convenience.
— Offer the customer a price estimate for work to be performed.
— Obtain prior authorization for all work done in writing or by other means satisfactory to the customer.

— Notify customer if appointments or completion promises cannot be kept.
— Furnish an itemized invoice for parts and services priced fairly which clearly identifies any used or remanufactured parts. Replaced parts may be inspected upon request.
— Furnish or post copies of any warranties covering parts or services.
— Maintain customer service records for one year or more.
— Exercise reasonable care for the customer's property while it is being serviced.
— Maintain a system for fair settlement of customer complaints.
— Cooperate with established consumer complaint mediation activities.

The institute is quick to point out that certification doesn't mean that every repair job will be perfect; but the institute does verify that each listed shop employ at least one certified mechanic.

We feel this book is well worth sending for, but as an alternative you can call various garages in your area and ask if they employ mechanics who are certified by the National Institute for Automotive Service Excellence.

Points to Remember

It is a good idea, when you take your car in for repair, to be as specific as possible in explaining the car's problem. "The car falters when I try to accelerate, even when it isn't cold," is far better than, "It doesn't run right." This will make diagnosis simpler and can lessen the repair time and possibly the cost.

Programs such as NIASE certification are meaningless unless consumers know about them and use them.

Remember, certification is not a panacea for all auto repair ills, but it does assure you that the mechanic is truly competent in the field or fields in which he's certified—and that certainly is a comforting thought when you are endeavoring to steer clear of unnecessary auto costs.

12
Taking Stock of Your Investments

It may be that you will never invest in the stock market. It certainly is not a necessity for financial survival. However, it is a subject that is important to understand because it is one method of increasing your income. You may be the purchaser of stocks, you may have inherited them, someone may have given you some at one time as a gift, or you may be considering entering the stock market for the first time. Whichever case applies to you, stock buying is not as mysterious as you may have been led to believe.

There are many people who spend a lot of time in front of the one-armed bandit or at the craps table in either Las Vegas or Atlantic City. This form of gambling has been likened to the stock market because there is risk involved. Sadly this is the part which is the most often publicized because it is where you can lose a lot of money. Good financial planning takes thought and work; it doesn't come from the roll of the dice.

To be a successful investor, rather than depend on Lady Luck to smile miraculously on selected investments, you should utilize your own common sense while you also employ the services of a stock-broker or other investment adviser, one that is known for integrity and has experience. As an investor you should avoid putting all your eggs in one basket. Plan a versatile investment portfolio with money you have not earmarked for necessities of everyday living. When you invest your hard-earned dollars in any type of securities, you should do so with the sole intention and reasonable assurance that there will be an increase in the original value of your invested capital.

In May 1975 *Family Circle* magazine contained an article about a woman who earned on the average $175 a week, yet expected to be worth more than $100,000 by the end of 1979. At the time the article was written, she was worth $84,000. She started investing in 1969. "She had just been extra-lucky," you say. You may feel this is an exception to the rule. If you plan carefully, however, you too can accomplish a similar financial objective.

What she did was to begin in a year when the stock market was at an all-time low. She invested consistently in blue-chip securities (the highest quality you can buy), never sold any stocks whether they had increased or decreased in value, and reinvested all her dividends in new stocks.

"Where do I begin learning about the stock market?" is probably the most common question a stockbroker hears. We have tried to simplify anticipated questions and their answers to their most basic forms.

What is stock? A stock is the name that represents a corporation. A share of stock represents ownership in a corporation.

Where are stocks traded (bought and sold)? Basically stocks are traded in three types of places: national exchanges, regional exchanges, and over the counter (OTC). The New York Stock Exchange (NYSE) is the oldest of our financial institutions and is a national exchange. This exchange had its beginnings in New York City as early as 1792. The American Stock Exchange (AMEX) is also a national exchange; until 1953 it was known as the Curb Exchange because brokers originally stood on curbs to transact business. Both these institutions are located in the lower Manhattan section of New York City still known as Wall Street. The difference between the two exchanges is one of prestige. Basically the companies which trade on the NYSE are older, more established corporations with larger capitalizations and more shareholders. Companies on the AMEX are younger and less seasoned, pay smaller dividends, and are more speculative.

The over the counter market is not really an organized exchange at all because it is not centrally located in a building similar to the NYSE or AMEX. It is an exchange formed by a vast communication system of telephone and telegraph lines which connect one brokerage house with another. This market is also known as the unlisted securities market or the off-board market because the securities traded are not usually listed on any other exchange. There are stocks, however, which have been dually listed on a national exchange and a regional one. Like all exchanges, the OTC market is highly regulated. It is a network of smaller companies throughout the country that specialize in investing in your local area's businesses. This OTC market is a negotiated market; that means you as the buyer can negotiate the price rather than automatically pay the quoted price, as you do on the NYSE and the AMEX.

State laws vary, but generally they require dealers in securities to be licensed and the securities offered for sale to be "qualified," or registered with the proper state authorities.

For example, let's say that you live in Indianapolis, Indiana, and want to purchase 100 shares of XYZ stock listed on the NYSE. A man in Savannah, Georgia, wishes to sell 100 shares of XYZ stock. Each of you makes those requests known to your broker. A ticket to buy or sell is written and transmitted by wire to the floor of the exchange. The brokerage firm's representative goes to the post (the place where XYZ is traded) and make known their requests—the bid (the price you receive if you sell) and offer (the price you receive when you buy)—and each representative carries out the respective order which he received from the brokerage offices (the one in Indianapolis and the one in Savannah).

When the tickets are executed, the results are wired back to the brokerage house. (With the advent of the new quote machines, some brokers have the capabilities to buy or sell securities right off their machines; these machines are usually located on a broker's desk Your broker then calls and tells you the execution price and how much money you have to pay for your purchase. Your purchase must be paid for within five business days. You may leave your stock with the brokerage house or have the certificates transferred to you. (This generally takes about three weeks.) The follow-up procedures for the OTC market, after the stock price is negotiated, are similar to those of listed stock.

What kinds of stock are there? Basically there are two kinds of stock: common and preferred. Common stock represents an ownership interest in a corporation. If you own 5 percent of a corporation's stock, you own 5 percent of the corporation. Common stock is also the foundation of corporate finance. Before a bank will lend money to a corporation, the company must have stockholders with a monetary interest in it.

Like common stock, preferred stock represents an ownership interest in a corporation, but to a different degree. Holders of preferred stock usually receive a high fixed dividend; that means the stock price does not rise as rapidly as common. Most preferred stock is issued by utility companies.

Some stock is also convertible. That means it can be exchanged for another form of stock. Let's say, for example, that you own some convertible preferred stock of XYZ Corporation which could be exchanged for common stock of XYZ under the terms of the original issuance of the convertible stock.

What would be the advantages of doing this? The convertible preferred stock could be an attractive investment because the price of the convertible preferred is linked to the earnings and growth of a company. If the common stock increases in price, so will the convertible preferred. The convertible preferred, however, will pay a higher current yield (percentage amount of money that is paid out) as a rule than a common stock of comparable quality will pay. Last, but certainly not least, a convertible preferred stock offers somewhat more safety and stability than a common stock because the preferred stock is required to pay dividends if the corporation can afford it, while the common is not. Hence, for an income-conscious investor, a convertible preferred offers the advantages of income and growth.

Brokerage houses own "seats" on exchanges. Although technically there are no longer seats, the word does have significant historical meaning. Years ago the members of the New York Stock Exchange would sit in chairs for roll call of the stocks as the trading sessions progressed. Today "seat" really means the privilege of standing on the floor of an exchange and trading securities at the various posts (a post is the place where a particular stock is traded). An individual who has a seat on an exchange may be there either because the firm for whom he trades has a membership, or because he may be an owner, independent of a firm affiliation.

What is the difference between one brokerage house and another? With respect to member firms for the New York Stock Exchange, there should be very little difference, except for the personnel involved. Some firms are much larger than others, but size alone is no assurance that any particular broker in a large firm is capable. In fact, about the only meaningful difference to you as an investor or a potential one is that some firms require a larger minimum account (amount of money invested) than others. The caliber of the broker you select is the most important consideration. If he/she services your account to your satisfaction and is the type of person with whom you like to deal, that should be your yardstick to measure the integrity of the firm.

HOW TO PURCHASE STOCK

If you have decided that the stock market might be worthy of your interest and development, the first thing you should do, if you live in a metropolitan area, is visit the brokerage houses in your city to shop for a broker. (You may decide that you would rather accomplish this by phone, and that is possible also—though not as thorough.) Talk with the manager of the office, and explain what your goals are and the type of broker you are seeking. Colleen Moore, the actress, who was heavily involved in the securities market, once wrote that a woman who is a stockbroker has to be twice as smart as the men who are her cohorts—even if it is just her first day on the job. If you are not pleased with the broker the manager has selected, you are not obligated to deal with that person. Personalities here do matter, and all brokers must pass the same brokerage tests, be schooled in securities information, trained to assist clients, and be licensed by the state where you reside.

Once you have a rapport establised with your broker, she/he should be your confidant. Your confidence in her/him should increase as you get to know each other through your business transactions. As we mentioned before, many brokers have the facilities to help you establish a good financial plan to follow. You certainly don't need to be financially well-off in order to have the proper attention. Remember, a good broker services her/his clients well. The newer broker is more likely to pay attention to a small account, in contrast with the broker who has been in the business for several years, because she/he does not have as many accounts as the seasoned broker.

Merrill Lynch, for example, has a small investors service department, which, for the little investor, in some respects does have an advantage over other firms. You can accumulate stock share by share rather than save your money to buy numerous shares at once. We're not recommending Merrill Lynch over other firms, but like other large brokerage houses, the company can provide services that a smaller house may not be equipped to handle.

Selma Warren has been a schoolteacher for many years and is getting ready to retire. She has built up a very good stock portfolio by dollar cost averaging. What this means is that over the years she acquired her securities on a periodic basis. She decided how much money she could afford to invest each month, or every other month, or maybe even at six-month intervals. Then, without fail, she purchased the same securities on a consistent basis, whether the price moved up or down. In this way, she acquired more shares for her investment dollars when her stocks were low and, of course, fewer shares when the stocks were higher. Over the period of years she invested, her average cost price was lower probably than if she had saved money and then invested it all at one time. For Selma this has been a good formula for buying. It should be for you also, if you are looking toward many years of investing.

Don't be afraid to take a conservative posture toward your stock portfolio. You can always allow the dividends to accumulate and reinvest them along with the other money you have set aside for investment purposes. Dividends are that something extra provided to the stockholder as a return on her/his investment in a particular corporation.

Dividends are usually declared quarterly but might be paid annually or even monthly. The declaring of a dividend means that the board of directors of the corporation has concluded that the company is relatively sound financially and can part with the money required to pay a dividend. The issuance of a dividend signals the investing public that the company has matured. Hence, as a rule, if you buy a stock which is dividend-paying, you know that management will probably take fewer risks and make more conservative decisions.

The obvious value of a dividend to the investor is the source of a reasonably consistent income. Barring unexpected downturns in the company's fortunes, most cash payouts will be continued on a long-term basis. Although cash dividends are far more common than any other type of dividend, some companies will issue stock dividends. A stock dividend is the issuance of additional common stock as a dividend by a company to its common shareholders. This form of dividend can be a percentage addition to the number of shares you now own in XYZ Company.

For example, Stacey Price owns 100 shares in XYZ Company. After a stock dividend of 5 percent, she owns 105 shares. In order for her to be entitled to the dividend on the stock, she had to be the registered owner of the 100 shares at least five business days before the record date (that is the date on which you already own stock in order to receive the dividend). Four business days before the date of record, stocks will trade ex-dividend, or without the dividend.

You own a stock on the day your purchase has been executed. This is true even though your trade does not need to be settled until the fifth business day after your purchase. For example, if you purchased XYZ Company on December 1, you would be entitled to a dividend declared on December 2 or later. Conversely, you would not be entitled to a dividend declared on November 30 or before. (The declaration date is the day the board of directors of XYZ Company meet and declare a dividend. Dividends are paid on a payable date, usually a month to six weeks after the declaration date. This gives the company ample bookkeeping time to prepare the necessary paperwork to distribute the dividends through the mail.

How is the price of stock determined? The price of stock is determined like that of any item sold in a competitive market—by supply and demand. If there is a demand for XYZ stock, but very few investors willing to sell, the price of XYZ will rise. Conversely, if many investors want to sell the same stock and there are only a few buyers, the price of stock will decline.

One broker told us about a former client of hers who thought she knew everything about this one company, and spent about $12,000 purchasing 300 shares, against the advice of her broker. What the client didn't know, however, were the latest financial problems of the company. Instead of the stock's rising, it dropped to almost nothing, since there were only sellers, not buyers of the stock.

Brokerage houses today are becoming so automated that many of them will simultaneously execute your purchase or sale right from equipment in the branch office while your broker is talking to you on the telephone or in person. If this happens, you will buy stock at the ask price, and if you are selling it, it will be at the bid price.

A friend of ours was complaining that he thought he had some great stock ideas, but his broker really discouraged him, saying that if the ideas were any good, his firm's research would have them. This is often true. However, independent research *is* a good idea. The more you become involved with your investment, the better feeling you would have about a stock's potential to rise in monetary value.

In looking for a company, decide on an area which may be greatly in demand. For example—and let us stress that this is *not* a recommendation—look at all the people who have taken up camping in the last few years. Or perhaps there is a special kitchen product you like or cosmetic you use. If you find a product that appeals to you, you may want to choose the company which manufactures that product as your stock candidate.

It is difficult to imagine any item in your kitchen or wardrobe, mass-manufactured, not being a product of a listed company. Your can of cleanser, your lipstick, your pantyhose, or the comfortable pair of jeans you are wearing right now all are products of a listed company.

Before you jump into an investment in any company, check two points about it: one, its financial position, and two, its capability to develop new products. If these two facets of the company's character look promising, you can talk to your broker about seriously investing in the company you have chosen.

Along with the stock market, there is the bond market, which is composed of many different types of bonds. A bond is an interest-bearing certificate of public or private indebtedness. There are corporate bonds, which are issued by corporations; municipal bonds, issued by cities, states, or local entities; and government bonds, which, of course, are issued by various agencies of the U.S. government.

As you may have noticed, stocks are equity interest (ownership). You own a piece of the corporation. Bonds are a debt of the corporation, meaning that the corporation eventually will have to repay the money that was paid for the bond, in other words, you lent money to the corporation. That is why bonds have a maturity date—the end of the period for which the debt is written.

Corporate bonds provide long-term debt financing for corporations since banks usually don't like to lend money for longer than a few years. Corporate bonds can have maturity dates as short as five years, but twenty to thirty years are the norm. These bonds pay a fixed rate of interest and pay back the principal on the maturity date. The bonds usually have face amounts of $1,000, although they can be issued in $100 or $500 amounts (these latter bonds are called baby bonds for the small face amount). The price of bonds is quoted in terms of percentage of face value. For example, a quote of 93 means the bond is selling at $930. Corporate bonds are backed by several different forms of collateral. The two most common are the mortgage bond, which is backed by specific real estate assets of the corporation, and the debenture. A debenture is a promissory note. Prices of corporate bonds change from day to day just as stock prices do. As general interest rates rise, market prices of bonds decline, and vice versa.

Corporate bonds are a good investment because there is a guaranteed return of principal if they are held to maturity, and corporate bonds provide fixed interest payments. When a bond is the senior debt of the company, it means that as debts are paid off, these bonds will be paid first. Naturally, junior means that the debt comes after senior debt is paid.

Most government securities are similar to corporate bonds, except that you will receive your interest by the discount price of the bond from its face value price. That discount produces an interest yield when the bond is held to maturity, at which time the government redeems it at face value. These securities are the safest you can buy, but they will offer you the lowest current yield available. Don't confuse government securities with the traditional government savings bond, which is a nonmarketable type of investment. Savings bonds have a fixed rate of return on your investment. What you are doing is lending the government immediate money. You give it one amount, and when your bond matures, it returns a larger amount to you. In the meantime, you have offered the government cash to run its operations. Marketable government securities are issued in the form of bonds, bills, notes, or certificates. (Each category signifies a different length of time before maturity date.) They bear interest on an annual basis.

When you purchase a bond, whether government, corporate, or municipal, the face value remains the same. The interest rate stays the same, but owing to market fluctuations and influences from the economy, the price of the bond will go up or down. One reason for the change in price is the change in interest rates. For example, a bond has an interest-bearing coupon of 8½ percent and its face value is $1,000. This means you will receive $85 for each $1,000 bond. If you paid less than $1,000, $900, let us say, your effective yield would be over 9 percent, but you would still receive the $85 per year, no more. Your investment would be a return of 8½ percent on $1,000, even though you paid only $900. The same thing is true if you paid more than $1,000 for your bond. You would receive $85 per year, but your effective yield would be less than 8½ percent because you paid out more than $1,000 to receive the $85 annually.

Municipal bonds are tax-free if they are issued by the state where you live. If you live in California, for example, and purchase a bond from New York, the bond will be federally nontaxable, but you will pay state tax. These bonds as a general rule can be divided into four categories: One form is *housing authority bonds*, which are issued by local authorities to finance low-cost housing projects. Bonds of this type not only are secured by the income from the rent of these projects but are subsidized by the United States Public Housing Authority. These bonds are backed by the credit of the United States government. *Revenue bonds*, another form, are payable only from the income or revenue of the authority that sold them. That may be income rent, tolls, or other phases of income which come from operating the particular facility for which the bonds were issued. Generally this type of bond will carry a higher interest rate because it exists on revenues, not on the obligation of a municipality or government. Although this category of bonds may sound a bit speculative, remember that some of the basic necessities of life can be included in this area—water, electricity, or gas. Therefore, in most instances, these bonds are good investments, since there is little chance of default.

Limited obligation bonds are basically revenue bonds which are partially secured by the taxing power of the bond issuer. Limited obligation bonds may be used, for example, to pay for highway bonds, with a portion of the revenue to pay the interest on the bonds coming from gasoline taxes. *General obligation bonds* are backed by the full faith and credit of the municipality or other authority which is issuing the bonds. School bonds are probably the best-known type of general obligation bonds.

Another common question frequently asked of a stockbroker is the current price of the stock. The answer can be readily given, right from the quote machine, which is usually on the broker's desk.

But what if you own a bond? If your bond is listed, which means that it trades on an exchange, your broker can probably also tell you the price of the bond from the quote machine. Bonds which aren't listed and trade over the counter may take more time for you to get an answer. A good reason for buying a listed bond, you may think. Just remember, if you're buying bonds for income, you should be more concerned in a constant income than in the market price of the bond.

Some bonds are callable—that is, the company may buy them back before their actual maturity date but not without a penalty premium. This means that the company will pay you more than the $1,000 you paid to redeem them. Callable features are good, but if you plan on holding your bonds till they mature, buy bonds that won't be called for at least five or ten years. When you consider buying a particular bond, your broker can tell you if the bond has a call feature, and if so, what it is.

Bonds are given ratings, just as children are given grades in school. AAA is the best you can buy. Banks and savings and loans will buy bonds that have a BAA rating or better, so this should also be your clue. The lower the rating of the bond, the higher the interest rate the company is paying to have investors buy their bonds. A company may be large, well known, and well capitalized, but because of the amount of debt outstanding versus annual earnings, the rating may not be as high as you might expect. A lower rating may offer

higher interest, but if you are security-conscious, go for the higher
rating.

You should expect your broker to be knowledgeable about all
elements of the market and keep you apprised of the varying aspects of your holdings. You should also learn how to read the financial pages of a newspaper. The *Wall Street Journal* is the best-known
financial paper, but a good major daily newspaper can also provide
sufficient information. One warning: There are sometimes errors in
printing so many numbers, so if there is a drastic difference in price
from one day to the next, it may just be a typographical error, and it
would be wise to check it out. This is what a typical column in the
newspaper will look like.

| 1978 | | | Sales in | | | | | Net |
High	Low	XYZ Co.	100's	Open	High	Low	Close	Chg.
53⅞	44	260	980	46	46⅜	45⅝	45¾	−1

The high stands for the highest the stock has been during the year,
and the low, the lowest. Then comes the name of the company,
usually abbreviated—e.g., XYZ, which stands for XYZ Company.
The money number is the amount of dividend. The sales in 100's
tells you how many round lots have traded (a round lot is 100
shares). On the day of the example, XYZ traded 98,000 shares.
"Open" means at what price the stock began trading when the
market opened. "High" means how high it went; "Low" means how
low the stock sold on that day of trading. "Net Change" means how
much the stock has gone up or down from the previous trading day's
close.

Another way to learn about investments is through an investment
club. The National Association of Investment Clubs produces a good
booklet for groups to use as a guideline. We have many friends who
play bridge once a week and have an investment club meeting once
a month. They pool their money and buy stock. The money invested
each month per person is anywhere from $25 to $100 or even more
sometimes, or it can be less. The women research stocks and then
select by vote which one to buy.

It's an easy, fun way to learn about investing, but it is more
educationally than monetarily rewarding most of the time. The address of the association, if you're interested in doing this with some
of your friends is: National Association of Investment Clubs, 1515
East 11 Mile Road, Royal Oak, Michigan 48068.

Another easy way to start acquiring stock would be through a
company stock purchase plan if you work for a substantial listed

company. One of the largest plans in the world is "Ma Bell" (American Telephone and Telegraph); and another good one is Sears. Lydia Jamison started with Sears when she was nineteen years old. Next month she'll be sixty. After several promotions over the years, she has accumulated almost $250,000 in her company's stock. Jane Parsons did the same thing at American Telephone and Telegraph.

Another form of investment sold through the securities industry is a tax shelter, or tax-advantaged investment. The better ones are usually real estate investments or an annuity (which we'll discuss later in this chapter). You can invest in almost anything through your broker—commodities, oil, cattle or gold. We're not going into tax shelters in depth, however, as they are usually, except for the annuity, highly speculative in nature, and in this book we are more concerned with women's security and survival. If you ever decide you want to purchase an investment of this type, make certain you discuss it with a reputable professional.

What we want to talk about is solid investments which can save you from paying income tax. For example, the interest on municipal bonds is exempt from state and federal income tax, and government securities interest is exempt from income tax. Each individual taxpayer is allowed $100 exemption on securities dividends.

There are preferred stocks in which part of the interest is nontaxable (there are also a few common stocks that have this feature). Actually this is because the nontaxable portion is a return of equity on the original investment. Ask your broker to find you some of these types of stocks if you are looking more for the income than for growth of your investments.

Just some words of advice if you plan to invest in the securities market. Brokerage houses have to make a profit; therefore, brokers necessarily have to reach sales quotas each month. This places a broker in the untenable position of having to sell. You should be certain that what you buy was not "sold" to you but was something which fitted into your investment plan. The broker's adage is: "Sell the sizzle, not just the steak! Convince the customer that the investment is what she/he wants and needs."

Don't believe every "growth" stock will double or triple in price. Take away the adjectives when you are listening to your broker describe a security. Once you have a working relationship with your broker, she/he can help you devise a plan so that whatever you buy will be helping you plan for a better future. Remember, also, that every investment may not work out as expected, so you should be prepared to withstand a loss if one should be incurred.

INVESTMENT COUNSELING

What can be said about investment counseling except that the people who are privileged to use it are probably in the higher tax brackets. A counselor, if chosen with care, will relieve the investor of the choice of investments and the timing of buying and selling those investments. Not only that, but bookkeeping chores will be lessened and, in many cases, tax forms completed. An investment counselor is an important adjunct of the securities market.

An investment counselor is a person who will invest money in various securities for a fee. She/He is not a stockbroker, and her/his orders for stock are placed with brokerage houses, for which you will also have to pay a commission. The typical minimum amount that an investment counselor will usually handle is $10,000. Some counseling firms will not handle accounts for less than a quarter of a million dollars. An advantage of using a counselor is that she/he is not partial to any particular brokerage house or stock. Her/His main objective is to see your capital increase. She/He may be an analyst or will have several analysts working for her/him.

A word of caution: Let us suggest that you do not walk blindly into selecting just anyone who advertises as an investment counselor, adviser, or consultant. Make inquiry of the nearest Better Business Bureau and Chamber of Commerce, as well as check her/his references. Of course, you should also confer with a reputable stockbroker.

Most investment counselors are honest and legitimate, but lately some smooth confidence men have appeared, advising the unsuspecting public that they can make a huge profit on a sure thing. Be wary of these types that are so anxious to get their hands on your money. Often they are without proper credentials. Check them out before succumbing to this type of shyster seduction, or they will quickly separate you and your money. Use your head as well as your dollars. Be selective in your choice of a legitimate investment counselor, and you won't be sorry.

MUTUAL FUNDS

Exactly what are mutual funds? Mutual funds are a combination of many things. Basically a group of financially oriented individuals get together and form a management company. What do they manage? They manage the buying and selling of stocks and bonds or money market instruments (money market instruments are securities such as certificates of deposit or U.S. government treasury notes which mature in a short period of time).

The goals of a management company can be varied. Some wish to achieve growth with the stocks that they buy and sell. That means the management company wants to increase the capital assets of the people whose money they manage. Some management groups want to keep money in its most liquid form, which is the easiest way to convert securities into cash. In between there are other management groups that seek a combination of any of the above.

Investors buy shares in the management companies. For this privilege, they may or may not pay a commission. If no commission is charged (called load), the fee taken by the management for managing the fund may be higher.

Mutual funds thrive or die on their performance. If it is good, more investors will purchase shares. If performance is poor, investors will redeem their shares. Performance ratings of the majority of funds are provided yearly by publications such as *Forbes* magazine. Mutual funds can offer a great many pluses to the small individual investor. They are the closest thing to an investment counselor. Because a mutual fund is "professionally" managed, you receive this professional service even though you perhaps only have a few thousand dollars invested. Some mutual funds have a minimum investment of only $25 or $50 each purchase or a minimum of $200 per year.

Mutual funds are an alternative to the stock market, and may be less risky, since the investor owns a small piece of many companies, not just a larger portion of one or two.

Irene Kaliday is seventy years old; her husband, George, is seventy-two. When they were twenty-six and twenty-eight, they wanted to start some type of savings plan with the small amount of money they could afford to set aside each month. They went to see a stockbroker, who advised them to start a systematic investment plan with a solid-quality mutual fund. They chose a combination fund the goals of which were income and growth. The fund could also be exchanged for other funds, managed by the same company. (When companies manage more than one fund, they are said to be a family of funds.) If Irene and George wanted to change their investment objectives, they could do so for a very small fee.

They purchased a mutual fund when the funds were just coming into vogue. In 1934 they invested $1,350 and from then on scrimped and scraped every month to invest $100 in their fund. Their fund is worth almost $1 million today. The fund, of course, has had its up and downs in the market, but it is basically stable and on the conservative side.

Today Irene and George are taking a 7 percent withdrawal on their money, and they receive almost $70,000 yearly in income.

We know this may seem an unusual case, but the point of the story is that the longer you can accumulate a good mutual fund, the better results your investment will have the opportunity to achieve.

Besides the advantage of professional management in investment decisions, a mutual fund might solve any number of required investment criteria. Diversification of your investment dollars among a number of stocks and industries can be important to you. A fund gives you the occasion to be part owner in many companies without having to worry about the growth of only one stock in a particular area. A mutual fund also provides a form of bookkeeping service for you because the company will handle all the details of managing your portfolio.

Margaret Hill started with $250 in 1968 and added $100 monthly out of her teaching salary. Her total investments in her particular fund has been approximately $12,000. She has had all her dividends reinvested, and they amounted to more than $2,500. (Her money was making money because she reinvested rather than spent the dividends.) The value of her fund today is approximately $18,500. The reason we are using Margaret's story is that she was continually investing even though there were several very bad years in the stock market during this particular period. A good mutual fund is capable of weathering bad markets and remaining relatively stable.

ANNUITIES

An annuity is an investment offered by insurance companies. Annuities are available through insurance brokers or agents, but they are just as commonly sold through securities dealers. An annuity will give you a guaranteed income with payments received at regular intervals. What happens is that you make an investment of a minimum number of dollars, usually $1,500, although there are annuities which will allow a smaller monetary investment. Your investment pays a guaranteed income of a specified percentage. However, if national interest rates rise, the interest your annuity receives can also go up. If interest rates go down, the annuity rate may also, but it will never go below a certain specified minimum rate.

The type of annuity we want you to be familiar with is the single premium deferred annuity. What makes this investment an attractive one is that you are not liable for income taxes on the earnings generated by the annuity until you begin drawing on those earnings when the annuity reaches its maturation stage or you wish to retire or receive its income. (They are generally sold in ten-year increments.) The value of such a program is that these tax-free earnings are reinvested to earn more interest, which still accumulates tax-free and generates more earnings. (Interest earned from a savings account is taxable.)

Since annuities, as a general rule, are designed to begin paying out at retirement, when you begin drawing its earnings, your tax liability is usually at a reduced level. Another positive aspect of such an annuity contract is that if you need to, you may make withdrawals of your principal, from time to time, just so you do not exceed your original investment in the annuity contract. As for principal, you would not be paying tax on it again because you would have invested after-tax dollars into your annuity contract, except in unusual circumstances. If you die before using the annuity, your beneficiary will receive it, and if it is put together correctly, there should be neither income taxes nor probate expenses, although there will be, of course, the possibility of estate taxes if your estate is large enough.

In the summer of 1978, *Best's Review*, a magazine for the insurance industry, contained a survey comparing seventy-six annuity plans presently available in the United States. The single premium deferred annuity can be used in Keogh, IRA, and pension plans as well as be just a method to save for your retirement or a conservative investment which also defers tax dollars.

Out of the survey, there were seven companies that did not charge commissions in order to buy the annuity. Of the seven, one stood out with higher interest rate than the other six. We looked at the pros and cons of many annuities. The plan, which is a product of the Anchor National Life Insurance Company, seems to meet all the requirements we feel are necessary. A plan is available for a $1,500 investment. There is a guaranteed cash surrender value prior to the annuity starting date even if you should die. There is no acquisition cost, and interest is credited immediately on 100 percent of your purchase. (Depending on the state where you reside, your annuity could be subject to any applicable state premium tax.)

Let's assume you purchase an annuity. All your interest accumulates tax-free, whereas, if you have money in a savings account, you will be taxed on your interest. When you deposit money in a certificate savings account, you expect your money to remain there for a predetermined specified period of time. It is the same with an annuity, with one difference: If you need the money for an emergency, you can withdraw a certain amount with no penalty. You cannot do this, however, if the annuity is for retirement purposes.

All retirement plans have to be approved by the IRS, in order to be tax-deductible or tax-sheltered for the individual who wants one. Mutual fund companies and annuity companies already have the proper forms approved, so there is no expensive outlay if you want to establish a retirement plan. A parent company contains a number of annuity programs and mutual funds.

This probably happened because the powers behind the scenes felt that besides being a sound practice for increasing business revenues, it would be worthwhile to offer prospective clients more than one investment program.

EXPANDING YOUR INCOME

Many books today stress the subject of expanding your income outside the stock market.

You'll find books on collecting art, buying Scotch whisky futures, trading precision metals, dealing in options, trading commodities, or purchasing diamonds.

There are people who make money investing and trading in any of these, but the majority of people lose because they don't know or have the proper information and are poorly advised. On the other hand, many people have purchased through their financial advisers, investments which have been excellent. We have a friend who took approximately $1,000 and purchased an interest in a real estate investment which has averaged better than a 25 percent return on her money. One of the things she said to us was that she trusts her adviser implicitly, and she knows he will not deliberately make any investment that could harm her financially.

If you want to learn about other forms of investments, you can, just by reading the newspapers in your area and attending all the free seminars that are available to you. Attending one or more of these seminars does not obligate you to purchase the products sold.

One form of investment we have not talked about is a second trust deed (seconds). There are third trust deeds (called thirds, naturally), but if you are of a conservative nature, as we are, you can dismiss them from your mind.

On many occasions when people want to buy a house, they are lacking several thousand dollars between the amount of money they have for a down payment and the amount of money that the lender will lend for financing purposes. In order to complete the purchase, the person handling the real estate transaction will tell the purchaser that she/he knows someone who will lend the money or that the seller will lend the money (this is called taking back a second for the seller or a second trust deed for the third party lending the money).

Second trust deeds can be extremely lucrative, but there are questions the answers to which you should consider before lending your money, such as: Does the borrower have the capacity to pay back the money? Is the home in a good area? Do you like the people you're dealing with?

Second trust deeds can also be purchased through home loan mortgage companies. It is here we feel you must be even more wary of the second trust deed of which you may be the holder. These trust deeds more often are of a lower caliber than one which is obtained through a private party. The rates of interest for a second trust deed vary from state to state.

If you are interested in this form of investment, you can talk with the manager of your bank or savings and loan. You may have a friend in the real estate business who might also be able to refer people to you. If you live in an area where there are large real estate firms, you could talk with the person who either manages or owns a real estate company. You can also buy second trust deeds through classified advertisements in your newspaper, but they should be checked out thoroughly before you make a commitment.

If investments are not a field which you are familiar with, all this newly acquired knowledge can be confusing. There *are* a lot of alternative investments out there. We cannot state strongly enough: Take small steps when you are choosing investments so that you thoroughly understand what you are doing, and why.

13
Planning for Your Retirement

When you think about the word "retirement," it should mean that time of life when you can loll in the sun all day, or you can take that long-awaited trip to Europe, or you can just sit in your backyard and enjoy your grandchildren. Whatever image fits you, then that is what you should aim for as your retirement life-style. For most people who retire, retirement probably means living, and, you hope, enjoying, a new way of life. If you were to retire today at sixty-five, you could easily expect to spend another fifteen, even twenty years in your new life.

According to the Social Security Administration, out of every 100 Americans who reach age sixty-five, 75 are dependent on relatives, friends, or charity; 23 are still working; and only two are financially independent. Another study showed that despite a long working period only 1 person out of every 500 winds up with more than $24,000 in liquid assets (money that is easily accessible for living expenses) at the age of sixty-five.

Establishing a sound financial plan early in life is the only way to maximize your retirement income, which must be stable and large enough to cover your retirement living expenses. Social Security and pension benefits will produce considerably less income than you received before you retired.

Social Security, if you are eligible, can provide only minimum subsistence. In 1977 the average income per month from Social Security, per couple, was $336; for a single individual, the average was $224. Inflation not only can but will erode the amount of spendable dollars you have when it comes time for you to retire.

If you are planning to move, and you own your own home, and you are close to age sixty-five, wait until you reach your sixty-fifth birthday to sell. Under our present tax laws the capital gains tax may be eliminated up to a profit of $35,000 if you sell after the age of sixty-five. However, you must have lived in the house for eight years prior to sale, and it has to be your principal residence. New legislation is pending which will allow anyone to sell his or her home one time without incurring the capital gains tax. Whether it will have passed by the time this book is published remains to be seen.

After selling their home, many retirees find that mobile home living offers an ideal solution to reduce living expenses, yet maintain a comfortable standard of living.

If retirement is many years away, you should be making decisions now that will affect your financial condition when you retire. Make certain your investments are keeping pace with inflation. If you have planned or are planning a family, will your children be on their own by the time you retire? If you have loans outstanding, plan to have them paid in full before you retire. Check to see if your life insurance plan has provisions for when you retire, and last, but certainly not least, check your employer's retirement plan.

CORPORATE RETIREMENT PLANS

If you are not part of a retirement plan where you work, you should establish one on your own. It is going to be important for you as a working wife or single woman to be able to draw on funds for living purposes.

Even as a nonworking wife, you are eligible to set up a retirement plan in conjunction with your husband, and you should do so. Many companies now offer as part of their fringe benefits a retirement plan that spouses can also join.

Helen Kearny's husband, George, is in the maintenance department of a large industrial company. The company recently modified its retirement plan to include spouses, allowing him to contribute to the plan on behalf of Helen. George's company would deduct an extra amount from his paycheck to contribute to the retirement plan. For each dollar deducted, George's company would also contribute one dollar on Helen's behalf. Helen went to see the benefits counselor at her husband's employer. He explained to her what would be done, and she signed the necessary papers and was enrolled immediately.

How can retirement plans differ from one company to another? Generally management will have as one of the provisions of the plan the requirement that you must be an employee for a specific length of time before you can be part of a retirement plan. As a rule, you must have worked for your employer a certain number of years before you are eligible to have your rights vested. Vesting means that benefits which have accrued to you, as a result of your employment, cannot be taken away from you and that if you leave, you can take your part of the retirement plan with you. Other companies use a profit-sharing plan for retirement purposes. This means that your company management is giving you and other employees part of the business profits. The funds are put into the plan by bonuses or excess profits at the end of the company's fiscal year. Sometimes you can make contributions from your own salary equal to that of your employer's contribution for you.

Included as a feature of retirement plans is the proviso that if your plan is terminated by the company, the amount of money which is yours may be reinvested into your own private personal retirement plan. This procedure is called a rollover. You have a total of sixty days in which to roll over your funds from a company plan to your own private plan after your plan is terminated, or there will be taxes to pay on the money you should have used for the rollover.

Marnie Rowan, fifty-nine, has worked as a secretary for the last nine years for a small service corporation. The company recently terminated its retirement plan, and Marnie received a check for a little under $2,000. She took her check and invested it in a deferred annuity. Now the $2,000 will continue to accumulate interest tax-free until she retires. Then, as one of the options available to her with an annuity, she can elect to have monthly payments with her annuity proceeds, commencing with her retirement. Even if she takes her accumulation in one lump sum, the fact that she will not be working after retirement means the money will be taxed at a lower rate.

IRA AND KEOGH PLANS

Let us assume you are employed by a company that has no retirement plan. Jan Mason is in the same boat, so she started an Individual Retirement Account (IRA) which allows her to take 15 percent of her net taxable income up to a total of $1,500 each year and place it in her IRA. The money she uses is deducted from her taxable income prior to paying taxes, so this also reduces her income tax liability, while it helps her prepare for retirement.

Jan's friend Barb Peters is self-employed. Under a Keogh plan, Barb can do the same thing as Jan, only instead of being limited to $1,500 she can take 15 percent of her income or $7,500 per year and invest it to earn money for retirement purposes. Barb has her choice of using an IRA or a Keogh plan, which is a retirement program for self-employed individuals. The plan was established by the federal government several years before an IRA plan. When it originally was instituted, the maximum contribution was $1,500, as is the IRA account today. Although there is a substantial difference between the contributions allowed under the two plans, the government will probably equalize them. Basically Keoghs and IRAs are very similar except that Jan works for someone else and Barb works for herself. With your own retirement plan, it is not necessary to invest the maximum dollar amount every year because some years could be leaner than others.

Zoe Adams is the wife of a gardener. She does not work outside the home. Les Adams started an IRA plan for himself, and now he wants to make Zoe a part of it. As of 1977, the total contribution was still 15 percent, but the maximum dollar limit was raised to $1,750 for the addition of a spouse. In order for Les and Zoe to deduct the contribtuions from their federal income tax return, the contribution for both of them must be equal amounts.

Either plan will allow you, however, to invest in mutual funds, annuities, U.S. Treasury retirement bonds, or savings accounts. There are also plans in which you can invest in securities of your own choosing. The latter method has not proved to be the most satisfactory because in most cases it is difficult to be objective about your own money. Also, there are very few outside trustees who have remained in business on a continuing basis over a period of time and who charge nominal fees.

Keep in mind the retirement benefits when considering a job change—those you may be giving up and those that are provided by your potential employer. At least one year before your retirement, make certain that you will have adequate health insurance available to you—as part of your retirement package or that insurance company will continue your policy without a physical, should you be the one responsible for obtaining health insurance.

A few months before the big R, you should initiate retirement proceedings at your company so that the proper paperwork can be completed on time. If you have a private pension plan, get in touch with your plan administrator to be certain your payments will begin according to your instructions. As a retiree you may also be eligible for supplemental Social Security income benefits and all kinds of "freebies," including checking accounts and discount tickets for theaters and travel. (Check your local merchants, banks, and savings and loans for these benefits.)

Edna Fargo works for a company that recently started a pension plan for its employees. She plans to retire in about ten years. In order for her to be better prepared financially, she plans also to make voluntary contributions. She will not be able to take any tax deduction on the money she contributes because they represent only after-tax-dollars, but she will have an important tax advantage. The income or capital gains which are earned on her "extra contributions" are not taxable until she withdraws the money or if she dies and the money from her plan is distributed to her beneficiaries.

If you are part of a corporate plan, like Edna's, the IRS will allow you as an employee to make your voluntary contributions in any amount you desire, so long as the amount doesn't exceed that of your employer.

ERISA

On Labor Day of 1974 a new law was enacted to protect the interests of employees who participate in retirement plan benefits connected with their jobs. Its title is the Employee Retirement Income Security Act of 1974, but it is more often referred to by its initials—ERISA.

ERISA requires plan administrators—the people who take care of your retirement plan—to tell you the most important facts you need to know, including a summary of your retirement plan benefits, in writing, and free of charge. Plan administrators must also let you look at plan documents and buy copies of them at a reasonable cost if you ask. ERISA says that retirement plans must give you certain minimum rights. For example, ERISA states that you are eligible for benefits after one year, if you are over twenty-five. Also, a great number of people have control over employee benefit plans. ERISA says that these people, called fiduciaries, must act solely in your interest and must be prudent in carrying out their plan duties. ERISA also has other special rules that limit what a fiduciary is allowed to do. Fiduciaries who violate ERISA are subject to dismissal and may have to replace any monetary losses they cause to the plan.

ERISA requires your plan's administrator to file certain information about your plan, a description of the plan's provisions, and an annual report with the U.S. Department of Labor. (You are also entitled to this information.)

Your plan administrator must make all the documents pertaining to your plan available to you for information and questioning. If you want copies of these documents, the administrator may charge you a small fee.

ERISA also requires the plan in which you are a participant to meet certain new standards for retirement plans. These standards state, for example, that you **must** be fully vested after ten years of employment with a company. If there are any changes made in, or any modification to, your retirement plan, your right to retirement benefits and the form and amount of your benefits may be affected. Regardless of your age, if you are thinking about changing jobs or retiring, you should contact your plan administrator about your retirement benefits before making any decisions. If you have any questions about your plan (or your husband's plan, for that matter), get in touch with the plan's administrator.

RETIREMENT PLAN SUPPLEMENTS

It is possible to supplement any retirement plan by purchasing annuities, since the interest does accumulate tax-free. Other ways to supplement are buying good-quality growth stocks or bonds and mutual funds or income-producing real estate. Annuities, however, are the most practical, if there is little money for doing any supplementing to your plan. Purchasing retirement bonds offered by the U.S. Treasury is another way to establish a retirement plan under either a Keogh or IRA. These bonds were authorized by the Self-Employed Individual Retirement Act of 1961.

Amy Morris purchased government retirement bonds for herself up to the annual maximum of 15 percent of her earned income from

her pottery shop, or $7,500, whichever was the lesser of the two. She deducts the entire amount of her purchase for income tax purposes. Upon her retirement she will begin to redeem her bonds purchased with tax-deferred income. When Amy does this, she must include in her income tax return the entire interest earned on the bond plus the amount of the purchase price that she took as a deduction for the year when the bond was originally bought.

If you are interested in the retirement bonds Amy purchased, you can write and find out more about them. *Public Debt*, Series No. 1-63, as revised, is available from the U.S. Department of the Treasury, Washington, D.C. 20226.

During the last five years, leisure counseling has begun to develop as a result of the increasing amount of spare time which has arisen as the result of shorter workweeks, longer vacations, and early retirement. You may be interested in taking a class on leisure time now being offered in some communities.

As you are looking toward your future or if you are already retired, you may also discover you are not the type of individual who can fully retire. The U.S. Government Printing Office has a booklet entitled *Back to Work After Retirement*, available from the Superintendent of Documents, Washington, D.C. 20402. It might give you some ideas for pursuing a second career, which might keep you from a retirement of boredom.

We have some thoughts about saving money during your retirement years. One interesting way to save is to barter services based on your prior business or profession. Perhaps your next-door neighbor's husband is a former accountant, and you are a practical nurse. His wife becomes ill. You trade nursing skills and time for having your income tax prepared. Both of you save money when it might have been necessary to spend it. In this way you can obtain a lot of useful services without reducing your income. You might also plan your meals by means of the specials each week which appear in your local newspaper ads. Buy foods that are in season—not strawberries in January or winter vegetables in July. Moreover, if you drive across town in order to save one cent or two cents for whatever item you wish to buy, the added cost to your gasoline bill makes the trek uneconomical. Also, most important, if an item is listed on sale at a lower price, to buy it when it is not needed is still a waste of money.

The most important step in planning for retirement is advance planning. The adage "A stitch in time saves nine" is more true than allegorical. The more thoroughly you do this preplanning, the easier it will be for you to adapt to changes, if they become necessary.

PLANNING YOUR RETIREMENT BUDGET

Where you want to retire—urban, suburban, or exurban—will necessarily dictate how much money you're going to need. In 1976 the budget of the average urban family (consisting of a thirty-eight-year-old husband, a wife who does not work outside the home, an eight-year-old girl, and a thirteen-year-old boy) averaged $16,236, and for a retired couple in that same urban area, two people over sixty-five, the average budget was $6,738. In a nonmetropolitan area, the budgets ranged from $14,625 down to $5,947.

The following chart will show you the 1976 average for retirement living in various parts of the country. You can also see the ranges from the high to low budgets for the urban, city, and country living.

COST OF LIVING
1976 - RETIREE BUDGET

City	1976 Budget
Austin, Texas	$6,285
Detroit, Michigan	$6,731
Portland, Maine	$7,168
N.Y., NE New Jersey	$7,929
Boston, Massachusetts	$8,017

	National Average Urban (Suburban)	National Average City	National Average Country
High	$10,048	$10,509	$8,669
Intermediate	$ 6,738	$ 7,002	$5,947
Low	$ 4,695	$ 4,807	$4,359

In order to determine how much you will have to live on when you retire, it is important for you to estimate ahead of time. Your actual monthly dollar amount on retirement from Social Security cannot be figured until you apply for your benefits. While you are still working, request an accounting of your Social Security account to determine its accuracy. You can use a form available through your post office or local Social Security office or the Social Security Administration in Washington, D.C.

Remember that if you earn 5 percent on your money, it will double every fifteen years. A return of 10 percent doubles every 7.2 years. If you invest $10,000 when you are thirty-five and do not touch it until you are sixty-five, you will have accumulated $40,000. You will have $40,000 by the time you are fifty if you can earn 10 percent on your money.

If by any chance you return to work after you started receiving retirement checks, your added earnings can often result in higher benefits when you again stop working. Social Security will automatically refigure your benefits after your additional earnings are credited to you.

If you work beyond age sixty-five, you receive a special credit that can mean a larger Social Security benefit. This credit will add 1 percent each year, or one-half of 1 percent each month from age sixty-five to seventy-two. (This applies only to people who were sixty-five after 1970.) If you should die during this time, however, your beneficiary does not receive this increase.

Rhoda Chapin worked very little and only at part-time jobs until retirement. Whatever work she did, however, she requested that money be deducted from her pay for Social Security. She is receiving a special minimum of $135 a month. Most people covered under Social Security receive more than Rhoda's special minimum. If Rhoda should work again, the automatic cost of living increase does not apply to her special minimum.

Retirement should be a great time of your life. Your child-rearing days are over. If you are properly prepared to retire, there can be an exciting time ahead for you. So plan and have the peace of mind, knowing you have done so. Then you can thoroughly enjoy it.

14
Protecting Your Estate

What is an estate? If you have possessions (assets), whether it be a gold ring or the deeds for an entire city block, you have an estate. While the words "estate plan" sound formidable, they are simply a method of protecting your property and sensibly disposing of your assets at the time of your death. The lack of a plan can lead to confusion and anguish for your heirs. Even if you, or you and your husband, are of modest means, estate planning is important. For according to the American Banking Association, while inflation forces prices up, it's also pushing up your total worth. Today a $120,000 estate is a middle-income reality. Federal estate taxes begin to apply when a married man or woman leaves an estate of $120,000 or more and when a single person leaves an estate of $60,000 or more.

Since every woman's situation is unique, we are not going to provide an estate plan for you but only give you guidelines, which you can suggest to your husband if you're married or consider for yourself if you are single. How can you simplify settling an estate? Many states have already helped you by updating their probate procedures and laws to allow a surviving spouse or next of kin to administer the disposition of the estate quickly and economically. In the last analysis, there is no magic solution for eliminating all the red tape involved in settling an estate. You can do more to simplify the process of settling your estate than anyone else. With careful planning, you can also keep your taxes and costs to a minimum.

Before you can plan your estate, you first have to know how much it is worth. Make a list of all your assets—your house (its current value even though it is only partially paid for), jewelry, Aunt Kate's portrait, bank accounts, life insurance, etc. Without a list of your assets you cannot begin to assemble an intelligent estate plan. The estimated value tells you several things—how much you can leave to your heirs; how best to reduce taxes on your estate; even how much you'll have available to live on when you retire. Once you've determined the value of your estate, you're ready to decide what you want to do with it all. We all know the road to hell is paved with good intentions, but intentions don't count when you're gone, so it is important to turn your plans into legal documents.

In a sound estate plan, you need written documents that state precisely your intentions and include the necessary provisions to execute them. The written documents that can help you accomplish your goals are a will, a trust, life insurance policy or policies (see insurance chapter), a buy-sell agreement if you are a co-owner of a business, and your employee benefits if you are employed by some-one else (see retirement chapter).

Once you have that list of assets, your next step is to prepare a will. Your will is your insurance that whatever you own will go to the person you want it to after your death.

A VALID WILL

Many an individual has drawn her own will in order to save costs. This is fine if properly done; but most of the time it isn't, and the costs involved in probating are many times more than the costs of having a lawyer draw up a proper will in the first place. Some important aspects to remember if you do write your own will: It *must* be in your own handwriting and legal in the state where you reside since some states do not permit a handwritten document as evidence of a will. If it does not, seek the services of an attorney. The cost is well worth it! Your will spells out in detail what you want done with your estate. In your will, you also appoint your executor. If you are married, you and your husband should both have wills— separate ones. What would happen, for example, if both of you were in a car crash and one of you died several hours after the other?

During that time your entire estate, depending on who died first, could change hands to the spouse without a will.

The person who implements your will is called an executor. His duties begin when the will is probated. Executors should be chosen for their ability to do a competent job for you and your family, not for friendship and loyalty. If you have made a will or are preparing one, you can choose your own executor.

The American Bankers Association has set forth the following guidelines to help you with your selection: She/He should comprehend and be capable of performing her/his duties and know why she/he is so important to the welfare of your family. You may select an individual executor or have several coexecutors to share a specific responsibility. A friend or relative will generally serve as your executor without a fee. If you appoint a bank as executor, the fee is set by the bank. If you have appointed no one in your will, the state's appointed executor will set the fee. The same is true if you appoint a lawyer. A bank trust department in some instances could be less expensive than a lawyer, should specialized services be required in the settlement of your estate. When you die, a probate court grants your executor authority to begin administering your estate.

If there is no will, the court will appoint an administrator in accordance with the law of your particular state.

Typically your executor accepts the responsibilities of (1) your assets (real estate, cash, securities, your business, bank accounts, royalties, art objects, and other property); (2) hiring a lawyer to handle the legal aspects of your estate; (3) collecting the money that is due your estate (salaries, pensions, VA benefits, profit sharing, Social Security, etc.); (4) seeing that life insurance companies are notified and everyone named in the policy or policies is paid; (5) paying off the valid debts owed by you to others; (6) preparing and filing all estate, income, and inheritance taxes; (7) arranging for your family's immediate living expenses; and (8) distributing portions of the estate to all people named in the will.

After all legacies are paid, property distributed, debts and taxes paid, and trusts operating, the court relieves the executor of her/his duties. Choosing your executor, therefore, is very important. It is up to the executor to fulfill your plans for your beneficiaries. Selecting an executor should be far more than a gesture of friendship. It's a tough, demanding assignment that should go only to a person you feel is qualified.

Preparing your own will and trying to lower death taxes may

cause hardship or confusion for your heirs. You should seek out a professional who can help you, not do it yourself. Make certain that you have an estate plan prepared and tailored to suit your needs, not one you copied from a friend.

Claire and Sam Darling were married for thirty-three years when Sam suffered a heart attack and died. A year prior to his death Sam consulted one of his friends about setting up some type of plan to take care of his family when he died. Sam copied his friend's trust and will, substituting his family's names for names in his friend's documents. Sam took the documents to a notary public and had them notarized and witnessed, then put the documents in the family safe-deposit box. When the documents were opened, they were written in such a manner that Claire would have been deprived of any money for her living expenses until she was sixty-eight years old (she had just turned fifty-nine). Luckily Claire's new son-in-law was a lawyer, and through the courts he had the documents revoked. All of Claire's problems could have been avoided if Sam had consulted a lawyer who specialized in estate plans or a trust officer of a bank or other trust institution who could have better advised him. Claire was lucky that she had a lawyer she could turn to, who helped her without cost.

If you die without a will and you live in a community property state (Arizona, California, Idaho, Louisiana, Nevada, New Mexico, Texas, and Washington), the surviving spouse will take her/his one-half of the community property outright, and the deceased spouse's share (her or his one-half of the community) passes as follows:

In California, Idaho, Nevada, New Mexico, and Washington that share passes to the surviving spouse.

In Arizona and Texas that share passes to her or his surviving children; if there are none, then to her or his descendants; if there are none, then to his or her spouse.

In Louisiana that share passes to the decedent's children; if there are none, then to his or her descendants; if none, then one-half of that share passes to the decedent's parents and the other one-half to the surviving spouse, who gets it all if the decedent's parents are dead.

With regard to the deceased's separate property, the exact rules vary from state to state; but generally the children get a fraction, and the surviving spouse gets a fraction.

Throughout the country there has been a conscious effort by individuals to avoid probate. To do so, many people have placed their assets in joint tenancy. With joint tenancy, regardless of whether your husband or you have a will, your property goes to the surviving spouse without probate. It may be that you wanted your child to receive your share upon your death because you may be living in a house that your ex-husband and you still own in joint tenancy. Under joint tenancy this is not possible. Joint tenancy at death is similar to a life insurance policy the proceeds of which are paid at the insured's death to the beneficiary named in the policy regardless of who is beneficiary of the decedent's will. Joint tenancy ownership can be established in any state except Texas, where it is illegal. *You cannot will away your interest in a joint tenancy.* If you want to leave your share of property to someone other than your spouse, you should hold title as tenants in common. It would be wise to check with a lawyer if you want to change the way you hold title on your property.

A TRUST

There are steps you can be taking now to assist in probate procedures. One of them is a trust. A trust is a document by which you convey all or any part of your assets to a third person, the trustee. A lawyer drafts a trust for you at the same time he draws up your will. The trustee is generally a trust officer from a bank, savings and loan, or private trust company, but he can be a friend if you wish.

There are two basic types of trusts: testamentary and living. A testamentary trust provides for the long-term management of your funds. A testamentary trust takes effect at the time of your death. A living trust is similar except a trustee manages your funds and property while you are still living.

The living trust may survive its maker and go on to furnish continuing financial security for a family. Both a testamentary trust and a living trust can provide tax-saving benefits. The primary difference between the two is that the assets of a living trust usually avoid probate, and the expenses of administering the trustmaker's estate can be significantly reduced. In both cases the estate taxes have been reduced since your assets have already been conveyed to the trust.

Most living trusts today are revocable, meaning they may be amended or even terminated at any time during life. This flexibility permits the trust maker to observe how the trust functions to meet his needs—and the future needs of the family—and then to make changes accordingly. An irrevocable trust is less apt to be challenged by the IRS and as a result is the best guarantee that your estate taxes will be lower.

Trusts are not necessarily just for husbands and wives. You might be single, with only your nieces and nephews as heirs, or you may want to leave your money to a cause you believe in. Miriam Rogers is sixty-seven years old, is single, and has accumulated a sizable estate during her working years. She wants to leave a substantial part of it to a large university when she dies since she has no close relatives. She went to see a trust officer who helped her establish a trust that pays her $9,000 a year as long as she lives. Upon her death the remainder will go to the university. This not only eases her money management worries now that she has retired, but also secures all her assets for the university at the time of her death.

You can put into your trust just about anything you would like, as long as the person who is your trustee will allow you to do so. You can start your trust with cash and have your trustee invest the money. You can have your trust manage property or other types of assets. The most important part of a trustee's job is to watch your investments carefully and make changes whenever it is in your best interests. Attention is focused on your income needs and the tax bracket of your heirs. Your trust can hold all your assets, or you can have a trust to hold only a portion of your assets—those designated for a particular person upon your death. There really is no limit to the kind of trust and no minimum size for a trust except what is practical. Banks and trust companies, however, will generally have a miminum size they will accept because it is impracticable for them to deal with smaller sums of money. If your estate consists largely of life insurance, you can even create a trust that will receive the proceeds on your death.

Where Do You Go to Learn About a Trust?

Most banks have trust departments, and there are also private trust companies throughout the United States. Either of these institutions can explain to you what a trust is, how it works, how much it may cost you. If you think a trust might be helpful to you, you should visit a trust officer. You will be provided with the answers to any questions you may have, and in so doing, you might do something very beneficial not only for you but for those you love.

LIFE INSURANCE POLICIES

You have already read the chapter on life insurance. By their very nature life insurance policies provide for the payment of their value on your death to the beneficiary you named. This may be an individual of your estate or a trustee under a will or trust agreement. The proceeds can also be held by the insurance company for payment of fixed sums on an installment basis.

Buy-Sell Agreement

If you are part owner of a closely held corporation or partnership business, you should have a buy-sell agreement. This will assure your other co-owners and partners that there will be money to purchase your interest in the business when you die. Frequently life insurance is purchased when the buy-sell agreement is made between you and your partners. The proceeds from the policy will be used to purchase your interest upon your demise. This type of agreement ensures an uninterrupted flow of business and allows your beneficiary to conclude your business transactions without delay. (See a further discussion of this in the insurance chapter.)

DEFERRED EMPLOYEE BENEFITS

An important part of your estate plan is the survivor benefits of your retirement plan because they have provisions for disposition after you die. You should check the provisions of your retirement plan with your company benefits counselor or employer to make certain that if you die, your accrued benefits will pass to your designated beneficiary. If you have been employed with a company for a long time, your deferred benefits are probably substantial and should be properly directed. Deferred benefits also include Social Security, naturally.

The objective in an estate plan is not tax evasion. That is illegal. Your goal should be to take advantage of available methods of minimizing your tax burden or the tax burden placed on your beneficiaries. One of the most important aspects to take into consideration is that while your estate plan may lessen your liability, it should also be a plan that is financially sound.

Estate planning is a vast and intricate field, which contains many pitfalls. No estate is too small to plan for the future. Take the time to make out a will and investigate the benefits of a trust. We hope this chapter will help you focus on your own estate and your responsibilities to it.

15

How to Avoid Being a Widow Without Assets

There are 12 million widows in the United States. Of these women 6 million are under sixty-five, and one out of four is under forty-five with young children living at home. After the husband's death the family's income, including all benefits, will be reduced by an average of 44 percent. Most wives will be widows for an average of five to ten years. Are you prepared for this eventuality?

Putting your head in the sand and saying, "This will never happen to me," is a dangerous premise to go on. The facts state otherwise, and as unpleasant as it may be to think about, you will in all probability be a widow.

Preparing yourself to be a widow doesn't imply that you are looking forward to it. It means you are being realistic. Don't you think it would make your husband happy to know his family is provided for if something happens to him?

In an excellent booklet, *The Financial Facts of Widowhood*, put out by Anchor National Financial Service, Inc., of Phoenix, Arizona, the following statistics are revealed: In a survey conducted among 1,744 widows, 32 percent encountered difficulty managing their family's finances following the husband's death, but difficulty was encountered by almost 63 percent of those whose husbands handled the family's finances before they died. The primary causes of difficulty revealed by the widows in this survey were lack of experience, unsureness, and income reductions.

The average of all death benefits left to a widow is only $12,000, including life insurance, veterans' benefits, and Social Security.

Other statistics show:

1. Fewer than three out of ten widows' husbands left a will.
2. Within eighteen months 52 percent of all widows studied had used up all the life insurance benefits of their husbands.
3. One of four had exhausted her life insurance money within only sixty days, mostly as a result of funeral and/or illness costs.
4. One out of four widows *never* received all of her husband's benefits because she didn't know about them.

What does all this mean to you? It means that there are certain steps you can be taking now which will help soften the blow financially if indeed you are widowed. We don't mean to imply that if you read this chapter, you will sail through widowhood. We realize it is emotionally devastating, but if you are financially prepared, you will have one less worry.

PREPARING TO BE A WIDOW

— Go to your local Social Security office and ask for the latest booklet, *Your Social Security Handbook—New Rates and Benefits*. Pay special attention to the death benefits sections. You may want to go over them with your husband to see what you will be eligible for. Write them down, and update them when need be, and keep them with your important papers.

— Discuss with your husband the possibility of his dying before you, and together devise a plan to be put into effect in that event. Have him tell you what benefits you are eligible for— pension, retirement, life insurance, GI insurance, etc. Naturally this is not a pleasant subject, and many people do not like to talk about it; but the facts cannot be ignored. Of course, you don't want anything to happen to your husband, but if you convince him that because of your love for him and your children, and his love for you and the children, it is a possibility that has to be prepared for. The subject of death is morbid, but it is unfortunately a morbid reality.

— Consider taking a financial planning class. More and more of these classes are being offered at day and evening colleges. Classes such as these will often even go into the particular financial problems widows face.

— Have your husband's insurance policy analyzed by an insurance consultant to see if you are under- or overinsured.

— Have someone in mind that you can go to, such as a life insurance agent, stockbroker, banker, trust officer, financial planner, or lawyer (preferably someone who knows your financial situation), and have him help you draw up a plan for your family's future in event of a death. Review your financial plan and situation at regular intervals.

— Become familiar, if you aren't already, with all the family finances—insurance owned, debts owed. Know where to find receipts, benefits you are eligible for through your husband's employment, how much money it would take to run the household.

— Keep a separate cash account, either savings or personal checking, in your *own* name. Some states "freeze" all accounts of a deceased person and all his other assets, including paychecks due. The freeze usually lasts until an executor has been named and an inventory of the deceased person's property has been presented to the court—a procedure that can take two to three weeks and even more. Social Security checks take on the average of four months to arrive. During this period a separate cash account will permit you to have some immediate funds.

— Take out mortgage insurance on your home. It is well worth the money. If your husband dies, your home is paid for. You can purchase mortgage insurance through your life insurance agent or through the lending institution that holds the mortgage on your home.

— Prepare a location list. Where is the deed to your house? Does your husband own shares in a mutual fund? Which one? Where are the shares kept? Who is his securities dealer? Do you contact the life insurance company or your insurance agent in the event of his death?

These and many other panic-filled questions can be avoided easily by preparing a simple location list of important documents now. One copy of the list should be kept at home; other copies might well be left with your financial adviser and, if you wish, a close relative. Your location list should include proof of ownership papers. All your bank accounts should be listed by passbook

numbers and branch; you should know where all insurance policies are located, including health and disability policies, union,
auto club policies, GI insurance, homeowner's package policies,
and group insurance contracts provided by your husband's employer. The location of all vital statistic documents (marriage,
birth, citizenship, and military records) should be included. You
should list the phone numbers and addresses of all financial and
legal advisers, including your attorney, insurance agents (for
both personal and casualty insurance), the individual or firm, if
any, who has prepared your family's tax returns in past years,
and, of course, the location of the family wills.

— Make sure you establish credit in your own name, via bank
accounts or charge accounts. This will eliminate a lot of problems with credit if you are widowed. (See the chapter on credit.)

— Make sure you, and especially your husband, prepare a will.
Every adult person who owns property should have a will because without a will the laws of your state direct how your personal or real property (real estate) will be divided and to whom it
will go.

For example, you might end up owning only half the family
home, with the other half owned by your minor children—a less
than satisfactory arrangement. Under the interstate laws of many
states, that's what would happen if your husband died without a
will.

Having a will prepared is usually quite simple. It takes only a
few hours and costs relatively little—an average of $50 to $75 for
the typical uncomplicated will—yet seven out of ten husbands
die without one.

You and your husband can have a joint will but make certain
that it is done through a lawyer. If you both write a will in own
handwriting (holographic), each of you must have a *separate
will* because the person writing a holographic will must be the
same person who signs it, or it will not be valid. Also, before
writing a holographic will, you should make certain that your
state will consider it *legal*. It really would be a much better
idea to have a will drawn up by a lawyer, even if you have to
save up the money to have it done.

When preparing a will, you and your husband will be asked
to name an executor. What exactly is an executor?

Simply stated, an executor is the person who is named in a
will to handle the job of settling an estate. (An estate is whatever
you have accumulated during a lifetime, from a grandfather clock

to a substantial income.) An executor can be the husband or wife, a friend, or a professional executor, such as a bank.

— After making up a will, investigate the advantages of a trust. All by itself a will is simply a set of instructions for your executor to divide up your property. A trust goes beyond a will; it provides for the management of your property as well as its distribution.

Properly designed, trusts and wills can work together very effectively, yet most people shy away from trusts, thinking they are only for the wealthy.

In the simplest terms, a trust provides another human being (the trustee) the authority to make decisions about your property after the maker of the trust (your husband) is deceased. (The chapter on estates goes into this in greater detail.)

— Consider the possibility of getting a job. Insurance can be of great help to a widow, of course, but according to an insurance industry figure, 80 percent of all widows have spent the proceeds from insurance policies within one year after the husband's death. One year—what then?

If you are not employed outside the home, and have not been, and have no marketable skills, you'd better look long and hard at your situation. If you feel that you will remarry, a cold, hard statistic shows that the older you get, the less chance you have to remarry.

We are not advocating that if you are a woman who is content at home—and many women are—you should rush out and get a job, but you should at least equip yourself with some marketable skills that could earn you a living. Let's be realistic: It would be exciting to be a news commentator on network TV, but if you can type or do basic bookkeeping, you can usually get a job at a fairly decent salary. We're not saying it's fair—we're saying that's the way it is—and we're not saying to take only typing and bookkeeping classes—we're just trying to get the point across that if you do go back to school, take classes that will give you a skill (such as radiology, not religions of the world). Remember, we are talking about a widow's having to go out and get a job— not preparing for a career or filling your spare time.

— If your state banking laws permit it, make sure any joint bank account you have with your husband reads: your husband's name or your name, not and. For example, John or Mary Smith, not John and Mary Smith. If you have an account that reads "and," you have to have both signatures to close out the account, so in the event of your husband's death, it can take considerable time

and red tape to get the money out. If you have an account that
says "or," you should have no problem.

FAMILY DOCUMENTS

We want to emphasize again the importance of knowing your
family's financial resources and the location of all your important
papers. If you only follow one piece of advice in this chapter, make
it this one.

Bank Accounts—Do you know where your passbooks are kept? The
location of your safe-deposit box, if any? Whether your accounts are
all in joint name or if they are in single-name accounts? Do you have
an inventory of the contents of your safe-deposit box and of other
valuables you may be keeping elsewhere?

Two lists should be made of the contents. If you own real estate,
your deed of trust or mortgage papers should be included in that
inventory. Keep one list in your safe-deposit box. When these steps
have been taken, sit down and write a letter to a close friend or your
lawyer or banker, informing him of the location of your safe-deposit
box with a copy of the inventory and the location of each bank
account. On the envelope, state that this letter is to be opened only
in the event of your death.

Insurance—A most important problem area is insurance. Talk about
your insurance with your husband. If he does not have any, urge
him to purchase some. Determine whether his coverage is adequate. One rule of thumb is that insurance should be ten times the
annual income needed to live without working. Statistics show that
on the average, all proceeds from an insurance settlement are dissi-
pated after three years. To prevent this from happening to you,
remember that insurance proceeds should not be used to pay off
current debts but should be used to allow the surviving family
members to continue to live a normal life without the husband's
support.

Many insurance companies and New York Stock Exchange member
firms have access to insurance analysts. Take advantage of the opportunity to have your existing insurance analyzed. There is no
obligation to purchase further insurance, but an analysis will certainly give you an insight into what insurance benefits you now have
and what additional protection you may need. As with the bank

information, all policies should be kept in one place, and their accessibility known by you.

The Lawyer—Wives frequently do not know their husband's lawyer (if they have one). Yet when the husband dies, the lawyer can be more important than any other adviser. A woman should be just as well acquainted with the lawyer as is the husband. Husband and wife should each have a will, which has been kept up to date. If both you and your husband should die in a common disaster, the will should indicate whom you want as your children's guardians if they are minors. The question of guardianship should be discussed beforehand with the people whom you have designated as guardians. No one would wish to create an excessive financial burden for guardians, so proper financial arrangements should also be considered.

Pension Plans—Are you entitled to benefits under the pension plan of your husband? If there is a survivor's option, has it been exercised? If the husband is entitled to group insurance, will the beneficiary be entitled to anything if he dies after retirement? You should know to what benefits you are entitled through your husband's employer.

Securities—If you and your husband own securities, find out how they are registered. Does your husband purchase securities in his name alone, or is your name on the certificates as well?

In settling the estate, if there are only a few odd lots (fewer than 100 shares of any issue of stock) that need a name change, it is probably easier for you to write directly to the transfer agent rather than your broker (call your brokerage house and find out who the transfer agent is) and ask for the shares to be transferred to your name. Although requirements vary from state to state, you generally will need a copy of the death certificate for each company in which you hold shares. In most cases, any New York Stock Exchange firm should make available for convenience all necessary papers and documents. If you hold the stock certificates or if the certificates are held in street name—that is, kept for you by the brokerage house and registered in its name—transfer procedures may vary. As with the lawyer, you should know the name of the registered representative and the brokerage house that has been executing transactions for your husband.

If you need to sell any stock, you will be helped with the necessary red tape involved. If you have a bond portfolio or stocks that pay dividends, a broker at your member firm can provide you with the dates the dividend payments or interest checks are due. Frequently you will find that all financial services can be provided for you under one roof.

Find out what Social Security benefits you and your children would be eligible for in the event of your husband's death.

When you have sat down with your husband, gone over your financial situation, and met all the people who are involved in the handling of your family finances, you have taken the first step toward avoiding becoming a widow without assets.

WHEN YOU ARE WIDOWED

Preparing to be a widow is of extreme importance, but equally important is what you should do in the event you are widowed. You will need to get copies of the death certificate. You must have one for the insurance company, for your husband's employer (to get your husband's pension), for Social Security, for any GI benefits, for putting real estate and securities in your own name, etc.

You should get in touch with the person you and your husband previously decided you should call—the insurance agent, financial planner, etc., and seek advice since this is the person who is familiar with your situation and can help you set up a new financial plan and budget.

Contact your husband's employer so your survivor's benefits can be processed immediately. Your husband may have vacation or sick leave, pension, or regular pay coming, and, in some cases, insurance benefits. Some companies have counselors for widows of employees who can be of great help.

Notify your insurance agent or company immediately, so the paperwork can be started and you can receive your money as soon as possible.

Go to your nearest Social Security office (it is listed in the phone book), and apply for the benefits you and your children are eligible for. To receive Social Security payments, you need to fill out an application with the Social Security office. The benefits from Social Security are not paid automatically unless you first apply for them. You should apply as quickly as possible because, as with any government agency, the paperwork can take weeks. When you go to the Social Security office to apply, you will need to take your Social Security card, if you have one, and your husband's card or number. If you do not know his number, call his place of employment. It should be on file there. You will also need to take your marriage certificate, your children's birth certificates, a copy of your last federal income tax return, and your husband's death certificate. *Do not delay* because you do not have any or all of these documents. The people in the Social Security office can tell you what other proofs may be used instead.

After you receive the life insurance benefits—which usually come in a lump sum, but sometimes in monthly increments—put the money into a savings account immediately. Widows are very often taken advantage of and are in no emotional state to cope. Your money will be safe and will be drawing interest while you and your financial adviser decide on the best way to utilize these funds—to invest the money in stocks or bonds, annuities or mutual funds, to leave it in the savings and loan to draw interest, to purchase real estate, the multitude of options you have available when you have money left to you, depending on your particular situation.

If you feel you cannot afford a paid financial planner or consultant, your insurance agent (if he/she is a good one) should help you assess your new financial picture. Often banks or savings and loans have this service available free to their customers.

Remember, you will need two-thirds of what you were living on when your husband was alive to continue to live in the same style, and the average budget for a family of four in 1976 was $16,236.

But let us reemphasize that while you are setting up your new financial plan, you should keep your money in the savings and loan. Do not be swayed by anyone's wanting to borrow or help you invest your money (except your adviser). Check out with your adviser any well-meaning advice you receive from friends. Widows sometimes are contacted by unscrupulous individuals with "get-rich-quick" schemes. Other individuals have been known to read the obituaries, call the widow, and tell her her husband owed him money and she should pay the debt. If someone should call, ask for proof of the debt, tell him you will check with your estate advisers and get back to him.

If you are unsure whether or not you want to invest your money, keeping your money in a savings and loan, drawing interest, is a very acceptable solution. In any event it would be advisable to keep (if possible) $2,000 to $3,000 in a passbook savings account for emergencies, and $1,000 in your checking account. Make sure the accounts are in your name (Mary Robinson Smith, not Mrs. John Smith), for this is an excellent way to establish credit. (See chapter on credit.) You will need to have credit in your name now to take out loans or make credit purchases.

You will also need to take out life, medical, and disability insurance on yourself since you are now head of the household. If you already have these policies, have them changed to read "Head of Household." Also, change the number of deductions on your paycheck if you work.

If your husband dies and he does not have insurance, and you cannot support yourself and the children, you may be eligible for state and federal aid. You should go to your local welfare office and see what programs, such as state or federal aid, you are eligible for. This will be based on your income (or lack of income) and the ages of your children.

One program which might help is the food stamp program. By law the program is operated through state and local welfare agencies. The federal government gives extra food-buying power to low-income families or individuals who decide to spend a specified amount of their own money for food coupons (commonly known as food stamps). Families with little or no income do not have a purchase requirement and get their stamps free. In order for a household to be eligible for food stamps, all able-bodied members (with certain exceptions) must register for and accept suitable employment. What most people refer to as a "family" becomes a "household" under the food stamp program. A food stamp household is a group of people who buy, prepare, and eat their meals together. A single individual can be a "household" if he prepares and eats his food at home. It is the total *net* income of all members of the household (over eighteen) that determines whether the household qualifies for food stamps. The other income may be from welfare checks, pensions, insurance benefits, Social Security, odd jobs, or other sources. If the total income is below the national eligibility standards, the household probably can get food stamps. It is most certainly a program a widow should look into to supplement her income. After all, you and your husband probably paid a lot of taxes into it.

It is extremely important for a woman who is left a widow to get her emotional state in at least workable condition. Mary Kay Higgins, regional sales manager of Merrill Lynch, Inc., stockbrokers told us, "Psychology and finance have a lot in common, although the definition of each doesn't put them in the same category. When a woman has to face the responsibility of handling her own financial affairs, she must also be in the psychological position to do so." Whether you opt for professional counseling or give yourself some time, you should make sure you are thinking rationally before making any major decisions such as selling your home and moving.

Mary Kay has been a widow herself, rearing two children alone. She commented, "When a woman first finds herself alone, she is usually in a catatonic state. The first thing she should do before making any financial decisions is to get herself in the proper frame of mind."

The most common problem she has seen is: "When a woman, and especially a widow, is seeking financial advice, she has no definite objectives and does not know how to begin to find them."

Thomas Garvey, partner of an insurance agency in Southern California, agrees that often a woman left alone by death (or divorce) is ill prepared to take over the family finances. He advises a woman not to sign anything until she not only reads it over carefully but has someone who is thinking more clearly also read it. "She should do everything quite slowly and be a bit wary."

Garvey states that if a widow is fortunate enough to receive a large sum of money from life insurance proceeds, one of the best ways to invest the funds could be in a conservative mutual fund.

HOW FOUR WOMEN HAVE COPED

When Cecilia Young's husband died, she did not have the foggiest idea of where she stood financially. She was not even certain she had enough to live on. She was desperate enough to write to a newspaper financial columnist for advice. Luckily the columnist printed Cecilia's letter and advised her:

1. Don't make any immediate radical decisions. Take your time, and go through your financial situation step by step. It is almost always more important for you to act wisely rather than quickly.
2. Take an inventory of all your assets. Bear in mind that money is not your only asset. Your home, your car, your education, your job skills are also assets.
3. Prepare a budget. Determine the minimum amount of money you need each month to maintain your standard of living. Next, look at your sources of income, including Social Security payments. If your income does not at least meet expenses, you have some difficult decisions to make, such as seeking employment, applying for aid, etc.
4. Even if you can afford to, do not buy stocks for at least six months (preferably nine to twelve months) after your husband has died because of your emotional state of mind. If you need

income (or want to put your money to work right away), buy
short-term government securities available through most banks.

5. Do not overuse your charge accounts.

6. Finally, talk with someone whose judgment you trust regarding your financial situation; preferably the person should be an
outsider, so that he can look at your financial situation objec-
tively. This person could be a lawyer, a banker, an investment
counselor, a trust officer in a trust company, or a stockbroker.
If you have little or no money, there are various volunteer
agencies which may be of help to you. This is your period of
transition, and you should explore all avenues that may be
open to you.

Fifty-seven-year-old Dorothy Farley's husband, Jack, was a carpet
installer for thirty-five years. He belonged to a union for almost ten
years until he was forced to go on full physical disability. Up to a
year before he died, he paid his dues regularly, but the doctor bills
were piling up so high he was forced to write the union and say he
could no longer pay. Dorothy and Jack went on welfare for day-to-
day living expenses, but it took six months before they received the
first check. Medicaid took care of part of Jack's doctor bills. When he
died the union disallowed all of Dorothy's claims for a widow's pension because, she was told, Jack had not been a member of the
union for fifteen years. Dorothy has been denied any Social Security
because she is not sixty years of age and has no dependent children.
Right now the only money Dorothy is receiving is a $117-a-month
check from the government through a service-related pension of her
husband's. Dorothy cannot get a job; otherwise she would lose her
$117. If it were possible for her to find a job, she would not be a
good employee because she suffers from constant migraine head-
aches. If Dorothy were not living with her daughter, she would not
be able to survive.

Joan McSweeney was widowed a year ago and left with two school-
age children. After her husband's estate was settled and all the
medical bills (incurred during her husband's illness) were paid, she
had $63,000 left. She had not worked while she was married, so she
decided to go back to college but was concerned about the best way
to invest the money to bring her a monthly income. She was advised
that she basically had two options: One was to buy a good-quality
mutual fund and receive a check each month until she had an earning
capacity of her own. The second was to purchase corporate bonds

and receive the interest from the bonds. She decided on the mutual fund because even though she was withdrawing a set sum each month, the mutual fund would probably continue to grow. The corporate bonds, however, would be strictly income. Joan plans to eliminate the withdrawal plan from the fund and continue to invest in it after she is through school as a means of saving for her children's education.

When Lorrie Blain's husband died of cancer, she was thirty-seven years old, with four children. She was, however, up to date on their finances since her husband had been ill for some time; besides that, she had always handled the money.

"Even so," she told us, "nothing quite prepares you for what you have to go through when your husband dies. You are in shock, yet you are immediately faced with decisions that will affect you and your children's lives. The first thing I did was to contact my insurance agent, but it still took three weeks before I received the benefits check. I applied for Social Security right away, and that took six weeks before I had a check. (Your case has to be studied, and they have to see a copy of the death certificate.) I did not receive my husband's pension check until a month after his death. On top of all this I had the ordeal of the funeral arrangements. I was very fortunate that my husband was a pastor and had known the funeral director, so I knew I could turn over the arrangements to him and I would not be taken advantage of. In some ways I think all the things a widow has to do is beneficial—you have to keep your wits about you."

Lorrie had not worked outside the home and was left relatively little insurance. Because the church had owned the home they lived in, she had no equity in a home to draw on.

"I knew trying to find a place to rent with four children would be next to impossible, so I took twenty thousand dollars of the insurance money and put it down on a home, financing another twenty-two thousand dollars. One of the members of the congregation, who was a loan officer at a bank, arranged a loan for me. That left me with enough insurance to live sparsely for two years.

"Fortunately another friend of mine operated a private school and, knowing I had taught Sunday School for years, let me join the staff as a teacher. Since it is a private school, I do not receive any benefits, such as insurance, and my salary is not large. My husband was ill for six years, and seeing first hand what medical bills can run into, I knew I must have medical insurance. All I can afford is a policy where all four of the children and myself have six hundred fifty dollars deductible. It was a good thing I purchased medical insurance since almost immediately one son had an emergency appendectomy and another son broke his foot. Even with the large deductible it certainly came in handy."

Asked what advice she would give to married women, Lorrie told us, "I would tell them to start to build a savings account, no matter what, and to get a degree in some field to fall back on. As a result of my husband's death, five of my friends went back to school and got their degrees. It is the best insurance you can have. If I hadn't had friends in the right places, so to speak, I don't know what I'd have done. It still isn't easy. I have had to take a second job, and if it weren't for that and Social Security, I wouldn't be able to make it. As it is, I'm barely making it now. With four children to raise and educate, I don't see much letup in my financial strain. As I said before, nothing really prepares you emotionally or financially for the loss of your husband or for the immediate decisions regarding the funeral arrangements you are faced with."

FUNERALS AND THE FUNERAL INDUSTRY

In preparing this chapter on widows, we had planned to mention funerals and funeral costs only briefly since these can put a sizable dent in your budget immediately after your husband's death. But in researching the information, we were so horrified by the way widows (and others) are taken advantage of by funeral homes and directors that we decided to discuss this subject more extensively.

The Federal Trade Commission's *Funeral Industry Practices Report* to the Bureau of Consumer Protections contains such vital information for widows and potential widows that we have included this information in the hopes it will spur you on to contact your congressman and urge him to support any federal regulations that are proposed as a result of this report.

The purchase of a funeral is one of the largest expenditures most consumers make in their lifetimes. But it is a purchase made out of necessity rather than choice. Frequently those forced into the role of funeral arranger are the grief-stricken spouses of the deceased. The emotional trauma of such a loss can profoundly influence the decisions that are made and the ability to make rational choices. Inexperience in making funeral arrangements and the unavailability of information contribute to a high level of consumer ignorance in this transaction. In addition, funeral decisions usually must be made under severe pressures. These factors make the funeral purchase markedly different from most other transactions.

The costs of funerals and the lack of laws regulating them are staggering. In the FTC's report, it took 526 pages to relate that there are virtually no federal regulations when it comes to licensing funeral homes and directors. There are state regulations in most states, but each state seems to go its own way. Finding out which state agency regulates funeral homes and directors is like figuring out a maze. The best you can hope for is to contact your state attorney general's office or your state capital and try to find out what agency regulates them in your state. Get in touch with that agency, and find out what is required by law in regard to funerals in your state.

At the core of state funeral regulations are the licensing requirements for funeral directors, embalmers, morticians (a combination funeral director/embalmer), and funeral establishments which can be found in every state. Different licensing schemes for each occupation have been adopted by most states.

Funeral Costs

There are $6.4 billion spent yearly on funerals in the United States. It is the third largest consumer purchase in this country. Funeral costs vary enormously according to the area of the country, the funeral home's individual price levels, the type of funeral services selected, and the specific merchandise and items purchased. These variations having been recognized, it is possible to outline generally what funeral costs are. It is important to realize, however, that these figures should not be interpreted as what a funeral *should* cost, only an approximation of what, on the average, typical funeral arrangements *do* cost.

The total cost of a funeral will be the sum of four different categories of charges. The first is the funeral home's basic charges for the services, facilities, casket, and several other items it provides in any "complete" adult funeral package. The second category consists of charges for products and services which the consumer may purchase from the funeral home, such as burial vault and burial clothing. The third category is comprised of the cemetery charges, including the charges for a grave site, monument, custodial care, and marker installation. The fourth category includes such items as an obituary notice and clergyman's services. It must be noted that funeral homes list these charges in many different ways. Read over what you are getting and the costs.

The most commonly selected form of funeral arrangements is the package of services and merchandise known as the traditional funeral. This package usually is priced as a unit and includes transporting and preparing the remains, a casket, use of the funeral home facilities and ceremony, the services of the funeral director and limousine, and other miscellaneous items, like guest book and memorial cards.

Surveys by funeral industry groups indicate that the average cost for the basic package and services associated with a traditional adult funeral is $2,000. Although consumers are likely not aware of it, the casket is the only real variable among the various packages offered since normally other services and facilities are about the same. Prices for coffins may range from $90 to $300 for a cloth-covered wood casket to thousands of dollars for bronze or copper sealer caskets.

This average cost of a funeral does not include expenses for final disposition, such as cemetery or interment charges. These run an average of $200.

These estimates also do not include the cost of the burial plot, which you must purchase *unless* you are having the body cremated. It is a good idea to purchase a burial plot before you are faced with a death. This allows you time to do some cost comparisons. Remember, if your husband was a veteran, he is entitled to be buried free. Check with the Veterans Administration.

You can usually pay funeral expenses off on the installment plan if your husband's insurance doesn't cover funeral expenses per se. Find out in advance if this is possible. Read over anything you sign carefully, and have someone you trust also read it over.

A fifty-eight-year-old widow who wished to remain anonymous told us that when her husband died three years ago, in a state other than where they lived, she was told she had to make arrangements to have the remains transported to her home state. She was informed of this not more than one hour after her husband's death. She had to call her hometown and make arrangements to have a funeral director there arrange to pick up the body the next morning.

Upon arriving back home, she was told to bring to the funeral home the clothes she wanted her husband buried in. At the same time she brought the clothes, she was to choose the casket and vault and to make arrangements to pay for it all. While she was still in a state of shock, the funeral director wrote up a contract, which she signed that morning. She could not pay cash because she had been left without insurance. She and her husband had not been able to afford it on the disability benefits which they had been living on for four and one-half years because of his illness.

About thirty days after the funeral the director came to her with the signed contract, saying a payment was due. She did not remember signing up for payments of $56.40 per month because she was unable to work, was on welfare, and was waiting for a widow's pension from the government. It took three months for the pension to come through, and it was for only $125 per month. There was no way she could make the payments of $56.40 on the funeral expenses even after she obtained a part-time job. (She cannot work full time because of her poor health.)

She is still being billed $56.40 a month and threatened with a lawsuit, but she pays only a little something on it each month. To this day she does not remember signing the contract. She asked us to advise a widow to turn the arrangements over to someone she trusts since it is virtually impossible to think clearly at a time like this.

In the *Funeral Industry Practices Report,* evidence and research in the area of bereavement make it clear that many funeral buyers are indeed disadvantaged and vulnerable when faced with funeral arrangements. This vulnerability has even been recognized by the courts. In a case involving the funeral bill as an expense charged against the estate of the deceased, one court contrasted the condition of consumer (buyer) and funeral director (seller).

One of the practical difficulties in such proceedings is that contracts for funerals are ordinarily made up by people in different situations. On the one side is generally a person greatly agitated or overwhelmed by deep sorrow, and on the other side persons whose business it is to minister to the dead for profit. One side is, therefore, often unbusinesslike, vague, and forgetful, while the other is ordinarily alert, knowing, and careful. The handicapped bargaining position of the funeral purchaser is the product of a number of different factors. The most significant of these are: emotional trauma, guilt, dependency and suggestibility, ignorance, and time pressure.

Dr. Collin Murray Parkes's study of recent widows noted that until the widow has taken in the fact of her bereavement, she seems, in the phase of numbness or shock, to be confused and disorganized. She has no plans that will enable her to cope with the situation and needs time and protection from intruders. In general, the first twenty-four hours are too soon for decisions to be made. The bereaved person is still in a state of numbness or shock and is not yet ready to come to grips with her confusion."

One woman told us, "As I think back on it, I had to be out of my mind. Don't you think you have to be in a state of shock? How else could I pick a coffin, decide what he should be buried in, and get through the funeral? Because I was in a daze, it was days before I realized I had agreed to an impossible financial obligation."

Psychologist and clergyman John Evans stated that "anyone . . . who has been responsible for making funeral arrangements for a close loved one knows that he is hardly aware of what he is doing."

Often it is during the height of this state of shock, numbness, and unreality that the widow must contact the undertaker and begin making funeral arrangements. During this immediate postdeath period, the bereaved will have to decide such questions as what funeral home to call, whether or not to have embalming performed, and if the disposition is going to be immediate or after several days of visitation and services. These decisions will be directly affected by the fact that the funeral customer may be experiencing the most intense of all human experiences.

Another symptom of bereavement which appears during this initial postdeath period and which may affect the widow's ability to make sound purchase decisions is guilt. In his study of the American funeral Dr. Leroy Bowman described the significance of guilt feelings in the funeral arrangements process in these terms:

> The most powerful, as well as the most universal force playing on the family at the time it meets the funeral director, is the sense of guilt. In the negotiations it is seldom, if ever, referred to and is undoubtedly unrecognized at the time as guilt. It is the inner drive, however, which responds most compulsively when the undertaker accuses the clients, by word or implication, of little love for the dead if the funeral falls short of most expensive outlay the family can scrape together.

The funeral industry has evidenced its recognition and use of the fact that the bereaved may seek to assuage guilt by providing a "suitable" funeral. The idea that the funeral is the last gift that can be given to the deceased has become a prominent bromide among funeral directors.

How the purchase will be viewed by friends and family is another dimension of the guilt reaction. It may be important to the funeral arranger experiencing guilt that others view his or her efforts as "having done right" by the deceased.

Thus, guilt feelings and related concerns may operate as the primary motivation for purchase of a particular type of funeral or specific products. Such feelings may lead to the purchase of an elaborate casket and services to impress the community or to an unwarranted expense for embalming, a sealer casket, and a vault in the belief that they will preserve and protect the remains. While the funeral purchase may provide an opportunity for resolution of these guilt feelings, it also creates a fertile field for exploitation.

Dr. Jeanne Quint Benoliel testified before the commission and cited the study by Glick, Weiss, and Parkes: "The bereaved person during the immediate post-death period often looks to other people for direction and guidance in making decisions about the funeral transactions." She noted further that "widows in particular were prone to look to the men in their immediate families for assistance in this matter, as well as to the funeral director from whom the purchase was made."

This tendency for the bereaved to rely on the funeral director is confirmed by other evidence. In a 1971 survey individuals were asked, "How did the funeral director assist you in making funeral arrangements?" Forty-one percent of the bereaved in this survey reported that they had asked the funeral director to "take over" all possible arrangements! The grief-stricken widow has also been described as having lost touch with social and economic reality in a way that is likely to lead to high expenditures on the funeral.

A former editor of *Mortuary Management,* one of the funeral industry's trade journals, testified that "those who are in a state of grief, of course, will not pay any attention to how they are led. They can be directed by the funeral director into what will be the most profitable for the funeral director. As a result of this suggestibility and dependency, the consumer may "select" a funeral by acquiescing to the suggestions and decisions made by the funeral director."

The vulnerability and suggestibility of the bereaved are compounded by the high level of consumer ignorance which characterizes the funeral transaction. In the ordinary consumer transaction the purchaser has available many kinds of information concerning prices, features, performance, durability, quality, general value, and alternatives to help make a decision. Available information varies among transactions. The consumer can usually defer the purchase decision until he acquires a level of information that is satisfactory.

The conditions in the funeral transaction are very different, for the consumer's access to relevant information is extremely limited.

Equally important is the consumer's lack of experience in making funeral arrangements. Since a funeral purchase is made infrequently, it is much harder for individuals to acquire useful, valid information by experience. One survey found that although most of the respondents had attended a funeral, 55 percent had never arranged a funeral before, and another 23 percent had done so only once.

Finally, at the time of a death, time pressures and the effects of grief severely restrict the time actively to seek out the necessary information. When a death occurs, therefore, the bereaved are forced to rely primarily on funeral directors as their source of information on prices, available alternatives, and what is practically or legally necessary.

A number of funeral directors acknowledged that consumers make funeral arrangements with limited information and knowledge. One funeral director stated: "It has been my experience that the bereaved are ignorant when making funeral arrangements. They know absolutely nothing about funeral costs. Usually they seem to think that the price and services stated are all that can be done and that they have no other recourse but to do what the funeral director recommends."

In a recent survey the findings showed 92 percent did not know whether (in their state) a casket was required by law, whether a burial vault was required by law, whether or not embalming (preserving the body) was required by law. For example, consumer testimony revealed that unknowledgeable funeral home customers have bought caskets when they did not need to. A Connecticut woman reported that while arranging a cremation, the funeral director showed her a $600 casket and told her the law required such a casket even with cremation.

Legal requirements for embalming have also been misrepresented. No state has an absolute legal requirement that the body must be embalmed in all circumstances. Yet countless consumers relate instances in which they were told by funeral directors that embalming was required by state law. A California consumer wrote: "My own experience included an undertaker who insisted that state law required embalming, which I later determined to be a gaudy lie."

At the end of the 526-page *Funeral Industry Practices Report*, proposed regulations for the industry are listed along with recommendations that they be adopted:

This report has shown that the proposed regulations will promote *consumer* choice of a particular funeral home, and selection of the method of final disposition and of the selection of merchandise and services. Consumers will be able to choose the type of funeral they want at a price that is consistent with their budget and desires.

This increased freedom to choose will greatly benefit the consumer, instead of the funeral director. Added to their gain in consumer welfare are the potential dollar savings which may be in the tens or hundreds of millions of dollars per year.

Moreover, the competitive environment forced by the rules may cause the geneal level of prices of funerals to decline. Thus, while exact calculations are impossible to make, the regulations have the potential to produce a tremendous increase in overall consumer welfare.

We certainly hope so, but in the meantime, if you are faced with a death:

First and foremost, realize that you are not required by law to have a funeral. You must have the body disposed of by cremation or burial, but you are not required to have a funeral.

Find out what agency in your state regulates and licenses funeral homes and directors. Contact that agency to find out what is required by law in your state.

If you wish a permanent burial site, purchase a burial plot before a death occurs, so you have time to do some comparison shopping and not have to purchase one hurriedly and under duress.

If you feel you cannot handle the arrangements yourself, pick someone you trust to do it for you, but make sure he is knowledgeable of the funeral laws in your state.

If you arrange to pay off the funeral in installments, take the contract home overnight, and read every word of it. Have someone you trust also read it.

Don't be talked into a larger or grander funeral than you can afford because of grief, guilt, or ignorance. To be brutally frank about it, your husband will not know the difference, and if he did, he would probably prefer you and the children to have food on the table.

16

Specifics for Specific Women

In preparing this book, we have included a lot of general information that can apply to a variety of women. But there are specific facts that particular women should keep in mind.

THE BACK-TO-SCHOOL WOMAN

If you have decided to go back to school but do not have any money, aside from the scholarships (which are mostly available to those under twenty-five), there are ways you can finance an education.

There are other sources of aid for you, as a woman, besides a government loan. Women's professional associations, foundations, civic groups, or service clubs all offer assistance in various areas, especially if you are a displaced homemaker. Check with the Women's Business and Professional Association or Chamber of Commerce in your area for women's groups in your community. Numerous cities across the country, colleges, and junior colleges have women's centers which can provide a wealth of financial information as well as the usual career guidance. Women's Opportunity Centers have information on financing an education.

Naturally the federal government is one of the largest sources of student financial aid in our country today. The government provides basic educational opportunity grants and national direct student loans, among others.

The most thorough way for you to learn about what type of loan is available to you is to make an appointment with the financial aid officer at the school you would like to attend. Or you can go to the reference librarian at your local library and request whatever information the library has on the subject of student loans. The former method will probably supply the more practical information, on how to apply, how the school is involved, etc.

If you have ever served in the armed forces, you have another source of aid. Irene Kendall was in the Air Force for four years. She is now using her educational veteran's benefits to pay the tuition at college toward her degree in psychology.

You should be aware that a scholarship gives you money that does not need to be paid back; a grant gives you money that is also a gift, and no repayment is necessary. A loan, however, will have to be repaid. Generally you will be allowed up to ten years to pay back the loan, and you are charged no interest rate while you are in school. Once you begin repaying after you are working, you will be charged a nominal interest rate on the unpaid balance.

We know of women who, because of their debt situation, although many times through no fault of their own, have been denied student loans or government financial aid. We don't have a remedy for this. We can only hope there will someday be an equitable solution. But if you feel you are in need of education, a higher degree, or a new career field, all we can say is that if you want it badly enough and strive toward that goal, you'll attain it.

Nine years ago Judithe Goldberg was thirty-one years old and a divorcée with two small children. She felt if she didn't have an education, she would not be able to support herself and her family adequately. She had been married to a very wealthy man who had had her not only unsuspectingly sign away her share of money in loan documents but made her solely liable for repayment. Her husband became addicted to drugs, and his fortune dwindled away. After Judithe divorced him, he left the country, saddling her with all the debts. She eventually declared bankruptcy. For four years Judithe and her children lived in student housing on a college campus, while she worked as a janitor, taught a class in slimnastics, and even became a go-go dancer for a short period of time in order to finance her education. Judithe has a successful business today as a financial planner, but at one point in her life her education was more than difficult to finance.

THE NEVER-MARRIED WOMAN

The days of the stereotyped Miss Dove, the old-maid school-teacher, are no longer applicable. Many women choose to remain single. The careers now open to women, in many cases, allow a woman the freedom of remaining single by choice. Yet there are facts which must be dealt with if you, the single woman, are to survive financially.

You must consider the need for a will. After you are gone, who will be responsible for disposing of your possessions? Do you want to leave your favorite piece of jewelry to your sister's daughter Penny? Do you want to set up a fund to provide a medical scholarship for a deserving student at your university? None of this will or can be done without a proper will. Moreover, if you die intestate and have no heirs, everything you own will escheat (go back) to the state.

So that you will not be a financial burden to anyone, you should have adequate health and disability insurance on yourself, enough life insurance to bury you, plus to pay your estate taxes when you die, and, of course, adequate auto insurance. Establish a retirement plan for yourself. Even if you have a retirement plan through your company employment, you can make investments in annuities, for example, which will shelter any income received through that annuity. If your company does not have a retirement plan available, start one yourself, using the Individual Retirement Account. If you are self-employed and have not already done so, start a Keogh plan. (See the retirement chapter.)

It is imperative that you establish credit as soon as you are financially able to do so. If nothing else, get some bank accounts started in your own name.

You should consult a tax expert in regard to the many changes that affect singles. Check into the possibility of purchasing property versus renting. You will not only be building equity but have a deduction for your income tax. If you are renting, read over any lease you sign carefully. Find out what it takes to break the lease, or for what reasons you can be evicted, *before* you sign. Get a receipt for any monies you put out for the first and last months' rent and cleaning deposit. Find out how much notice you must give in order to move and how much notice you will be given if you are requested to do so.

Be sure to establish some kind of savings plan either through a passbook account at a savings and loan or through your credit union. You have only yourself to look to for an income, so in case of emergency it would be nice to have a fund to draw on.

Learn to make simple home and car repairs yourself so you are not at the mercy of unscrupulous repairmen. Keep adequate records of all your financial dealings.

Pia van der Hiede is thirty-four and lives in New York City. She is single and has no plans for marriage. Happy with her life-style, Pia is contemplating buying some real property, either a condo in the city or a house in the country. She earns $19,000 a year, has $12,000 in savings accounts, and has a securities portfolio worth just about that much. "I learned a long time ago I wanted to stand on my own two feet, and I established financial goals to help me get there. Since my financial situation is secure, I'm pleased to be in a position of being able to choose whether I want to marry or not, not having to for financial security."

THE MARRIED OR ABOUT-TO-BE-MARRIED WOMAN

If you are planning to be married, have all your ideas regarding money, work, and bank accounts and changing your name established prior to "tying the knot," or marital bliss may become marital blight. The matter of changing your name or not changing your name is really a matter of choice. Legally and financially there is not any great legal advantage to keeping your own name except it is easier if you already have credit under your own name, and it is more convenient if the marriage breaks up. If you opt to go by your married name, notify any agencies or companies where you do business. Keep some credit standing in your maiden name and married name—June Wendover Smith, not Mrs. James Smith, and if you do change it, notify the Social Security Administration immediately; otherwise, your earnings may not be properly credited.

If you are a married nonworking wife, become aware of what your husband is doing in the way of finance whether or not you handle the money. Don't think it is cute not to be able to do such

things as balance the checkbook. It is extremely important for you to
establish credit in your own name; it will save you time and effort if
you do divorce or are widowed. Know where your important papers
are kept. Know the name of your lawyer (if applicable), insurance
agent, tax consultant, and any other financial people you and your
husband deal with. Know what retirement and insurance benefits
your husband has through his work. Don't sign anything without
reading it, even if your husband has already done so. Be aware that
it is a good idea to have life and disability insurance on yourself. You
are a valuable commodity to your family, and your services as a
homemaker would be costly to replace. Look into establishing your
own retirement plan. In many cases this can be done through your
husband's employment. To put it in a nutshell, the most important
thing for you is to "tune in" on the family finances. We have given
you numerous examples throughout the book of women who failed
to do this and have paid dearly for it.

If you are a married working woman, along with the advice above,
you will want to discuss with your husband and a tax consultant
whether it is more to your advantage to file a single or joint income
tax return. This can make quite a difference in the refund or amount
of money you pay. Remember, according to law, your income as
well as your husband's must be considered when you purchase
property. Check on mortgage redemption insurance. If you or your
husband should die, the home would be paid for free and clear.
Women who have not been employed long enough to earn pensions
of their own are becoming eligible for benefits under their husbands' retirement plan. The Pension and Reform Act of 1974 requires all employees covered by retirement plans to be allowed to
sign up for spousal benefits as soon as they are eligible for the plan.
You or your husband could receive lifelong pension benefits even if
one of you dies before retirement. Check with the benefits or personnel department of your and your husband's place of employment. It is a good idea to have your own insurance program through
your employment. If you do have a change in marital status, you
will have your own plan already established.

If you are a married woman who has learned next to nothing
about finance and has begun to think about what would happen if
your husband should predecease you, you should discuss with him
the possibility of setting up a trust to manage the assets he accumulated during his lifetime with you. The trustee (person who takes
care of your trust) will attend to all the routine but vital chores that
have confronted your family, from making investment decisions to
paying hospital bills.

THE "LIVING-TOGETHER" WOMAN

If you and your man have decided to skip marriage and live together, you should consider setting up a few safeguards for yourself in case the bloom wears off and you go your separate ways. It is a very good idea to keep separate financial arrangements. Keep your checking and savings accounts, credit cards, loans, and property in your own name. *Have a written agreement concerning finances* (who will pay what, will you split the costs, etc.). More and more lawyers are drawing up living-together agreements for couples who do not wish to marry. For example, California attorney Paul Garber and Roger Renfro, pension consultants, have devised a living-together contract they call an Unmarriage Agreement. They are now specializing in this area and have formed a business called Unmarriage Unlimited.

If you are not working and will be depending on your man for your livelihood (a poor idea in our opinion), it is a *must* that you have a written contract with some financial provisions in it for you. If you are doing his cooking, cleaning, laundry, etc., your services are worth something—especially if you have given up a job to stay home and do them.

It is important to establish these arrangements before you move in together.

You may remember the case of movie star Lee Marvin and his live-in actress Michelle Triolo, who gave up her career for him. When he left her for his childhood sweetheart, she sued him, claiming she had performed the duties of a wife and should be entitled to some compensation. While she did not receive what she asked for, she was awarded $140,000, setting a precedent in the state of California. Though aspects of this case are still pending, it established the groundwork for some financial guidelines for couples who do not wish to marry but would like to cohabitate.

One reason couples are deciding to live together (besides personal life-style choice) may be due to our tax structure. Often a couple is better off, taxwise, living together rather than marrying. (If you'll excuse the pun, marriage can often be taxing.) This is especially true when both partners earn roughly the same income. However, the tax advantages decrease when one partner earns a great deal less than the other. Marriage is the less expensive option—taxwise— when one member of the couple earns nothing at all.

Other points to remember when you decide to live with someone else:

Don't cosign any contract papers that put you in debt, because you will be responsible for the debt if your partner decides not to make the payments. If you have a joint checking account, remember he can write a check and close out the account. Have your own insurance plan on yourself, and list yourself as the head of household. At the risk of sounding unromantic, relationships can be "here today and gone tomorrow," so you must be realistic.

Danielle R. wishes she had faced reality. "I was 'in love,' so I wouldn't have dreamed of talking about money. What emotions can do to your intelligence is amazing! I met Patrick in my line of work—advertising sales—when we both happened to call on a prospective client at the same time. He was just getting started in this line of work, while I was my company's top sales representative. We were attracted to each other immediately, and even though he was living with a woman, we began a relationship. Before long he moved in with me. As he was just starting out, and sales is an off-again, on-again business, I agreed to pay the rent and lend him money for a car. We had such an 'honest relationship' that I believed him when he told me he would start paying me back. I even got him a job with my firm and—you guessed it—after a few months he began to take over my clients, then moved in with one of them who owned her own business.

"I did manage to have him fired, but I figure all in all he cost me almost ten thousand dollars. It was an expensive but excellent lesson. I don't care how hard I 'fall in love' next time; I'll get the financial arrangements in writing. If a man really loves me, he is not going to object, and if he does object, I need to know that about him. Who knows? I may even change my mind about marriage. At least I would have more legal rights."

THE ABOUT-TO-BE OR
ALREADY DIVORCED WOMAN

Divorce laws vary too widely from state to state for us to give you specific divorce advice. Also, individual situations are unique to the particular couple involved. There is, however, some general advice for women who are about to be, or already are, divorced.

Dr. Pamela Bigelow, executive director of the Women's Law Center in Tustin, California, stated, "A woman who is suing, or being sued, for divorce, should not sign any document without seeing a lawyer—her own lawyer, not her husband's. This is true even if the divorce is a so-called friendly one. Women very often allow themselves to be intimidated and sign away what is rightfully theirs. Unfortunately, to be realistic, you should view your husband as your adversary from the minute you contemplate divorce. This does not mean he is your enemy, but he is your adversary when it comes to financial matters.

"The *average* lawyer's fee for an uncontested divorce is sixteen hundred dollars. Who pays this varies, depending on your settlement, but often a woman's first moment of freedom includes a lawyer's fee to be paid. A woman should find a lawyer she is comfortable with—and remember, you can fire a lawyer if you are not comfortable with him/her.

"A woman can call her local chapter of the National Organization for Women (NOW) for a recommendation of a lawyer. A woman who wishes to get a divorce, but cannot afford one, should also contact NOW or a law clinic if she is fortunate enough to have one in her town."

Ms. Bigelow also feels that a woman should ask for enough support money in her settlement to continue her education toward a career. "If you just get a 'job,' you will be locked into it until God knows when. Also, a woman should ask her husband to keep medical insurance on the children under his place of employment so he will be responsible for paying the premiums. It is a good idea to get life, medical, and disability insurance on yourself and list yourself as head of household. If you are contributing more than half the support of the children (and most divorced women are since the *average* child support payment is fifty dollars per child per month), you should claim the children as dependents at your place of employment."

Ms. Bigelow feels women should be aware that divorce is very costly for women. "Most women, contrary to what you hear, do not receive much in a divorce settlement. It infuriates me when people say this is a result of the feminist movement. It is male legislators who are still 'punishing women' for getting a divorce."

For the woman contemplating divorce, she advises, "Get some credit in your own name, and open a separate checking and savings account. In a community property state your husband can claim part of the funds in any joint account, or he can clear out an entire account. In general, I would say to all married women, 'Start being realistic. Know your financial situations, and have some safeguards to protect yourself. It's not that you should expect a divorce at any time, but it is a possibility in any marriage.'" Ms. Bigelow went on to relate, "I see so many women who are caught totally off guard.

One woman we helped at the center had never even grocery shopped. Her husband had done all that. When he left her high and dry, we had to teach her literally how to make change. Though it is an extreme case, we commonly see cases such as that of a woman I met a year or so ago when I was speaking to a women's group on the subject of finance and credit, urging them to establish credit in their own names. She sat in the front row and was obviously not interested in what I was saying since she was talking quite loudly to her friend next to her. I stopped my speech and asked the woman if she was listening. She replied, 'Not really. I'm talking about what kind of pie I'm going to make for my husband when I get home.' I was rather perplexed why she had come in the first place.

"Several months later this same woman was in the law center distraught. Her husband had left her for another woman. She did not have the least idea of what to do or of her financial status. She did admit, 'I never thought it would happen to me. I should have listened to you, and at least I would have known what was going on financially in my own home.'"

Some general advice we would add or reiterate for the divorcée is: Realize you will be in a traumatized state even if you are the one that wants the divorce. Try not to make any major financial decisions until you can emotionally cope. Get into a retirement plan. Change your insurance and tax status to read "Head of Household." Consult a tax expert or the IRS to find out the new and ever changing laws regarding child support and alimony. If at all possible, develop a savings plan. Put any monies you have received in a settlement in a savings account to draw interest. Then get some reliable investment advice. Don't rush into major decisions, such as selling your home (if you receive it in a settlement), until you are sure it is what you need or want to do. If you haven't done so already, change any bank accounts and charge accounts to your own name. We could go on and on with examples of women who have had terrible financial experiences in divorce proceedings; but let us just say again: Get your own lawyer, and do not sign *anything* without his/her approval.

EVERYWOMAN

There are certain specifics we sincerely hope every woman will remember and apply:

1. Take the time and the effort to be aware of your financial situation whether you are single or married.

2. Keep up-to-date financial records, and know where all your important papers are kept.
3. Establish a regular savings plan.
4. Establish credit in your own name.
5. When seeking a job, prepare yourself for filling out the job application and being interviewed.
6. If you face job discrimination or sexual harassment on the job, take the proper steps to rectify it.
7. Provide yourself with adequate insurance—life, health, disability, auto.
8. Don't sign any documents without reading, and understanding, them.
9. Ask for credentials and references from any financial expert you consult.
10. Consider purchasing a home so you can begin to build equity.
11. Be a financially aware wife, so you will not be a financially uneducated widow or divorcée.
12. Take the time and effort to make out a will.
13. Know what your Social Security will provide for you, so you can help augment plans for your future.
14. Set up a retirement plan.
15. Do some homework before you purchase a car.
16. Either learn to prepare your own income tax, or find a reputable expert to do it for you.
17. Learn about the stock market and other forms of investments whether you decide to invest a dollar or thousands of dollars.
18. Balance your checkbook and statement regularly.
19. Set up and stay on a budget.
20. Familiarize yourself with financial terms.

BECOME A FINANCIALLY AWARE WOMAN

The many women we interviewed for this book told us, without exception, that they wished they had been more financially aware at an earlier date. In conducting interviews with many people who deal with finance, we found that as always, the experts tend to disagree. But they, too, felt that women must play, or continue to play, an ever-increasing role in financial matters. To quote financial planner Judithe Goldberg, "Men are conditioned to be wise in the ways of the world, women have not paid much attention and they must start."

Glossary of Financial Terms

abstract | A summary of the history of the legal title to a piece of property.

accrue | To grow, accumulate; to become one's permanent right, such as the interest earned on money in savings accounts.

acquisition | Something obtained, such as a piece of property.

amortize | To pay off a debt through periodic payments of equal amounts.

annuity | A type of investment offered by insurance companies, providing a guaranteed income for life, with payments received at regular intervals.

applicant | An individual who applies for credit.

appraisal | An impartial determination of property value.

appraiser | An expert in establishing current market value for property such as a house, jewelry, or antiques, depending on his specialty.

appreciation | Increase in the dollar value of an asset over time.

assets | All forms of property, real and personal, owned by a person or a business.

balloon payment	A final loan payment which is substantially larger than any previous payments.
basic coverage	A type of homeowner's insurance policy that covers property against losses caused by perils such as fire, windstorm, explosion, smoke, vandalism, and theft.
beneficiary	The recipient of the death benefits of a life insurance policy.
benefits	The amount of money left to a surviving relative (or friend) by the deceased.
bequeath	To give or leave property by means of a will.
bill of sale	A receipt that shows how much money was paid for an item.
bonding	A guarantee through an insurance policy of protection from any losses which one might suffer during the building or remodeling of one's home.
capital assets	Stocks, bonds, automobiles, household furnishings, and jewelry.
cash flow	The cash surplus generated from an investment irrespective of the amount of taxable profit involved.
cash surrender value	The amount of money one is entitled to if cash value life insurance premiums are discontinued; not used to buy protection, but held by the insurance company as one's savings.
certificate of deposit	A time deposit requiring a stated minimum to invest, which yields a higher return than a passbook savings account.
chain of title	The record of previous ownership of a property.
chartered institution	Financial organization that has received either state or federal approval for its existence.
charitable remainder trust	A trust that has a qualified charity as its beneficiary.
claim	A policyholder's demand for benefits in accordance with his insurance contract or another person's contract.
closing	Period when real property changes ownership from seller to buyer.
closing costs	The cost of necessary transactions when a real estate purchase or sale is completed.
co-insurance clause	For property insurance, a provision informing the insured that he must buy insurance coverage

	for at least 80 percent of the value of the property being insured in order to receive full payment of claims up to the face amount of the policy. For health insurance (usually major medical policies), a provision requiring the insured to share with his insurance company expenses arising from a claim.
collateral	Assets which may be used to pledge repayment of (secure) a loan.
commission	A fee paid to an agent or employee for transacting some business or performing a service, usually a percentage of the money involved in the transaction.
community property	Personal and real property held jointly by a husband and wife. In a community property state, it is property accumulated during a marriage and belonging equally to each spouse, unless it was an inheritance or a gift to a particular spouse.
concealed costs	Costs that are not clearly stated in a buying contract for which the consumer will ultimately have to pay.
condominium	A type of homeownership; a home unit where one or more walls may be common with another unit.
co-signer	An individual who signs someone else's loan and becomes equally responsible for it.
consumer	One of the buying public.
contract	The signed document which is drawn up when two parties agree to certain contingencies and obligations.
contractor	Person who supplies materials or performs services in building or home construction.
conventional loan	A loan made without government assistance.
convertible term insurance	A term policy that can be converted into a whole life policy or other cash value type of plan without a new medical check. Most insurance companies offer term policies that are both convertible and renewable.
credit	(1) Ability to purchase or borrow on trust; (2) Loans of money or goods on the promise of ability and willingness to repay.
credit bureau	An agency which collects consumer credit information from its members and provides this in-

formation to members for use in evaluating credit applications.

credit history
The record of an individual's borrowing and payments.

creditor
An individual or company to whom money is owed.

credit union
An organization composed of members with a common interest who bind together to offer loans to each other at rates lower than they might be able to obtain otherwise.

credit worthiness
Ability and willingness to repay as shown in credit history.

deductible clause
A provision in a property, auto, or health insurance contract that directs the insured to pay the amount of any loss up to a certain limit above which the insurance company will pay the balance.

deduction
Expenditures that can be subtracted from income when computing taxes.

deed
A document used to offer proof of ownership of property.

deferred annuity
An annuity in which the income is not payable until several years in the future.

deferred employment benefits
A program whereby a company sets aside a small percentage of funds and each employee is credited with a portion of the fund according to his wage or salary level and/or length of employment.

depositor
Person who puts money into an account.

depreciation
Decline in the dollar value of a car over a period of time, and amount of wear through use.

discount
Monies deducted from the original asking price or value price of consumer goods.

disposable income
Income available for personal spending after payment of taxes.

diversification
The principle of reducing risk by spreading money among several different types of investment.

dividend
A share of profits, distributed to a person as a stockholder.

down payment
The monies put down as a deposit toward the purchase price of real property.

easement
A right or privilege a person or entity may have to one s property.

endowment insurance	A type of cash value life insurance in which savings accumulate more rapidly than in other types of similar insurance.
ERISA	Employee Retirement Income Security Act of 1974.
escrow	In some states the process by which property is placed in the safekeeping of a third party until the first and second parties to a transaction have successfully completed it.
escrow company	The company which acts as the third party.
estate	Financial resources and personal assets left upon death; also one's ownership interest in all forms of property.
estate tax	A tax levied on the transfer of rights to property in an estate.
executor	The person appointed in a will and appro ʒd by a probate court to administer the disposition of an estate according to directions in the will.
exemption	The amount a taxpayer is allowed to deduct for oneself and for each dependent, including certain circumstances: the total of which is deducted from income to determine taxable income.
face value	The dollar value that expresses coverage limits; it appears on the front of the policy.
FICA	Abbreviation for Federal Insurance Contributions Act; the Social Security payroll deduction.
fiduciary	Person who controls employee benefit plans and makes investment decisions; a trustee.
finance charge	The amount paid by a purchaser for interest on money borrowed and charges for the carrying costs of the money lent.
financial district	Area where there is a concentration of firms that deal with money.
financial plan	A methodical arrangement for investing and saving money.
financial position	The monetary condition of a company.
fiscal year	The accounting year for a company, which is not necessarily January 1 to December 31.
fixed expenses	Expenses, such as monthly rent or mortgage payments, that must be paid at regular intervals and in fairly set amounts.

fixed rate	The set amount of interest one pays during the lifetime of one's mortgage.
foreclosure	The legal process which can force the sale of one's property in case of default on payments.
gross income	The amount of income earned before deductions.
group insurance	Insurance (either health, life, auto, liability, or property) written for a specific group of people. A master policy is issued by the insurance company covering the whole group; members of the group are issued agreements that tie them to the master policy. Reduced administration costs and savings caused by favorable loss experience for the group as a whole generally make these policies less expensive than individually written policies.
guaranteed insurability option	An option, sold with cash value policy, that allows the policyholder to purchase additional insurance at specified ages and amounts without having to meet medical qualifications. The option is designed to assure the policyholder that she/he will be able to obtain more insurance at regular rates even if his/her health fails.
guild	Group of persons that join together to pursue common interests.
holographic will	A will written entirely in the handwriting of the person making it.
impound account	Special account which withholds a portion of money to be used for the payment of insurance and property taxes.
inflation	A rise in the general level of prices caused by an increasing demand for commodities and services that are available.
interest	The cost of borrowing money, or the payment an investor receives from a bank or similar institution for lending it his/her money.
interest rate	The percentage charged for borrowing money, or the percentage received for lending money.
intestate	Leaving no will.
invalid will	A will that is improperly drawn or is lacking some conditions.
investment portfolio	The combination of stocks and bonds a person may own.

IRA	Individual Retirement Account, which can be established by any person who is employed and does not have a company retirement plan.
IRS	Abbreviation for the Internal Revenue Service.
joint tenancy	A way to own property in which two or more persons each own a percentage but not a specific piece of said property.
Kelly Blue Book	A book available at financing institutions that lists the book value (resale value) of cars by year.
Keogh	The name of the retirement plan which can be set up by a self-employed individual. It is also known as an HR-10 plan.
legacy	A gift of personal property made in a will.
lending institution	Savings and loan, or commercial bank, where real estate loan may be obtained.
lending policy	The established criteria for making loans.
liability	The extent to which one may be subject to punishment under the law for interference with another person's rights as recognized in the Bill of Rights. Also, an obligation to pay one's current debts—i.e., bills, loans, balances due on charge accounts, or mortgages on a home.
liability insurance	A form of coverage that protects a policyholder against claims derived from any sort of negligence on his/her part.
lien	A claim, recorded against property, as security for payment of a debt.
line of credit	The maximum amount of credit a lender will extend to a borrower at any one time.
liquid assets	All property owned by a person or a business that can easily be converted into cash at a readily determinable fair market price—e.g., savings accounts, stocks and bonds, cash value of life insurance.
listed security	A stock or bond that trades on an organized exchange.
living trust	A trust that is put into use during one's lifetime.
long-range planning	Charting a course of financial action for later years.
management company	Company that manages a mutual fund.
maturity	The period of time for which a mortgage is written.

Medicare	The popular name of a government health plan for financing medical care for persons sixty-five years of age or over. It consists of hospital insurance and supplementary medical insurance.
modification	A small adjustment.
money market	Colloquial term for the large pools of lendable funds that exist in the economy.
mortality rate	A set of statistics indicating how many people per thousand die at various ages. It can be used to determine one's life expectancy at any age.
mortgage	The amount of money owed on your real property.
mortgage market	A phrase coined by the real estate and banking industry used to describe the economic conditions for real estate loans.
multiple listing service	Listing service which is organized for members to share real estate listings with other members.
mutual fund	An investment company that uses the proceeds from the public sale of its shares to invest in various securities for the benefit of its public shareholders.
net income	Income, minus expenses, taxes, interest, and depreciation.
notary public	A licensed person who verifies a signature.
odometer	The device on a car that records the amount of miles traveled in said car.
optional features	Items, such as radio, heater, air conditioning, that one may not wish to purchase when buying a car.
overdraft	The difference between money on deposit in the bank and the amount of money checks have been written for.
overinsurance	Insurance in an amount that exceeds the amount of potential loss.
package policy	An insurance contract (normally property) that combines several types of coverage. A homeowner's policy, for example, combines property coverage with liability and medical coverage.
passbook account	Standard savings account offered by a bank or savings and loan association, which offers interest.

pension	The amount of financial resources set aside to provide income benefits at a future date, usually upon retirement.
personal property	Any asset owned that does not include real estate —e.g., money, furniture, stock certificates.
plan administrator	Person who handles a retirement plan.
points	A point is 1 percent of the amount of the loan paid at the time the loan is made or when the loan is paid off ahead of due date.
prepayment penalty	A clause in a note which provides for a penalty in the event of an early payoff of the note.
prequalifying	Meeting of requirements before they are necessary, e.g., filling out a loan application and knowing one is eligible for a loan before one needs to take out a loan.
principal mortgage	First mortgage; senior security in the form of real property offered by borrower to lender to obtain a loan on a piece of property.
private lender	Any individual or institution other than the U.S. government from whom one can obtain a loan.
probate	The legal procedure that establishes the validity of a will and ensures that the will's provisions will be carried out.
profit sharing	A plan some companies have that enables an employee to share in the company profits.
proof of ownership	A written statement or copy of a document that proves that one owns something.
provision	The part of an agreement referring to one specific contingency.
real estate agent	Person licensed to buy and sell real estate.
real estate market	The listings of property which are available for sale.
real property	Any real estate owned—e.g., a home, a vacant lot.
reducing or decreasing term	A term policy the face amount of which is reduced in stages over a prescribed period. The reduction is usually scheduled so as to leave enough face amount at any point to pay off a debt, such as a mortgage or installment loan, or to provide a certain minimum income to the beneficiary.

replacement value	The amount of money that would have to be paid today to replace an object with a new one; this value is acceptable to property insurers only when used to determine the amount of insurance needed for physical structures, such as the home. Also called replacement cost.
resale	Real property which has had a previous owner.
reverse annuity	The process whereby one mortgages one's home to a lending institution in return for which it pays him/her a fixed monthly amount for a period of years. One resides as a tenant during that time.
revolving credit	A continuing line of credit.
rollover	A process whereby funds from a terminated retirement plan may be placed in a private individual retirement account.
sales contract	Purchase agreement.
sales documents	Papers used as evidence of purchase and sale.
scheduled property	Personal property that is described and given an appropriate value, article by article, on the face of an insurance policy rather than lumped together under general property coverage.
second mortgage	A loan secured by an interest in real property. This loan is subordinate to the principal mortgage.
securities	Stocks, bonds, notes.
securities industry	The name given to those companies that buy and sell stocks, bonds, and mutual funds.
separate property	Real or personal property which belongs to only one spouse.
special coverage	A type of homeowner's insurance policy that covers all risks to a house with the exception of personal property.
sticker price	The price posted on a new car (usually on a sticker on the side window).
stock certificate	A document which is evidence of ownership in a company.
subcontractor	Person hired by a contractor to supply materials or perform services in building or home construction.
"take back"	A phrase used in the real estate industry to describe the seller holding a second mortgage rather than the buyer having to go out and find the necessary money.

tax liability	The amount of tax one is responsible for paying.
tax shelter	An investment that offers certain income tax advantages; tax-exempt, not subject to federal or state income tax.
tax write-off	An investment loss which can be offset against gross income.
tenants by entirety	Joint owners of property who are husband and wife.
tenants in common	Two or more owners of a piece of real property.
term insurance	A policy that insures one's life for a specified number of years and then must be renewed to be kept in force. Term sells for considerably lower premiums than whole life.
testamentary trust	A trust which is created by provisions of a will and goes into effect upon the death of the person who made the will.
tight money	Words used to describe the scarcity of loanable funds. This scarcity contributes to high borrowing costs.
title	The evidence of one's legal right to possession of property, usually in the form of a deed.
title insurance	Insurance to protect one against any loss if the title to one's home is imperfect.
title search	The process of checking title records to make sure that one is buying a home from the legal owner and that there are no liens or defects in the title.
town house	A type of home, generally one that has little or no outdoor landscaping or upkeep. It can be either a condominium or planned unit development type of ownership.
trade-in	The car turned in as down payment on another car.
transfer agent	An institution—e.g., a bank—that is authorized by a corporation to administer and record the transfer of its stocks or bonds between investors.
treasury bill	A negotiable debt obligation issued by the federal government.
trust	A legal contract for the management and control of certain assets held by one person for the benefit of another.

trustee	An individual or organization legally responsible for managing a trust.
vested	One's right to money accumulated for retirement purposes that cannot be taken away from one.
warranty	An assurance by the seller that the car is, or shall be, as it was represented or promised to be at the time of sale.
W-4 Form	A form an employee fills out which indicates how many deductions are to be made from his/her paycheck.
W-2 Form	Record received by an employee from his/her employer showing the amount of income earned and the amount withheld from his/her earnings during the year for income tax purposes.
zoning	City or county rules which restrict the use of specific pieces of real property.

Bibliography

Abstracts of State Day Care Licensing, Part 1; Family Day Care Homes. Department of Health, Education and Welfare, Office of Child Development, 1971.

Abstracts of State Day Care Licensing and Requirements, Part 2; Day Care Centers. Department of Health, Education and Welfare, Office of Child Development, 1971.

Booth, S. Lees. a research paper. *Industrial Banking Companies*, Washington, D.C., October 1978.

Common Sense to Buying a New Car. Office of Public and Consumer Affairs, U.S. Department of Transportation, April 1978.

Common Sense to Buying a Safe Used Car. U.S. Department of Transportation; February 1976.

Control Your Debts Booklet. National Association of Chapter 13 Trustees, 1976.

Copley News Service; reprints of *You and Your Money;* columns by Judith Rhoades.

Department of Health, Education and Welfare, Social Security Administration; various pamphlets.

Educational Attainment of Workers, Special Labor Force Report 209. United States Department of Labor, Bureau of Labor Statistics, March, 1977.

Employment in Perspective; Working Women, Report 531. United States Department of Labor, April 1978.

The Family Banker Newsletter, published by Continental Bank, Chicago, Illinois.

Federal Home Loan Bank Board Journal, July 1978.

Federal Interagency Day Care Requirements. United States Department of Labor; 1968.

Financial Facts of Widowhood. Anchor National Financial Service, Inc.; 1977.

Financing an Education. United States Department of Health, Education and Welfare.

The Food Stamp Program. United States Department of Agriculture, Washington, D.C., 1978.

Funeral Industries Practices. Bureau of Consumer Affairs, Federal Trade Commission, Final Staff Report, June, 1978.

A Guide to Budgeting for the Family. United States Department of Agriculture, 1978.

Information on balancing your checkbook, reprinted from Bank of America NT & SA, *How to Balance Your Checkbook*. CONSUMER INFORMATION REPORT No. 1, Copyright 1975.

The Labor Force Patterns of Divorced and Separated Women. Special Labor Force Report 198. United States Department of Labor, Bureau of Labor Statistics.

Marital and Family Characteristics of the Labor Force, Special Labor Force Report 206. United States Department of Labor, July 1978.

Mature Women Workers: A Profile. United States Department of Labor, Employment Standards Administration, Women's Bureau, 1976.

Occupations in Demand. United States Department of Labor, July 1978.

Policy Issues in Day Care, Summaries of Twenty-one Papers. Center for Systems and Program Development, Inc., November 1977.

Prepared Statement of Bruce A. Hubbard, Esq.; The Harlem Lawyers Association, Inc.; Hearings before the Assembly, Standing Committee on Banks, The Assembly, State of New York, on Alternative Mortgage Instruments, New York, N.Y., October 18, 1977.

Savings and Loan Fact Book. Savings and Loan League; 111 East Wacker Drive; Chicago, Illinois 60601.

Selecting and Financing a Home. United States Department of Agriculture Home and Garden Bulletin, No. 182, 1977.

Smith, Dr. David L. *Alternative Mortgage Instruments, an Invited Paper*. Federal Home Loan Bank Board, San Francisco, California.

Some Sources of Information, Planning for Retirement, prepared jointly by the Administration on Aging, HEW, and the Consumer Information Center, GSA, Washington, D.C.

Starting and Managing a Small Business of Your Own. Small Business Administration; Washington, D.C., 1973.

United States Department of Health, Education and Welfare, Social Security Administration; Washington, D.C.; various brochures and pamphlets.

Wall Street Journal, Archives, University of California at Irvine.

Wise Home Buying, United States Department of Housing and Urban Development, June 1976.

A Woman's Guide to Buying a Used Car. Hertz Corporation pamphlet.

A Woman's Guide to Social Security. United States Department of Health, Education and Welfare.

Women: To Your Credit, published by Commercial Credit Corporation, Baltimore, Maryland, 1976.

Women's Rights Handbook. California Department of Justice Information Services, Los Angeles, California.

Work Experience of the Population in 1975, Special Labor Force Report 192. United States Department of Labor, Bureau of Labor Statistics.

Your Social Security Number. United States Department of Health, Education and Welfare, January 1978.

Appendix

Common Financial Forms

JUDY JONES AGENCY

Date _____ (Maiden Name) _____ Counsellor _____ Inv. # _____ Class _____

Name in Full (Print Last Name First)

Home Address — City — State — Zip

Give as much information as possible below.
We can help you best with complete information.
✓ check for actual experience
✓✓ for best ability

Phone Number — Home — Message

Soc. Sec. No.

How long in Orange County
Car for own use

Are you over 18 years of age?
☐ Own Home ☐ Rent ☐ Live with family

How did you learn of this Agency?
☐ Newspaper Ad ☐ Yellow Page
☐ Other (specify) ☐ Personally recommended by

In order to avoid duplication, please list all other agencies and companies where you have applied:

Position Desired: Salary
1.
2.

Type	Bkpg. Mach. Kind
WPM Elec	Kardex
WPM Man	Good at Figures
Shorthand WPM	Acct'g
Transcriber Kind	Bkpr. F/C
Duplicator Kind	Bkpr. Asst.
Addressing	Cost Clerk
Mach. Kind	Payroll
Teletype	Credit & Collection
PBX Kind	Cashier
Adding Mach.	Order Desk
Calculator	Inventory
Comptometer	Control
Biller	Accts. Receivable
Kind	Accts. Payable
Key Punch	Other:
Tab No's	

EDUCATION Spouse's Name and place of employment

	Name of School - City & State	Course	Graduate? Degree Held	Grade Average	Years Attended
High School					
College					
Business or Other					

TEST SCORES

Typing _____ Shorthand _____

PLEASE GIVE THREE PERSONAL REFERENCES

Reference 1: _____ Ph. Number _____
Address _____
Reference 2: _____ Ph. Number _____
Address _____
Reference 3: _____ Ph. Number _____
Address _____

EMPLOYMENT RECORD (Present or Most Recent First)

From	Firm Name	Business	Duties (Do not print)	Reason for Leaving (Do not print)
To	Address / Supervisor	Salary		
From	Firm Name	Business	Duties	Reason for Leaving
To	Address / Supervisor	Salary		
From	Firm Name	Business	Duties	Reason for Leaving
To	Address / Supervisor	Salary		
From	Firm Name	Business	Duties	Reason for Leaving
To	Address	Salary		

REFERENCE CHECK FORM

I UNDERSTAND THAT ANY OFFER OF EMPLOYMENT IS CONTINGENT UPON SATISFACTORY VERIFICATION OF MY REFERENCES, PAST EMPLOYERS AND EDUCATION.

I HEREBY AUTHORIZE ABIGAIL ABBOTT PERSONNEL AGENCY AND DESIGNATED EMPLOYEES TO CONTACT PERSONAL REFERENCES, PAST SUPERVISORS, EDUCATIONAL INSTITUTIONS.

REFERRALS:

DATE	COMPANY NAME	ORDER NO.	N/H	HIRED

PLACEMENT INFORMATION:

EMPLOYER _____ full & exact name: co., corp., inc., div., etc. _____ phone

ADDRESS _____ exact#, st., suite # _____ city _____ zip

APPLICANT _____ last name _____ first _____ middle _____ phone

SEND INVOICE to: _____ first & last _____ TITLE _____

COMPANY _____ full & exact name

BILLING ADDRESS _____ exact#, st., suite# _____ city _____ zip

START DATE _____ SALARY _____ FEE _____

VERIFIED _____ POSITION _____ ORDER# _____

ROSE ADDRESS: _____

BANK REFERENCE _____

BY _____ j/o counselor _____ BY _____ p/l counselor

JUDY JONES TEMPORARIES
EMPLOYMENT APPLICATION

Date_____

Full
Name_____

Address_____ Apt._____

City_____ State_____ Zip Code_____

Social Security No. | | | | | | | | | |

Your Phone_____ Message Phone_____

Position Desired_____
_____

Height_____ Weight_____ U.S. Citizen?_____

Have You Been a Temp. Employee Before?_____ Where_____ When_____

Do You Have Transportation?_____

Available for work ☐ Days ☐ Evenings ☐ Sat. ☐ Sun.

Available for How Long?_____

If You Cannot Work a Full Week- Check Which Days You Can Work

MON	TUE	WED	THR	FRI	SAT	SUN

Type Name (Last Name First)   Type Phone No.

Type Name

Date Inactive _____ In Pencil _____ Reason _____ In Pencil _____

INDICATE: ☑ SOME EXPERIENCE   INDICATE: ☒ BEST ABILITIES

SPECIAL MACHINES
☐ MTST
☐ Vari-Type
☐ Multilith
☐ Addressograph
☐ Graphotype
☐ Ozalid or Blue Print
☐ Mimeograph
☐ Ditto
Other_____

STENOGRAPHIC
☐ Shorthand
☐ Steno Type
☐ Court Reporting
☐ Conference Reports
☐ Foreign Language
Which Ones_____

TRANSCRIBING MACHINES
☐ Stenorette
☐ Dictaphone
☐ Ediphone
☐ Audograph
☐ Soundscriber
☐ Tape Recorder
Other_____

TYPING MACHINES
☐ Manual Typewriter
☐ Electric Typewriter
☐ I.B.M. Executive
☐ I.B.M. Selectric
☐ Auto or Robotype
☐ Wide Carriage
☐ Billing Typewriter
☐ P.S.M. Typewriter
Other_____

MATERIALS TYPED
☐ Duplimats
☐ Stencils
☐ Policies
☐ Scripts
☐ Specifications
☐ Invoices
☐ Shippers
☐ Pur. Orders
☐ Ditto Masters
☐ Tax Return
☐ Bal. Sheet
☐ Statements
☐ Statistical Reports
Other_____

BUSINESS BACKGROUND
☐ Legal
☐ Medical
☐ Banking or Finance
☐ 1-Girl Office
☐ Accounting
☐ Engineering
Other_____

CALCULATOR
☐ Comptometer
☐ Burroughs
☐ Friden
☐ Marchant
☐ Monroe
☐+☐-☐X☐÷

ADDING MACHINE
☐ 10 Key
☐ Touch
☐ Full Bank

BOOKKEEPING
☐ Full Charge Bookkeepers
☐ Accts. Rec. ☐ Accts Payable
☐ Inventory Records
☐ Payroll-System?

BOOKKEEPING MACHINES
☐ Burroughs Model_____
☐ National Cash Model_____
☐ Und. Ell. Fish._____
☐ Rem. Rand_____
☐ Billing Mach. Model_____
Other_____

GENERAL SKILLS
☐ Mailing, Stuffing, Folding, etc.
☐ Posting or Pricing
☐ Cashier

FILING (CHECK BELOW)
☐ Alphabetic ☐ Subject ☐ Numeric
☐ Sales
☐ Demonstrations
☐ Market Surveys

COMMUNICATIONS
☐ Switchboard ☐ One Position ☐ Two Position
☐ PBX ☐ Cordless
Trunks_____ Exts._____
☐ Relief Work Only
☐ Teletype
☐ WU ☐ TWX
Other_____

TABULATING
☐ Key Punch Models
☐ I.B.M.
☐ Rem. Rand
☐ NCR_____
☐ Mohawk_____
☐ Acct. Mach. Models_____
☐ Programming

INSURANCE
☐ Life ☐ Broker
☐ Casualty ☐ Agency
☐ General ☐ Home Office
Other._____

BANKING
☐ Teller Yrs._____
☐ Credit Invest. Yrs._____
☐ Stock transfer Yrs._____
☐ Proof Mach. Opr. Yrs._____

➤ IMPORTANT PLEASE TURN OVER AND COMPLETE EMPLOYMENT RECORD ON REVERSE SIDE ◄

ORDER NUMBER	CUSTOMER NAME	DEPT AND EXTENSION	START DATE	APPROX LENGTH	FINISH DATE	PAY RATE	BILL RATE	SKILL CODE	CUSTOMER COMMENTS
1									
2									
3									
4									
5									
6									
7									
8									
9									
10									
11									
12									
13									
14									
15									

TYPE NAME

ON ASSIGNMENT

ORDER NUMBER	CUSTOMER NAME	DEPT AND EXTENSION	START DATE	APPROX LENGTH	FINISH DATE	PAY RATE	BILL RATE	SKILL CODE	CUSTOMER COMMENTS
16									
17									
18									
19									
20									
21									
22									
23									
24									
25									
26									
27									
28									
29									

TYPE NAME

ON ASSIGNMENT

EMPLOYMENT RECORD (LAST EMPLOYER FIRST) — YOU MAY CHECK MY REFERENCES _____
(SIGNATURE)

DATES		COMPANY	TYPE BUSINESS	DUTIES	REASON LEFT
FROM	TO				
SALARY					
	CITY				
FROM	TO				
SALARY					
	CITY				
FROM	TO				
SALARY					
	CITY				

YEARS OF EDUCATION: HIGH SCHOOL _____ COLLEGE _____ COLLEGE NAME _____

OTHER _____ MAJOR _____ MINOR _____

		S	R	W	HAVE YOU EVER HAD SECURITY CLEARANCE? ☐ YES ☐ NO
FOREIGN					WHERE _____
LANGUAGES					HAVE YOU EVER BEEN BONDED? ☐ YES ☐ NO
MASTERED					WHERE _____

IN CASE OF EMERGENCY NOTIFY { NAME _____ ADDRESS _____

TEL _____

EMPLOYMENT APPLICATION   Date_____

Name
in Full (print)_____ Social
                                        Security No._____

Street
Address_____ City_____
                                           (Zip)

Own Phone: _____ Neighbor: _____

Do you have any physical condition which may limit your ability to perform the job(s) applied for?_____

Kind of work desired_____ Wages expected_____

In case of emergency or accident, notify_____ Phone_____

Address_____ City_____ State_____
                                                     (Zip)

PREVIOUS EMPLOYERS (Address and Tel. No.)	TYPE OF WORK	FROM	TO	REASON FOR LEAVING

SIGNATURE: _____

(For references see reverse side)

(Reverse side)

REFERENCES (other than immediate family):

EDUCATION: High School Graduate_____ Yes or No

           College _____ Yes or No

           Other:_____

REMARKS:

Checking Account Application

1st	ADDRESS (NO. AND STREET)		CITY	STATE	ZIP CODE
	CITY AND STATE OF BIRTH	HOME PHONE NO.	MOTHER'S MAIDEN NAME		
FOR BANK USE					

2nd	ADDRESS (NO. AND STREET)		CITY	STATE	ZIP CODE
	CITY AND STATE OF BIRTH	HOME PHONE NO.	MOTHER'S MAIDEN NAME		
FOR BANK USE					

STATEMENT MAILING ADDRESS	
EMPLOYER	POSITION
BUSINESS ADDRESS	BUSINESS PHONE NO.
FOR BANK USE	MGR.'S INITIALS
BANK REFERENCE	DATE THIS A/C OPENED	INITIAL DEPOSIT
OPENED BY	DATE ORIGINALLY OPENED	DATE CLOSED
INTRODUCED BY	REASON CLOSED

(Reverse side)

Account Name	ACCOUNT NO.
	Soc. Sec. or Taxpayers Iden. No.

The undersigned hereby agree with BANK OF NEWPORT that the account specified below shall be subject to all its by-laws, rules, regulations, practices, interest, service charges, etc. now in effect or hereafter established. This account shall be carried as a ☐ CHECKING ☐ SAVINGS account All funds now on deposit or which may hereafter be placed on deposit in said account shall be owned by the undersigned as ☐ INDIVIDUAL ☐ JOINT TENANTS (with right of survivorship) ☐ TRUSTEE(S) and shall be subject to withdrawal by any.................of us, except that in the event of conflicting demands of the undersigned the Bank may require all signatures of the undersigned. The undersigned, jointly and severally, agree to pay said Bank on demand the amount of overdrafts on this account, however created.

The Bank may supply endorsements for any of us on checks and drafts presented for deposit unendorsed. The Bank is hereby authorized on a JOINT TENANCY account to accept for encashment and/or deposit to said account all checks and drafts payable to any or all of the undersigned when endorsed by any of us, or by one for the other.

Said Bank is hereby authorized to:
☐ MAIL all statements, notices and vouchers to the statement mailing address shown on reverse side.
☐ HOLD all statements, vouchers and notices until called for; if not called for within 10 days after preparation said Bank may mail statements, etc. to the statement mailing address shown on reverse side.

Bank may deliver statements, vouchers and notices to any representative of the signatories hereto and is relieved of liability for items lost in delivery by U.S. Mail or otherwise, or not called for by signatories hereto or their representatives.

NA 104

1.	Signature
2.	Signature

CALIFORNIA FIRST BANK | 1ST

Credit Application

CHECK APPROPRIATE BOX

CREDIT CARD ACCOUNT: ☐ MASTER CHARGE ☐ VISA

OVERDRAFT PROTECTION PLAN: ☐ MASTER CHECKING PLAN ACCOUNT ☐ CASH RESERVE ACCOUNT

☐ AUTO LOAN YEAR_____ MAKE_____

☐ PERSONAL LOAN—PURPOSE_____

☐ OTHER—PURPOSE_____

AMOUNT REQUESTED $_____ FOR_____ MONTHS_____

C.F.B. Branch

Mr. Jack G. Perkins
474 16Th Pl
Costa Mesa, CA 92627

1

WHETHER MARRIED, UNMARRIED, OR SEPARATED, YOU MAY REQUEST INDIVIDUAL CREDIT BY APPLYING ALONE. PERSONS MARRIED TO EACH OTHER MAY REQUEST JOINT CREDIT BY APPLYING TOGETHER ON ONE APPLICATION. PERSONS NOT MARRIED TO EACH OTHER MAY REQUEST JOINT CREDIT BY COMPLETING SEPARATE APPLICATIONS AND SUBMITTING THEIR APPLICATIONS TOGETHER.

YEARS AT PRESENT ADDRESS	HOME PHONE	DATE OF BIRTH	SOC. SEC. NO.

NO. OF DEPENDENTS OTHER THAN SELF OR SPOUSE | MARITAL STATUS ☐ MARRIED ☐ UNMARRIED ☐ SEPARATED

PREVIOUS ADDRESS, if at above less than 5 years (No., Street, City, Zip) | YEARS THERE | DRIVER'S LICENSE NUMBER

ADDITIONAL SPACE FOR PREVIOUS ADDRESSES (including zip codes)

NAME AND ADDRESS OF NEAREST LIVING RELATIVE NOT LIVING WITH YOU (OTHER THAN SPOUSE) | RELATIONSHIP | PHONE NUMBER

CURRENT EMPLOYER | ADDRESS (No., Street, City, Zip) | PHONE & EXTENSION

OCCUPATION | HOW LONG THERE | MONTHLY EARNINGS (gross) $ | BADGE NUMBER

NAME AND ADDRESS OF PREVIOUS EMPLOYER (INCLUDING ZIP) | HOW LONG THERE | POSITION HELD

SOURCE OF OTHER INCOME (ALIMONY, CHILD SUPPORT, OR SEPARATE MAINTENANCE INCOME NEED NOT BE REVEALED IF YOU DO NOT WISH TO HAVE IT CONSIDERED AS A BASIS FOR REPAYING THIS OBLIGATION) | OTHER INCOME PER MONTH $

Credit Information

BANK NAME—ADDRESS	CHECKING ACCOUNT NUMBER	SAVINGS ACCOUNT NUMBER

SAVINGS AND LOAN | ADDRESS

CREDIT UNION | ADDRESS

HOME OWN☐ RENT☐ | MONTHLY PAYMENT OR RENT $ | FIRST MORTGAGE HOLDER/LANDLORD | ADDRESS

LOAN NUMBER	CURRENT ESTIMATED VALUE $	DATE OF PURCHASE	PURCHASE PRICE $	AMOUNT OWING $

SECOND MORTGAGE HOLDER	ADDRESS	LOAN NUMBER	AMOUNT OWING $	MONTHLY PAYMENT $

AUTO MAKE & YEAR	FINANCED BY—NAME	ADDRESS	LOAN NUMBER	AMOUNT OWING $	MONTHLY PAYMENT $

AUTO MAKE & YEAR	FINANCED BY—NAME	ADDRESS	LOAN NUMBER	AMOUNT OWING $	MONTHLY PAYMENT $

PLEASE LIST ALL OTHER DEBTS AND OBLIGATIONS, INCLUDING LIABILITY TO PAY CHILD SUPPORT, ALIMONY, OR SEPARATE MAINTENANCE (ATTACH SEPARATE SHEET IF NECESSARY)

NAME OF CREDITOR	ADDRESS	ACCOUNT NUMBER	BALANCE OWING $ (Show Date if Closed)	MONTHLY PAYMENT
		TOTAL MONTHLY PAYMENTS	$	

Spouse Information

SPOUSE'S NAME	SPOUSE'S ADDRESS (No., Street, City)	ZIP

SPOUSE'S EMPLOYER | ADDRESS (No., Street, City, Zip) | PHONE & EXTENSION

OCCUPATION	HOW LONG THERE?	MONTHLY EARNINGS	BADGE NO.	SOC. SEC. NO.	DRIVER'S LICENSE NUMBER

HOME PHONE | DATE OF BIRTH | SOURCE OF OTHER INCOME (ALIMONY, CHILD SUPPORT OR SEPARATE MAINTENANCE INCOME NEED NOT BE REVEALED IF YOU DO NOT WISH TO HAVE IT CONSIDERED AS A BASIS FOR REPAYING THIS OBLIGATION) | OTHER INCOME PER MONTH $

Applicant's Signature _____ Date _____

Spouse's Signature _____ Date _____

1078

Spouse sign ONLY if this application is for joint credit with applicant.

Personal Financial Statement

ASSETS [List market value]		LIABILITIES [List balances due]	
CASH IN THIS BANK	$	NOTES/LOANS PAYABLE	$
CASH IN OTHER BANKS	$	BANKS	$
STOCKS OR BONDS	$	RETAIL STORES	$
REAL ESTATE (list below)*	$	CREDIT CARDS (BANK)	$
AUTOS/TRUCKS	$	OTHERS	$
OTHER ASSETS	$	REAL ESTATE LOANS	$
	$	OTHER PAYABLES (total balance only)	$
	$		$
	$		$
TOTAL ASSETS	$	TOTAL LIABILITIES	$

Real Estate Owned

NET WORTH $

ADDRESS	DATE PURCHASED	PURCHASE PRICE $	CURRENT VALUE	INCOME (if rental property)

*TRANSFER TOTAL CURRENT VALUE TO REAL ESTATE LINE ABOVE $

General Information

LIST ALL NAMES IN WHICH YOU HAVE PREVIOUSLY RECEIVED CREDIT. EACH CUSTOMER MUST MAINTAIN ALL CREDIT AND ACCOUNTS WITH THIS BANK IN THE NAME SHOWN ON THE FRONT OF THIS APPLICATION.

APPLICANT _____ SPOUSE _____

Are you an endorser or co-maker of notes of others? _____ Explain: _____

Are you a defendant in any legal action? _____ Explain: _____

Are there any unsatisfied judgments against you? _____ Explain: _____

Have you ever declared bankruptcy? _____ Explain: _____

Do you know of anything which may interrupt the income shown on the front of this application

or your ability to repay the credit amount? _____ Explain: _____

For bank use only

	ASSN. CODE		
NAME		LOAN APPROVED BY	
NAME		DATE OF NOTE	
STREET ADDRESS		RATE	
CITY ___ STATE ___		BORROWER REQUIRES $	
ZIP ___ PHONE ___		INSURANCE PREMIUM $	
CO-SIGNER		D.M.V. FEES $	
STREET ADDRESS		USE TAX $	
CITY ___ STATE ___		$	
ZIP ___ PHONE ___		$	
SOURCE OF REPAYMENT		CR. LIFE INSURANCE $	
		NET FUNDS $	
		$	
PURPOSE OF LOAN		FINANCE CHARGE $	
		GROSS LOAN AMOUNT $	

PAYABLE IN ___ INSTALLMENTS OF $ ___

COLLATERAL AND COMMENT ___

AND ___ OF $ ___ ON THE ___

DAY OF EACH MONTH BEGINNING ___

AND CONTINUING TO (MATURITY) ___

ANNUAL PERCENTAGE ___

MONTHLY PAYMENT SOURCE:
☐ 35-Day Chart ☐ 45-Day Chart
☐ Other ___

ASSOCIATION CODES:
1-Individual   5-Co-maker
2-Joint   7-Maker

Form **W-4** (Rev. May 1977) Department of the Treasury Internal Revenue Service	**Employee's Withholding Allowance Certificate** (Use for Wages Paid After May 31, 1977) This certificate is for income tax withholding purposes only. It will remain in effect until you change it. If you claim exemption from withholding, you will have to file a new certificate on or before April 30 of next year.

Type or print your full name		Your social security number

Home address (number and street or rural route)

Marital Status
☐ Single ☐ Married
☐ Married, but withhold at higher Single rate

City or town, State, and ZIP code

Note: If married, but legally separated, or spouse is a nonresident alien, check the single block.

1 Total number of allowances you are claiming . . . . _____

2 Additional amount, if any, you want deducted from each pay (if your employer agrees) . . . . $ _____

3 I claim exemption from withholding (see instructions). Enter "Exempt" . . . . _____

Under the penalties of perjury, I certify that the number of withholding exemptions and allowances claimed on this certificate does not exceed the number to which I am entitled. If claiming exemption from withholding, I certify that I incurred no liability for Federal income tax for last year and that I anticipate that I will incur no liability for Federal income tax for this year.

Signature ▶ _____ Date ▶ _____ , 19 _____

---- Detach along this line ----

▲ Give the top part of this form to your employer; keep the lower part for your records and information ▲

Instructions

The explanatory material below will help you determine your correct number of withholding allowances, and will assist you in completing the Form W–4 at the top of this page.

Avoid Overwithholding or Underwithholding

By claiming the number of withholding allowances you are entitled to, you can fit the amount of tax withheld from your wages to your tax liability. In addition to the allowances for personal exemptions to be claimed in item (a), be sure to claim any additional allowances you are entitled to in item (b), "Special withholding allowance," and item (c), "Allowance(s) for credit(s) and/or deduction(s)." While you may claim these allowances on Form W–4 for withholding purposes, you may not claim them under "Exemptions" on your tax return Form 1040 or Form 1040A.

You may claim the special withholding allowance if you are single with only one employer, or married with only one employer and your spouse is not employed. If you have unusually large itemized deductions, an alimony deduction, or credit(s) for child care expenses, earned income, or credit for the elderly, you may claim additional allowances to avoid having too much income tax withheld from your wages. Please note that alimony is no longer an itemized deduction, but rather is an adjustment to gross income. It may be to your benefit to take the standard deduction in lieu of itemizing deductions because of this change.

If you and your spouse are both employed or you have more than one employer, you should make sure that enough has been withheld. If you find that you need more withholding, claim fewer exemptions or ask for additional withholding or request to be withheld at the higher "Single" status. If you are currently claiming additional withholding allowances based on itemized deductions, check the worksheet on the back to see that you are claiming the proper number of allowances.

How Many Withholding Allowances May You Claim?

Use the schedule below to determine the number of allowances you may claim for tax withholding purposes. In determining the number, keep in mind these points: if you are single and hold more than one job, you may not claim the same allowances with more than one employer at the same time; or, if you are married and both you and your spouse are employed, you may not both claim the same allowances with your employers at the same time. A nonresident alien, other than a resident of Canada, Mexico, or Puerto Rico, may claim only one personal allowance.

Completing Form W–4

If you find you are entitled to one or more allowances in addition to those you are now claiming, increase your number of allowances by completing the form above and filing it with your employer. If the number of allowances you previously claimed decreases, you must file a new Form W–4 within 10 days. (If you expect to owe more tax than will be withheld, you may increase your withholding by claiming fewer or "0" allowances on line 1, or by asking for additional withholding on line 2, or both.)

You may claim exemption from withholding of Federal income tax if you had no liability for income tax for last year, and you anticipate that you will incur no liability for income tax for this year. You may not claim exemption if your joint or separate return shows tax liability before the allowance of any credit for income tax withheld. If you are exempt, your employer will not withhold Federal income tax from your wages. However, social security tax will be withheld if you are covered by the Federal Insurance Contributions Act.

You must revoke this exemption (1) within 10 days from the time you anticipate you will incur income tax liability for the year or (2) on or before December 1 if you anticipate you will incur Federal income tax liability for the next year. If you want to stop or are required to revoke this exemption, you must file a new Form W–4 with your employer showing the number of withholding allowances you are entitled to claim. This certificate for exemption from withholding will expire on April 30 of next year unless a new Form W–4 is filed before that date.

The Following Information is Provided in Accordance with the Privacy Act of 1974

The Internal Revenue Code requires every employee to furnish his or her employer with a signed withholding allowance certificate showing the number of withholding allowances that the employee claims (section 3402(f)(2)(A) and the Regulations thereto). Individuals are required to provide their Social Security Number for proper identification and processing (section 6109 and the Regulations thereto).

The principal purpose for soliciting withholding allowance certificate information is to administer the Internal Revenue laws of the United States.

If an employee does not furnish a signed withholding allowance certificate, the employee is considered as claiming no withholding allowances (section 3402(e)) and shall be treated as a single person (section 3402(l)).

The routine uses of the withholding allowance certificate information include disclosure to the Department of Justice for actual or potential criminal prosecution or civil litigation.

Figure Your Total Withholding Allowances Below

(a) Allowance(s) for exemption(s)—Enter 1 for each personal exemption you can claim on your Federal income tax return[*] . . . _____

(b) Special withholding allowance—Enter 1 if single with 1 employer, or married with 1 employer and spouse not employed[**] . . _____

(c) Allowance(s) for credit(s) and/or deduction(s)—Enter number from line (k) on other side[**] . . . . . . _____

(d) Total (add lines (a) through (c) above)—Enter here and on line 1, Form W–4, above . . . . _____

[*]If you are in doubt as to whom you may claim as a dependent, see the instructions that came with your last Federal income tax return or call your local Internal Revenue Service office.

[**]This allowance is used solely for purposes of figuring your withholding tax, and cannot be claimed when you file your tax return.

235-038-1

(Reverse side)

Form W-4 (Rev. 5-77)

Table for Determining Number of Withholding Allowances Based on Tax Credits

Estimated salaries and wages	Number of additional withholding allowances for the amount of tax credits for child care expenses, earned income, or credit for the elderly from the appropriate column (see line (c) on other side). For an explanation of these credits, see the Instructions for Form 1040.												
	0	**1**		**2**		**3**		**4**		**5**		**6**	
	Under	At least	But less than	At least	But less than	At least	But less than	At least	But less than	At least	But less than	At least	But less than

Part I — Single Employees

Under $5,000	NO ADDITIONAL ALLOWANCES												
5,000– 7,000	$75	75	200	200	300	300 or more							
7,001–10,000	125	125	260	260	400	400	530	530	650	650	770	770 or more	
10,001–15,000	175	175	370	370	550	550	700	700 or more					
15,001–20,000	200	200	450	450	670	670 or more							
20,001–25,000	250	250	525	525	800	800 or more							
25,001–30,000	400	400	700	700 or more									
30,001–35,000	800	800 or more											

Part II — Head of Household Employees

Under $5,000	NO ADDITIONAL ALLOWANCES												
5,000–10,000	$90	90	210	210	340	340	475	475	600	600	710	710 or more	
10,001–15,000	50	50	210	210	400	400	560	560	725	725 or more			
15,001–20,000	1	1	190	190	400	400	610	610	800	800 or more			
20,001–25,000	1	1	120	120	350	350	630	630 or more					
25,001–30,000	1	1	75	75	375	375	640	640 or more					
30,001–35,000	75	75	350	350	620	620 or more							
35,001–45,000	475	475	750	750 or more									

Part III — Married Employees (When Spouse Is Not Employed)

Under $7,000	NO ADDITIONAL ALLOWANCES												
7,000–15,000	$125	125	250	250	390	390	525	525	660	660	800	800 or more	
15,001–20,000	180	180	375	375	540	540	700	700 or more					
20,001–25,000	210	210	420	420	630	630	800	800 or more					
25,001–30,000	240	240	480	480	720	720 or more							
30,001–35,000	270	270	550	550	800	800 or more							
35,001–45,000	425	425	750	750 or more									

Part IV — Married Employees (When Both Spouses Are Employed)

Under $8,000	NO ADDITIONAL ALLOWANCES												
8,000–10,000	$150	150 or more											
10,001–12,000	220	220 or more											
12,001–14,000	300	300 or more											
14,001–16,000	450	450	590	590	670	670 or more							
16,001–18,000	560	560	710	710 or more									
18,001–20,000	650	650 or more											
20,001–25,000	800	800 or more											

Determining Withholding Allowances for Itemized Deductions and Payments of Alimony

The worksheet below will be helpful to you in determining whether your expected itemized deductions and adjustment to gross income for alimony payments entitle you to claim one or more additional withholding allowances

(a) Total estimated annual salary or wages (from all sources) . . . . $

(b) Total estimated itemized deductions . . . . $

(c) Enter $3,200 for joint return or $2,200 for all others . . . .

(d) Line (b) or line (c), whichever is larger . . . .

(e) Total estimated deduction for alimony payments . . . .

(f) Add lines (d) and (e) . . . .

(g) Appropriate amount from column (A), (B), or (C) in the table below . . . .

(h) Balance (subtract line (g) from line (f)). If less than $1, you are not entitled to additional withholding allowances and may be having too little tax withheld. You can generally avoid this by claiming 1 less allowance than the total number to which you are entitled for each $750 by which line (g) exceeds line (f) . . . . .

(i) You are entitled to 1 allowance for each $750 or fraction thereof that line (h) exceeds $1. Enter number here . . . .

(j) Withholding allowances from Part I, II, III, or IV . . . .

(k) Total of lines (i) and (j). Enter here and on line (c) on the other side . . . .

Table for Determining Number of Withholding Allowances Based on Deductions

Estimated salaries and wages	(A) Single Employees (With One Job) and Head of Household Employees	(B) Married Employees (Wife or Husband is Not Working)	(C) Married Employees (Both Husband and Wife Working) and Employees Working in More Than One Job
Under $10,000	$2,500	$3,500	$4,300
10,000–15,000	2,500	3,500	5,100
15,001–20,000	2,500	3,600	6,000
20,001–25,000	2,600	3,600	6,600
25,001–30,000	2,800	3,600	7,300
30,001–35,000	3,600	3,600	8,000
35,001–40,000	4,700	3,900	8,900
40,001–45,000	6,000	4,600	9,800
45,001–50,000	7,600	5,600	10,900
Over $50,000	21% of estimated salaries and wages	15% of estimated salaries and wages	24% of estimated salaries and wages

1 Control number	222	2 Employer's State number					

3 Employer's name, address, and ZIP code	4 Sub-total ☐　Cor-rection ☐　Void ☐	For Official Use Only
	7 Employer's identification number	Make No Entry Here See Note on the Back of Copy D

10 Employee's social security number	11 Federal income tax withheld	12 Wages, tips, other compensation	13 FICA tax withheld	14 Total FICA wages
15 Employee's name (first, middle, last)		16 Pension plan coverage? Yes/No	17 *	18 FICA tips
		20 State income tax withheld	21 State wages, tips, etc.	22 Name of State
19 Employee's address and ZIP code		23 Local income tax withheld	24 Local wages, tips, etc.	25 Name of locality

Wage and Tax Statement　　　**1978**　　COPY A For Social Security Administration
*See Instructions for Forms W-2 and W-2P and back of Copy D

Form **W-2** ▼　　　　　　　　　　　　　　　　　Department of the Treasury—Internal Revenue Service

---

1 Control number	222	2 Employer's State number					

3 Employer's name, address, and ZIP code	4 Sub-total ☐　Cor-rection ☐　Void ☐	
	7 Employer's identification number	Make No Entry Here

10 Employee's social security number	11 Federal income tax withheld	12 Wages, tips, other compensation	13 FICA tax withheld	14 Total FICA wages
15 Employee's name (first, middle, last)		16 Pension plan coverage? Yes/No	17	18 FICA tips
		20 State income tax withheld	21 State wages, tips, etc.	22 Name of State
19 Employee's address and ZIP code		23 Local income tax withheld	24 Local wages, tips, etc.	25 Name of locality

Wage and Tax Statement　　　**1978**　　Copy B To be filed with employee's FEDERAL tax return

Form **W-2**　　This information is being furnished to the Internal Revenue Service.　　　Department of the Treasury—Internal Revenue Service

1 Control number 222	2 Employer's State number	
3 Employer's name, address, and ZIP code	4 Sub-total ☐ Cor-rection ☐ Void ☐ 7 Employer's identification number	**Make No Entry Here**
10 Employee's social security number 11 Federal income tax withheld	12 Wages, tips, other compensation 13 FICA tax withheld	14 Total FICA wages
15 Employee's name (first, middle, last)	16 Pension plan coverage? Yes/No 17	18 FICA tips
	20 State income tax withheld 21 State wages, tips, etc.	22 Name of State
19 Employee's address and ZIP code	23 Local income tax withheld 24 Local wages, tips, etc.	25 Name of locality
Wage and Tax Statement 1978		Copy C For employee's records

Form **W-2**   This information is being furnished to the Internal Revenue Service.   Department of the Treasury—Internal Revenue Service

(Reverse side)

Notice to Employee:

File Copy B of this form with your Federal income tax return for 1978. Attach Copy 2 to your State or local income tax return you file for 1978. Please keep Copy C for your records. You can use it to prove your right to social security benefits. If your name, social security number, or address is incorrect, please correct Copies B, C, and 2, and let your employer know.

If you have non-wage income of more than $500 and will owe tax of $100 or more, you should file Form 1040ES, Declaration of Estimated Tax for Individuals, and pay the tax in installments during the year.

Credit for FICA Tax.—If more than one employer paid you wages during 1978 and more than the maxi-mum FICA (social security and hospital insurance) employee tax, railroad retirement (RRTA) tax, or combined FICA and RRTA tax was withheld, you can claim the excess as a credit against your Federal income tax. (Please see your Federal income tax return instructions.) The social security (FICA) rate of 6.05%, under Public Law 93-233, includes 1.10% for hospital insurance benefits and 4.95% for old-age, survivors, and dis-ability insurance.

Box 16.—If you were covered by a government em-ployee plan, a qualified pension or profit-sharing retire-ment plan, or a tax sheltered annuity plan, box 16 will show YES. Otherwise, box 16 will show NO. Armed forces reservists, national guard members, or volunteer firefighters, who have a retirement savings arrangement, should see Form 5329.

1 Control number	222	2 Employer's State number	

3 Employer's name, address, and ZIP code

4 Sub-total Cor-rection Void
☐ ☐ ☐

7 Employer's identification number

Make No Entry Here

10 Employee's social security number	11 Federal income tax withheld	12 Wages, tips, other compensation	13 FICA tax withheld	14 Total FICA wages
15 Employee's name (first, middle, last)		16 Pension plan coverage? Yes/No 17		18 FICA tips
		20 State income tax withheld	21 State wages, tips, etc.	22 Name of State
19 Employee's address and ZIP code		23 Local income tax withheld	24 Local wages, tips, etc.	25 Name of locality

Wage and Tax Statement   1978   Copy D For employer

Form **W–2**   Department of the Treasury—Internal Revenue Service

(Reverse side)

Instructions for Preparing Form W–2

Note: The information requested in boxes 5, 6, 8, and 9 of the prior version of this form is no longer needed because of a change in law. Make no entry in this space.

The 6-part wage and tax statement is acceptable in most States. If you are in doubt, ask your appropriate State or local official.

Prepare Form W–2 for each of your employees to whom any of the following items applied during 1978.

(a) You withheld income tax or social security tax.

(b) You would have withheld income tax if the employee had not claimed more than one withholding allowance.

(c) You paid $600 or more.

(d) You paid for services any amount, if you are in a trade or business. Include the cash value of any payment you made that was not in cash.

By January 31, 1979, give Copies B, C, and 2 to each person who was your employee at the end of 1978. For anyone who stopped working for you before the end of 1978, you should give copies within 30 days after the last wage payment. Send Copy A to the Social Security Administration by February 28, 1979. (For more information, please see Forms 941, 942, W–3, or Circular E. Farmers, see Circular A.)

See separate Instructions for Forms W–2 and W–2P for more information on how to complete Form W–2.

1 Control number	222	2 Employer's State number		
3 Employer's name, address, and ZIP code		4 Sub-total ☐ Cor-rection ☐ Void ☐		**Make No Entry Here**
		7 Employer's identification number		
10 Employee's social security number	11 Federal income tax withheld	12 Wages, tips, other compensation	13 FICA tax withheld	14 Total FICA wages
15 Employee's name (first, middle, last)		16 Pension plan coverage? Yes/No	17	18 FICA tips
		20 State income tax withheld	21 State wages, tips, etc.	22 Name of State
		23 Local income tax withheld	24 Local wages, tips, etc.	25 Name of locality
19 Employee's address and ZIP code				
Wage and Tax Statement		**1978**	Copy 1 For State, City, or Local Tax Department Employee's and employer's copy compared. ☐	

1 Control number	222	2 Employer's State number		
3 Employer's name, address, and ZIP code		4 Sub-total ☐ Cor-rection ☐ Void ☐		**Make No Entry Here**
		7 Employer's identification number		
10 Employee's social security number	11 Federal income tax withheld	12 Wages, tips, other compensation	13 FICA tax withheld	14 Total FICA wages
15 Employee's name (first, middle, last)		16 Pension plan coverage? Yes/No	17	18 FICA tips
		20 State income tax withheld	21 State wages, tips, etc.	22 Name of State
		23 Local income tax withheld	24 Local wages, tips, etc.	25 Name of locality
19 Employee's address and ZIP code				
Wage and Tax Statement		**1978**	Copy 2 To be filed with employee's State, City, or Local income tax return. Employee's and employer's copy compared. ☐	

CROCKER NATIONAL BANK
RESIDENTIAL LOAN APPLICATION

YOU MAY APPLY SEPARATELY OR JOINTLY WITH YOUR SPOUSE

MORTGAGE APPLIED FOR	Type ☐ Conv. ☐ FHA ☐ VA	Amount $	Interest Rate %	No. of Months	Monthly Payment Principal & Interest $	Escrow/Impounds (to be collected monthly) ☐ Taxes ☐ Hazard Ins. ☐ Mtg. Ins. ☐

Prepayment Option

SUBJECT PROPERTY

Property Street Address	City	County	State	Zip	No. Units

Legal Description (Attach description if necessary)	Property is: ☐ Fee ☐ Leasehold ☐ Condo ☐ PUD ☐ DeMinimis PUD	Year Built

Purpose of Loan: ☐ Purchase ☐ Construction-Perm. ☐ Construction ☐ Refinance ☐ Other (Explain)

Complete this line if Construction-Perm. or Construction Loan	Lot Value Data Year Acquired $	Original Cost $	Present Value (a) $	Cost of Imps. (b) $	Total (a+b) $	ENTER TOTAL AS PURCHASE PRICE IN DETAILS OF PURCHASE

Complete this line if a Refinance Loan Year Acquired	Original Cost $	Amt. Existing Liens $	Purpose of Refinance	Describe Improvement [ ] made [ ] to be made Cost: $

Title Will Be Held In What Name(s) | Manner In Which Title Will Be Held

Source of Down Payment and Settlement Charges

This application is designed to be completed by the borrower(s) with the lender's assistance. The Co-Borrower Section and all other Co-Borrower questions must be completed and the appropriate box(es) checked if ☐ another person will be jointly obligated with the Borrower on the loan, or ☐ the Borrower is relying on income from alimony, child support or separate maintenance or on the income or assets of another person as a basis for repayment of the loan, or ☐ the Borrower is married and resides, or the property is located, in a community property state.

BORROWER		Age	School Yrs	CO-BORROWER*		Age	School Yrs
Name				Name			

Present Address Years at present address ☐ Own ☐ Rent	Present Address Years at present address ☐ Own ☐ Rent
Street	Street
City/State/Zip	City/State/Zip
Former address if less than 2 years at present address	Former address if less than 2 years at present address
Street	Street
City/State/Zip	City/State/Zip
Years at former address ☐ Own ☐ Rent	Years at former address ☐ Own ☐ Rent

Marital Status ☐ Married ☐ Separated ☐ Unmarried (incl. single, divorced, widowed)	DEPENDENTS OTHER THAN LISTED BY CO-BORROWER NO. AGES	Marital Status ☐ Married ☐ Separated ☐ Unmarried (incl. single, divorced, widowed)	DEPENDENTS OTHER THAN LISTED BY CO-BORROWER NO. AGES

Name and Address of Employer	Years employed in this line of work or profession? years Years on this job ☐ Self Employed*	Name and Address of Employer	Years employed in this line of work or profession? years Years on this job ☐ Self Employed*
Position/Title	Type of Business	Position/Title	Type of Business
Social Security Number***	Home Phone	Business Phone	Social Security Number***	Home Phone	Business Phone

GROSS MONTHLY INCOME / MONTHLY HOUSING EXPENSE / DETAILS OF PURCHASE

Item	Borrower	Co-Borrower	Total	Rent	PREVIOUS	PROPOSED		
Base Empl. Income	$	$	$	First Mortgage (P&I)		$	a. Purchase Price	$
Overtime				Other Financing (P&I)			b. Total Closing Costs(Est)	
Bonuses				Hazard Insurance			c. Prepaid Escrows(Est)	
Commissions				Real Estate Taxes			d. Total (a+b+c)	
Dividends/Interest				Mortgage Insurance			e. Amount This Mortgage	( )
Net Rental Income				Homeowner Assn. Dues			f. Other Financing	( )
Other † (Before completing, see notice under Describe Other Income below)				Other			g. Present Equity in Lot	( )
				Total Monthly Pmt	$	$	h. Amount of Cash Deposit	( )
				Utilities			i. Closing Costs Paid by Seller	( )
Total	$	$	$	Total	$	$	j. Cash Reqd. For Closing(Est)	$

DESCRIBE OTHER INCOME

NOTICE † Alimony, child support, or separate maintenance income need not be revealed if the Borrower or Co-Borrower does not choose to have it considered as a basis for repaying this loan.

◁▷ B—Borrower C—Co-Borrower

	Monthly Amount
	$

IF EMPLOYED IN CURRENT POSITION FOR LESS THAN TWO YEARS COMPLETE THE FOLLOWING

B/C	Previous Employer/School	City/State	Type of Business	Position/Title	Dates From/To	Monthly Income
						$

THESE QUESTIONS APPLY TO BOTH BORROWER AND CO BORROWER

	Borrower Yes or No	Co-Borrower Yes or No
If a "yes" answer is given to a question in this column, explain on an attached sheet.		
Have you any outstanding judgments? In the last 14 years, have you been declared bankrupt?		
Have you had property foreclosed upon or given title or deed in lieu thereof?		
Are you a co-maker or endorser on a note?		
Are you a party in a law suit?		
Are you obligated to pay alimony, child support, or separate maintenance?		
Is any part of the down payment borrowed?		

	Borrower Yes or No	Co-Borrower Yes or No
Do you have health and accident insurance?		
Do you have major medical coverage?		
Do you intend to occupy this property?		
Will this property be your primary residence?		
Have you previously owned a home?		
Sales Price of previously owned home?	$	$

* FHLMC requires self employed to furnish signed copies of one or more most recent Federal Tax Returns or audited Profit and Loss Statements. FNMA requires business credit report, signed Federal Income Tax returns for last two years, and if available, audited P/L plus balance sheet for same period.

** All Present Monthly Housing Expenses of Borrower and Co-Borrower should be listed on a combined basis.

*** Neither FHLMC nor FNMA require this information.

FHLMC 65 Rev. 3/77
91-6148 (Rev. 4-77)

FNMA 1003 Rev. 3/77

(Reverse side)

This Statement and any applicable supporting schedules may be completed jointly by both married and unmarried co-borrowers if their assets and liabilities are sufficiently joined so that the Statement can be meaningfully and fairly presented on a combined basis; otherwise separate Statements and Schedules are required (FHLMC 65A/FNMA 1003A). If the co-borrower section was completed about spouse, complete this statement and supporting schedules about spouse also.

☐ Completed Jointly ☐ Not Completed Jointly

ASSETS		LIABILITIES AND PLEDGED ASSETS				
Indicate by (∗) those liabilities or pledged assets which will be satisfied upon sale of real estate owned or upon refinancing of subject property.						
Description	Cash or Market Value	Creditors' Name, Address and Account Number	Acct. Name, if Not Borrower's	Mo. Pmt. and Mos. left to pay		Unpaid Balance
Cash Deposit Toward Purchase Held By	$	Installment Debt (include "revolving" charge accounts)		$ Pmt./Mos. /		$
Checking and Savings Accounts (Show Names of institutions/Acct. Nos.)				/		
				/		
Stocks and Bonds (No./Description)				/		
				/		
Life Insurance Net Cash Value Face Amount $		Automobile Loan		/		
SUBTOTAL LIQUID ASSETS	$			/		
Real Estate Owned (Enter Market Value from Schedule of Real Estate Owned)		Real Estate Loans (Itemize and Identify Lender)				
Vested Interest in Retirement Fund				✕		✕
Net Worth of Business Owned (ATTACH FINANCIAL STATEMENT)						
Automobiles (Make and Year)		Other Debt Including Stock Pledges (Itemize)		/		✕
Furniture and personal Property		Alimony, Child Support and Separate Maintenance Payments Owed To		/		✕
Other Assets (Itemize)						
		TOTAL MONTHLY PAYMENTS		$		✕
TOTAL ASSETS	A $	NET WORTH (A.−B.) $			TOTAL LIABILITIES	B $

SCHEDULE OF REAL ESTATE OWNED (If Additional Properties Owned Attach Separate Schedule)

Address of Property (Indicate S if Sold, PS if Pending Sale or R if Rental being held for income)	Type of Property	Present Market Value	Amount of Mortgages & Liens	Gross Rental Income	Mortgage Payments	Taxes, Ins. Maintenance and Misc.	Net Rental Income
		$	$	$	$	$	$
TOTALS →		$	$	$	$	$	$

LIST PREVIOUS CREDIT REFERENCES

B−Borrower C−Co-Borrower	Creditor's Name and Address	Account Number	Purpose	Highest Balance	Date Paid
				$	

List any additional names under which credit has previously been received _____

AGREEMENT: The undersigned applies for the loan indicated in this application to be secured by a first mortage or deed of trust on the property described herein, and represents that the property will not be used for any illegal or restricted purpose, and that all statements made in this application are true and are made for the purpose of obtaining the loan. Verification may be obtained from any source named in this application. The original or a copy of this application will be retained by the lender, even if the loan is not granted.

I/we understand that periodically you may receive information and answer questions and requests from others, like credit reporting agencies, about me/us and my/our transactions with you.

I/we fully understand that it is a federal crime punishable by fine or imprisonment, or both, to knowingly make any false statements concerning any of the above facts as applicable under the provisions of Title 18, United States Code Section 1014.

_____ Date _____   _____ Date _____
Borrower's Signature   Co-Borrower's Signature

VOLUNTARY INFORMATION FOR GOVERNMENT MONITORING PURPOSES

If this loan is for purchase or construction of a home, the following information is requested by the Federal Government to monitor this lender's compliance with Equal Credit Opportunity and Fair Housing Laws. The law provides that a lender may neither discriminate on the basis of this information nor on whether or not it is furnished. Furnishing this information is optional. If you do not wish to furnish the following information, please initial below.

BORROWER: I do not wish to furnish this information (initials) _____ **CO-BORROWER:** I do not wish to furnish this information (initials) _____

RACE/ NATIONAL ORIGIN	☐ American Indian, Alaskan Native ☐ Asian, Pacific Islander ☐ Black ☐ Hispanic ☐ White ☐ Other (specify) _____	SEX ☐ Female ☐ Male	RACE/ NATIONAL ORIGIN	☐ American Indian, Alaskan Native ☐ Asian, Pacific Islander ☐ Black ☐ Hispanic ☐ White ☐ Other (specify) _____	SEX ☐ Female ☐ Male

FOR LENDER'S USE ONLY

(FNMA REQUIREMENT ONLY) This Application was taken by _____, a full time employee of

Interviewer

Crocker National Bank, in a face to face interview with the prospective borrower

FHLMC 65 Rev. 3/77   REVERSE   FNMA 1003 Rev. 3/77